P9-EGJ-926

Don Messer
The Man Behind the Music

787.21620092 Messe -B

Bertin, J.
Don Messer.

(CDN)

PRICE: $19.95 (3559/he   )

1

Also by Johanna Bertin

*Sable Island: Tales of Tragedy and Survival
from the Graveyard of the Atlantic*

Sir Charles Tupper: The Bully Who Battled for Canada

*Holiday Misadventures:
Tragedy, Murder, and Mystery*

*Strange Events and More:
Canadian Giants, Witches, Wizards, and Other Tales*

*Strange Events:
Incredible Canadian Monsters, Curses, Ghosts, and Other Tales*

Don Messer

The Man Behind the Music

JOHANNA BERTIN

Copyright © 2009 by Johanna Bertin.

All rights reserved. No part of this work may be reproduced or used in any form or by any means, electronic or mechanical, including photocopying, recording or any retrieval system, without the prior written permission of the publisher or a licence from the Canadian Copyright Licensing Agency (Access Copyright). To contact Access Copyright, visit www.accesscopyright.ca or call 1-800-893-5777.

Every effort has been made to secure permission for photographs reproduced in this book from the rightful copyright holders. We regret any inadvertent omission.

Edited by Laurel Boone.
Cover photo of Don Messer, photographer unknown.
Cover design by Zachary Atkinson.
Book design by Kent Fackenthall.
Printed in Canada.
10 9 8 7 6 5 4 3 2 1

Library and Archives Canada Cataloguing in Publication

Bertin, Johanna
    Don Messer: the man behind the music / Johanna Bertin.

Includes index.
ISBN 978-0-86492-531-2

    1. Messer, Don, 1909-1973. 2. Fiddlers — Canada — Biography.
I. Title.
ML418 M584 B54 2009   787.2'1620092   C2008-907198-0

Goose Lane Editions acknowledges the financial support of the Canada Council for the Arts, the Government of Canada through the Book Publishing Industry Development Program (BPIDP), and the New Brunswick Department of Wellness, Culture, and Sport for its publishing activities.

Goose Lane Editions
Suite 330, 500 Beaverbrook Court
Fredericton, New Brunswick
CANADA E3B 5X4
www.gooselane.com

To all who allow themselves to have a dream
and then work hard to make it come true,
and to fiddlers everywhere,
thank you for the music.

And of course, to Bruce, Geoff, and Catharine . . . love you lots!

"Yes, I realized that Naomi and Dawn were home alone in Saint John. I was just as lonesome for them as they were for me, but I just couldn't bring myself to give up the violin; it had become part of me."

—Don Messer, 1936
From *Canada's Don Messer*, by Lester Sellick, 1969

CONTENTS

ACKNOWLEDGEMENTS

Thirty years ago, when I first moved to Harvey Station, New Brunswick, I considered writing a biography of Don Messer. A friend of mine lived in his boyhood home in Tweedside, just a few kilometres from my home, and as we spoke of Don's accomplishments, it seemed to me they warranted recognition and celebration. I didn't write the book then — children and jobs were a priority — but the desire to record his story never left me.

I have a penchant for feel-good stories, for stories of people who have a dream and set out to achieve it despite almost insurmountable difficulties. The story of Don Messer is one of these. I wanted to explore why this particular man from a farm in Tweedside, New Brunswick, had, amongst all the talented fiddlers of his era, been able to rise to the top of Canadian television and performing stardom. What set him apart? Obviously he had talent, but there had to be a great deal more.

As I searched for that elusive quality, there were many times when I felt like giving up, but each time I did, something would happen to encourage me to press on. I would receive a letter from a fan in Grande Prairie, Alberta, saying how glad he was that I was writing the book, or I would get a phone call from someone answering one of the mysteries in Don's life. I would also recall Don's daughter, Dawn

Messer Attis, telling me, "Dad just never gave up." It seemed the least I could do was persevere.

There are so many people to thank. First of all, I am especially grateful to many members of the Messer family: Dawn Messer Attis, John Clifford, Dallas Davis, Jack Gray, Lorraine Hickey, Brenda Hill Hudson, Shirley Messer Jamieson, Muriel Martin, Lucille McCrae, Hayes Messer, Vaughan Messer, and Grace Smith, and to two very special friends of the Messers, Jeannie Miller and Ruby MacLean.

The story of Don Messer's accomplishments is also the story of Charlie Chamberlain, Marg Osburne, and the other performers in the band, all talented musicians in their own right. It was apparent that without them Don would not have been able to accomplish what he did, and without him it is doubtful that they would ever have come together as a group. So thank you to the families of these musicians: Ann-Marie Chamberlain Doyle, Donny Chamberlain, Sandi MacKinnon, Ruth Munro, Dorothy Nielsen, Jessie Ryan, Shirley Simmons, Austin Squarebriggs, David Squarebriggs, and Melody Squarebriggs White.

People who were involved with the show or tours gave me generous help, for which I am grateful: Jane Edgett, Art Fabean, Johnny Forrest, Bill Guest, Ned Landry, Bill Langstroth, Catherine McKinnon, Vic Mullen, Ken Reynolds, Don Tremaine, Joe Wallin, and Mary Wile.

I am thankful to everyone who phoned or wrote or met with me to share their memories: George Breckenridge, Thomas Brown, Vera Busshoff, F. Vincent Clark, Harold Cleghorn, Mary Conlon, Gary Copeland, Jim Dolmage, Edwin Doyle, Doug Eidt, Sandra Ferris, John Forbes, Carol Gowan, Grace Guevin, Betty Hanson, Jean Hawkins, Ivan Hicks, Jane Higgins, Shirley Hunter, Barbara Laird, Joyce Langley-Murphy, Walter Learning, Valerie Lee, Ron MacInnis, Eva MacLean, Ambrose McGee, William McLaughlin, Lottie Messer, James Morrison, Bill Murdock, Matilda Murdock, W. G. Murdock, Ron Noiles, Tom Oldenburg, Barb Patriquan, Doug Perrin, Lorne Perry, Wyville Reeves, Norm Ripley, Brenda Robitaille, Stewart Romans, Patricia Ross, Doug Salton, Jim Santa Lucia, Nancy Schofield,

Phyllis Shannon, Ken Smith, Leon Stachnyk, Jean Storie, Jerry Taylor, Bonnie Ventrasca, Jerry Viel, Barbara Vincent, Richard Wadge, Robert Wasykowski, Khris Weeks, Myrel White, Glenna M. Wilson, and Doreen Wooder, and all the others who told me their stories.

For help with research, I would like to thank: Janet Bishop, New Brunswick Museum; Christine Cadotte, Doug Kirby, and Nick Tustin, all with CBC Archives; Diane Ota, Boston Public Library; Tim Patterson, Ottawa-Carleton Geoscience Centre; Sheldon Posen, Canadian Museum of Civilization; Brock Silversides, University of Toronto Libraries; Chip Sutherland, lawyer; Philip Hartling and Gail Judge, Nova Scotia Archives and Records Management (NSARM); Helen Jean Newman, Tourism New Brunswick; and Harold Wright, Heritage Resources Saint John.

For help with tracing elusive photographs I would like to thank: Tom Beckett, Leo Burnett Company Ltd.; Brenda Carroll, CBC Image Research Library; Gary Craswell, Craswell Portrait Studio; Lena Goon, Whyte Museum; Wanda Lyons, Provincial Archives of New Brunswick; Lisa Olson, General Mills; Terry O'Reilly, CBC; Dawn Sugimoto, *Lethbridge Herald*; Marnie Peters and Laura Harkness, *Chatelaine*; and Trish Purkis, Galt Museum and Archives.

To my editors, Laurel Boone and Paula Sarson, I offer a note of gratitude for their discriminating eyes in detecting weaknesses in the manuscript and the gracious way in which they guided me to accept their suggestions for improvement. To the team at Goose Lane Editions: Susanne Alexander, Akoulina Connell, Julie Scriver, Kent Fackenthall, Susan Baker, and Angela Williams, I extend my heartfelt appreciation for their belief in the importance of this book and for their contribution in bringing it to fruition.

Finally, for their support and encouragement, I owe so much to Judy Hagerman and Elle Andra-Warner; Ana Watts and other members of the Central New Brunswick Branch of the Professional Writers Association of Canada; my co-workers at the Social Work Department, Dr. Everett Chalmers Regional Hospital; Rachelle Levesque for help with typing transcripts; my husband, Bruce Pendrel; and my children, Geoff and Catharine, who, as always, make me so proud to be their mum.

A final note: throughout the book, I have used fiddle and violin interchangeably. They are the same instrument, though customarily identified differently, depending on the type of music played. Classical musicians prefer the term "violin"; all others tend to use "fiddle." Don Messer always referred to his instrument as the violin.

— Johanna Bertin
www.johannabertin.com

Don Messer

The Man Behind the Music

Don Messer, 1949. Courtesy: John Clifford [Craswell Portrait Studio].

Mourners file into Calvin Presbyterian Church in downtown Halifax. They respect the exclusivity of the front rows roped off for family, but they edge as far forward as they are able, wanting a good seat for this last public appearance of Don Messer, whose performances in community halls and arenas and then on radio and television have been a part of their lives for more than fifty years.

The men and women scoot sideways on the bare wood pews, cramming against strangers, soon becoming overheated in such close confines. Wedged tightly together, there is not even room to man-oeuvre an arm out of a coat sleeve, so they settle for removing their scarves and letting their coats hang open. Funeral home attendants bring chairs from the basement, lengthening each row and providing seats for those standing near the door. Still more people come into the church, and they tuck themselves into corners and alcoves or remain standing against the wall at the back. Calvin Presbyterian is overflowing, but there is no lessening of the crowd trying to get in.

People are respectful, but they can't resist murmuring in excitement as they recognize some of the attendees and question the absence of others. They point out Walter Fitzgerald, the Mayor of Halifax, and Tommy Hunter, known as the Gentleman of Country Music. CBC announcer Don Tremaine is there, present because of his personal affection for the man with whom he has worked for so many years.

There are the members of his band, his family on the road, each of them an accomplished musician, each of them playing a significant part in the success of the group. A few of them have been with Don Messer for more than thirty years; none have been with him for less than twenty-one years: bassist Duke Nielsen, clarinettist Rae Simmons, pianist Waldo Munro, fiddler Cecil McEachern, drummer Warren MacCrae, and the perennial sweetheart of the audiences, Marg Osburne. Their grief is palpable, and they make no effort to hide it.

Two of them have travelled long distances to be here today. Gunter Buchta, director of the dance group that has entranced show audiences since 1959, has flown in from Grenada to be present with his dancers at this difficult time, and kilted Johnny Forrest, an accordion player and singer on the show for the last seven years, has arrived from Vancouver to say farewell to his old friend and mentor whom he always called "Wee Donald." Nobody else in this circle, with the exception of Marg, ever called Don anything but Mr. Messer.

Then, of course, there are the Chamberlains, the widow and children of that bigger-than-life personality that was Charlie Chamberlain. The family has come to pay their respects. Their presence emphasizes the absence of the golden-voiced balladeer who started with Don in 1934 and remained with him for thirty-eight years, through difficult times and good times, until his death. They have come out of love for Don, apparently not slighted that none of the cast were there for Charlie's funeral the previous year. That absence had been as noticeable as if blood sisters and brothers had stayed away. Equally stark today is the absence of Bill Langstroth and Ken Reynolds, the CBC producer and Don Messer's Jubilee tour promoter respectively, arguably the two people whose careers benefitted the most from their association with Don Messer.

Though many in the church have been fans of Don Messer for years, others never had an opportunity to meet this icon of Canadian music. They are here as fans of old-time fiddle music, to show their respect for the man who worked so hard to keep the traditional Irish and Scottish tunes alive, to say thank you and goodbye to the man they spent time with each week when they sat down and watched his show on television.

Don Messer was only sixty-three years old, and his death two days earlier, on March 26, 1973, came as a shock. The news rippled across the nation as different time zones broadcast the story over the breakfast hour, and it spread from cities to villages to houses to kitchens. Messer had been performing since the age of seven, for so long in fact that many had been aware of his music their whole lives. His work ethic was the stuff of legend. As Don Messer and His Islanders and then Don Messer's Jubilee, he and his musicians toured Canada twenty-three times, bringing his brand of old-time fiddle music to large towns and small, to hockey rinks and dance halls, barn dances and racetracks.

He was an innovator: the first Maritime fiddler to perform live on radio in 1929, the first Maritime fiddler to record music onto vinyl in 1934, the first to travel to gigs by chartered aircraft, the first whose band performed live on television in 1956, and, very significantly, the first Canadian to sell a million records. He was one of the first artists to be a recording star, a star of radio and TV, and a live-concert star, all at once. *Don Messer's Jubilee*, his weekly TV show, ran for thirteen years; for ten years, it was ranked in the top eleven, and for two of those years it was number one, above both *Hockey Night in Canada* and *The Ed Sullivan Show*.

The congregation at Don's funeral knew about these public achievements. Unknown to anyone in the crowd was an important private achievement: the amassing of one of the finest collections of rural, folk, Celtic, and old country music scores in Canada.

The mourners queuing outside are no longer able to enter the church; the crowd at the door spills out into the churchyard. They don't seem to mind. The March day is clear and sunny, though snow still lingers at the edges of the lawn, and they are content to gather in clusters, talking quietly amongst themselves, sharing favourite memories. Everybody has a story: the fiddler who once played as a guest on the stage; the fan who received a response to a letter he had written; the family who had a photo taken with Don Messer when his tour bus came to town.

A frisson goes through the churchyard. Despite the din of traffic, they have heard a rustle of clothing and the creak of old wood. Those inside have stood to acknowledge the entrance of the grieving family. Though they cannot see them, they feel that they know them well, can list who is walking in. Those fortunate enough to be inside expect to recognize the individuals, and some of the faces do seem familiar, similar to those seen in the photographs accompanying articles in *Maclean's* and *Chatelaine* during the last few years. They are changed now in grief, gracious smiles nowhere in evidence.

Naomi comes first, dark rings under her eyes, shaken by the change in her status from wife to widow. She will say later that she has no memory of anyone who was present that day. She is followed by her three surviving daughters, Dawn, Lorna, and Janis, and her adopted son Gray. None of the grandchildren are present; Naomi does not want them exposed to the media crush. She wants them to remember their grandfather as they last saw him.

There are sisters and brothers who have travelled from Don's hometown of Tweedside, New Brunswick, extraordinarily proud of their youngest sibling and somewhat amazed at his accomplishments. They are accustomed to well-attended funerals; people in rural communities naturally support each other in times of need. The TV cameras and sound trucks have disconcerted them, as have the print journalists eager to speak with them about their famous brother. They are proud that Don is so well respected, but this intrusion into their grief makes them uncomfortable.

The Reverend Dr. Allison MacLean moves to the pulpit. He glances at the coffin, against which leans a violin made of flowers, a tribute from Don's musicians. This service will not be easy for him. His acquaintance with Don's family began when he was their pastor and friend at Knox Presbyterian Church in Harvey Station, New Brunswick. Now the minister at Calvin Presbyterian, he has continued to be Don's spiritual leader; indeed, he has baptized two of the children. He speaks eloquently of Don, his love of music and church and community. He uses words like decency and generosity, common enough in a eulogy, but there is substance behind his words. He knows that there is much more to this man than was apparent in the figure people saw on television.

He pronounces the benediction and people rise from their seats, glad for the chance to move, to stretch and shift in the straight-backed pews. They feel they have been present at a historic event and are eager to share the experience with friends and family. Suddenly, without introduction, a voice rises from their midst. A man begins to sing alone, his voice so powerful and rich that it reaches every nook and cranny of the church and reverberates off the walls. The mourners hesitate, unsure now whether the service is indeed over. They seat themselves, confused and a little embarrassed that they may have appeared overeager to leave. Jammed together again, they try to crane their heads around to see who is singing.

The commanding tenor voice comes from a man three-quarters of the way back. He is the only one standing now in this crowd of several hundred, but it is difficult to see his features, dressed as he is in a long black trench coat with his hat pulled low over his brow. He sings "How Great Thou Art" in a voice so strong that mourner Bill Guest says, "It could probably have been heard a mile away." Don Tremaine looks at Bill and asks him who the man is, a question that is circulating throughout the church. No one seems to know. That is odd for they are sure they recognize the voice.

The man sings all the verses, his voice rich and pure and beautiful, the voice of a young Charlie Chamberlain before cigarettes and lung disease had taken their toll. The effect on the congregation is like a jolt of electricity. As soon as she is able, with the aid of her family, Mrs. Chamberlain hurries to the back of the church in the hope of speaking with the man, of finding out who he is.

"But the person never came out," says Ann-Marie Chamberlain Doyle, Charlie's eldest daughter. No one remembered him coming in, no one remembered seeing him in the crowd before he began to sing, and no one could find him after the service. Few that knew the group really well had any doubt: it was the spirit of Charlie Chamberlain, come to bid farewell to his friend, to present the final song in the final Quiet Time of Don Messer's final Jubilee.

"You Don't Get Something for Nothing"

The small child creeps up the steep stairs, clinging to the banister, keeping as close as he can to the outer edge of the steps where the boards don't creak. In his wool stockings, he treads carefully on his tiptoes. He is not generally a sneaky child, but today he is on a mission, and he must not be caught.

He reaches the top stair and gazes across the large attic His eyes are blue and trusting, usually full of excitement and just a hint of mischief. Today excitement predominates. He glances at the two doors on the far wall that lead to his sisters' bedrooms. He knows that they are empty, for he can hear Emma, Alice, and Doris in the kitchen with his mother. His brothers are busy milking.

The attic is sparsely furnished, with two beds tucked under the slope of the ceiling — one on the west wall, the other on the east. There is a row of hooks for overalls and wool shirts, farm clothing that never makes its way into the chest of drawers reserved for Sunday best and school clothes. Braided rugs soften the wide pine plank floor, and behind him, what little light there is filters through the window in the peak above the stairs. He can see the yard from here, buried deep in snow, and he checks to make sure that no one is coming from the barn.

Reassured, he scampers across the room to Andrew's bed against the west wall. He ducks down and slithers under the cot. Stretching out his fingers, he touches only air. Momentarily, he fears that Andrew has outsmarted him, has hidden it somewhere else. He wriggles further under the bed, his wool shirt catching on the uneven boards, his fingers probing deep into the dark recesses. He touches something that isn't floor or wall. He has found it, and he lies there, his forehead flat on the boards, as relief and joy flood through him.

Donald Charles Frederick Messer has found his brother Andrew's violin. He knows he is not to touch it, has heard Andrew ask their mother to keep him away from it. That doesn't matter now. He drags the wooden box towards him, backs out from under the bed, and then kneels over the container. It is locked, but he is prepared for that.

Taking the penknife out of his pants pocket, he sets to work removing the screws that hold the hinges in place. In his eagerness, he scratches the shiny brass. He continues unfazed, carefully placing each screw in the candle saucer on the dresser. He knows that, to keep up the deception, he will have to replace them before Andrew returns home. Finally he raises the lid and lifts the violin from its bed of newspapers and old rags. Holding it against his chest as he has seen Andrew do, he takes the bow and drags it across the strings, heedless of the noise that carries down the stairs and into the kitchen.

"The first time he played, I guess he made an awful squawking," said Muriel Martin, his niece.

☙

Donald was five years old when he broke into his brother's violin case in 1914, not even old enough for school. Doing the forbidden thing is not unusual for a five-year-old, and being told not to touch the instrument might have induced him to do just that. Yet Donald's interest was not in the defiance, it was in the violin itself: he wanted to make it sing for him as it did for Andrew. He had been trying to get at it for weeks, ever since Andrew left it behind when he went to work in the woods for the winter.

"It wasn't his first attempt," said Hayes Messer, the son of Donald's brother George. "He was always in where Andrew kept his violin, and his mother would tell him to come out of there."

Margaret and John Messer, Don's parents. Date unknown.

Courtesy: Lorraine Hickey/Messer Family.

Margaret Messer, his pretty and sweet-tempered mother, sympathized with Donald's love of the fiddle. She had a cheerful nature and a lovely voice, and she sang Scottish and Irish tunes as she worked at the endless tasks that consumed her time on an active farm that, in all, had housed eleven children. Though two of her daughters had married young and two of her sons worked away, there were still seven at home, still meals to make and rugs to braid, pickles to prepare and meat to can.

Usually, there would be a quilt in the frame in the parlour. Margaret and eighteen-year-old Alice worked away at it in the afternoons when the sun shone through the window, and they could see to make the tiny stitches. They would hear Donald upstairs in the attic directly above them, running Andrew's bow across the strings, tentatively at first, discouraged perhaps by his lack of skill. Alice went up once to ask him to bring the fiddle into the parlour where it was warm, but he refused, saying he was fine where he was. It seemed he wanted to make the fiddle work the way it did for Andrew, but he wanted to do it privately.

"He'd put the fiddle away," said Hayes Messer. "But he went back to it three or four times, and one day, my gosh, he was hitting a tune, and Margaret could tell that he was kind of touching on some of those old Scottish and Irish tunes she loved so well." They grew very close, Donald and his mother, sharing their fondness for "Haste to the Wedding," "Gloria Moore," "Bonnie Dundee," "Top of Cork Hill," and other traditional melodies.

ↄ

The Messer family had been in Canada for more than seventy years when Donald was born in 1909. William and Alice (Alyson) Messer, his great-grandparents, had embarked from Berwick-upon-Tweed, England. Sailing on the maiden voyage of the *Cornelius of Sunderland*, they arrived at Saint John, New Brunswick, on July 12, 1837. They brought with them four children: nine-year-old Elizabeth, five-year-old Walter, three-year-old William, who eventually became Donald's grandfather, and nine-month-old Thomas. Three more children were born in Canada.

The Cornelius Settlers, as they and their fellow travellers came to be called, started off as part of a larger group seduced by the promises and extravagant inducements put forth by the New Brunswick Land Company. The NBLC had purchased large tracts of land in the Stanley area, but it was in no position to fulfill its commitment to the settlers it had attracted — a year earlier, many settlers of the Skye Party had actually perished. So terrible was that disaster and so outrageous was the disparity between what was promised and what was provided that the Government of New Brunswick put a stop to the NBLC's operation until a new commissioner could be appointed. The Cornelius Settlers wanted no future dealings with the company, and instead they petitioned Governor Sir John Harvey directly, seeking to "be allowed to clear a tract of land . . . to be sold to them at as reasonable a rate as practicable, to be paid for by instalments within a given period." They were not seeking grants; they sought land at a fair price, to be purchased through labour.

The scheme worked out well for all concerned. The governor allocated them land along the new highway he was building from Fredericton to St. Andrews and supplied them with a man to teach them to fell trees. They in turn built the road and used their wages to pay for the land. They named their village Harvey Settlement, after the governor; the name changed to Harvey Station when the railway arrived.

The three generations separating William and Alice Messer and their great-grandson Donald did not dampen the family's love for the music of the border country. Living as they did among the descendants of the Cornelius Settlers only solidified their Anglo-Scottish heritage. Fiddling was a central and important part of that tradition.

こう

The immediate problem for Donald, with Andrew due home from the woods any day, was getting the fiddle and its wooden container back to rights. He polished the instrument to remove any fingerprints and placed it back in the case. Then he carefully replaced all the screws in the hinges. He knew he had scratched the brass, but he hoped rather wistfully that Andrew might think the marks had been there already. He waited and worried, a little frightened of Andrew's reaction.

On his first evening home, Andrew pulled the violin case out from under his bed. He'd missed the instrument and was eager to play. The lock looked sound, but he noticed immediately that the hinges were scratched. He tramped down the stairs to ask his mother, "Has Donald been at my fiddle?" Margaret admitted that indeed he had and that Andrew would be doing him a kindness if he would leave the case unlocked in the future.

Andrew reacted far better than anticipated. "He didn't want to see it broken," said Hayes Messer. The fact that Donald was the youngest in the family probably helped. His brothers and sisters doted on him, warmly teasing him as the "runt of the litter," not just because he was the baby but also because he was tousle-haired, small, pink-complexioned, and the furthest thing from rowdy. Donald (who was never called Don until he became a bandleader and remained Donald to his family his entire life) knew to be careful. Andrew was a very good fiddler, and he treasured that instrument.

Donald also knew that if Andrew went out west that summer as planned, he would likely take the fiddle with him. A lot of the local boys boarded the train in Harvey Station, just sixteen kilometres away, and rode more than four thousand kilometres to Regina to work the wheat harvest. Andrew would be gone from August into the fall, returning in time to head to the woods for the winter. Donald recognized that soon the fiddle would be gone for good. He needed his own.

"But there wasn't much money in those days," said ninety-nine-year-old Emma Treadwell when she was interviewed in 1995 about her brother Donald. "We had a good home, but my father took every cent he could earn to feed his cows and his horses and his pigs. We weren't paupers, but we had no great amount of money. He [Donald] thought he'd buy his own fiddle, so he sent away and got a bunch of chewing gum, and he was going to go around and sell it," she recalled, "to earn enough to buy a fiddle from Eaton's. A dollar ninety-eight it cost. He had pretty good luck selling gum, and he got his fiddle and he learned how to play. He was clear full of music."

That is one version of the story. The other is that Donald's older brothers and sisters got together and bought him that first instrument. Either way, $1.98 didn't buy a good-quality violin, and Donald looked for a better one. He heard of a competition sponsored by a seed company that offered the choice of a violin or a box camera as a prize for selling quantities of seeds. With characteristic determination, he trudged the roads, selling packets of seeds to neighbours and relatives. When he had sold the requisite amount, he sent for his prize. The violin that arrived had been shipped in a cardboard box; it was in splinters, utterly unusable. Donald cried when he opened the package, and then he went back to his Eaton's special.

The Messers may not have had much money, but they were industrious. John Messer, Donald's father, was well respected as a builder. If a barn needed building, John was the man everyone wanted. Almost single-handedly he would trim the logs, lay out the framing, and do the mortise and tenon work to make the posts fit together. When he was ready to erect the frame, all the men in the community would gather to help.

"Same thing with a barn roof that needed shingling, that same group of men would all hit the roof and tear the old shingles off and put the new ones on in a day," said Hayes Messer.

These were the frolics, the times when the whole community assembled to do in one day what it would take fewer men a week to accomplish. They

John Messer, Don's father, date unknown.

Courtesy: Dallas Davis/Messer Family.

worked hard from dawn till the work was done, the barn ready to house the livestock. Afterwards, the meal would begin, a feast with pancakes and pork and pies. Where there was food, there was music. Music in this community meant fiddling and piano playing that got people's toes tapping and heads bobbing, old-time dance music that lifted the heart and brought a smile to everybody's face.

Donald first performed before a crowd at a frolic in 1916. That afternoon, he had ridden with his father in the buggy the ten kilometres to his brother's farm to attend a barn dance. He brought his fiddle with him, and once they settled the horse in the pasture, his father picked him and his fiddle up and carried them through the crowd to the front of the dance floor. There he settled Donald on a box on top of a trestle table so he could be seen and heard. The seven-year-old knew only one song well enough to perform in public, and he played "The Harvey Quadrille" over and over again until the early hours of the morning, when the women served a meal of baked beans, pork, biscuits, and fried potatoes.

Donald Messer as
a twelve-year-old
at Tweedside,
New Brunswick.
Courtesy: Messer Family.

Donald enjoyed performing and people loved the novelty of the child fiddler. With time, he would learn other tunes from his Uncle Jim Messer, his cousins Jimmy, Sandy, and Edison Messer, and his brother-in-law, Margaret's husband, Charlie Bell. When they were still very young he and his sister Emma, an accomplished pianist, were in demand to play at weddings. While the wedding itself was usually held at the church, the party and supper would be at the family home, where a platform for dancing would be specially built next to the house. Sometimes this platform had a roof in case of rain and boards around the base to keep people from falling off. A piano would be rolled onto it, and there Emma and Donald would play. Many years later, Donald recalled that he spent much of his youth looking as if he had the measles as he couldn't swat mosquitoes and play the fiddle at the same time.

"I wish I had five cents for every dance," said Emma Treadwell. "Donald was a good little fiddler. He and I were kept on the hop. We played for dances and took up a collection, a lot of five-cent pieces" that would be put in a felt hat set on the sill.

As small as the take was, Donald was making money from his fiddling. He knew the value of work, was surrounded by people who knew and taught him that you don't get something for nothing; you have to work for what you want. He may have recognized at this time that his fiddling, not farming or sales, might be the means by which he would buy a better fiddle. Borrowing money was out of the question, a principle so ingrained in the family that even as adults they avoided debt.

John Messer instilled other values in his family. While the house might be lightened with the sound of Margaret's singing in the daytime and Emma's and Donald's duets in the evening, the Sabbath was a day of quiet reflection and churchgoing. First they attended the morning service five kilometres away at Knox Presbyterian Church in Manners Sutton, a one-hour trip each way by horse and buggy when the roads were bad. The Messers always sat in the last pew, uncomfortable, though not ashamed that they seldom had a coin to put in the collection plate. After lunch at home, the children would head to Sunday school at the local church, right next to the schoolhouse in Tweedside, and later the entire family would attend evening service there.

Sometimes they might be allowed to swim in the evening, or sing and play instruments, but only sacred music was allowed. "John Messer did not even permit whistling on the Sabbath," said Muriel Martin, his granddaughter. His daughter Emma told how she and Donald broke the rule.

> I always remember one Sunday. I forgot it was Sunday. Usually after we'd had our dinner, Donald would say, 'Let's go and have a tune.' He wanted me to play the piano or the organ, and he was going to play the fiddle. It happened to be a Sunday, but I never thought of it being one. I said 'Okay.' So the two of us went into the parlour to the organ, a great big square Dominion. It was like a piano-cased organ, but it was an organ — you had to pump it. The organ was kept in the parlour, the best room in the house.
>
> We went in and we shut the door, pretty nearly shut it, but didn't close it right up. Of course, when Donald picked the fiddle up, the first thing he would play would be a jig or a reel. Boy, did he ever go for the old jigs! Well, I was right with him, and all of a sudden, the biggest bang came on the door, and that door came right open.
>
> Dad was there, and he says, 'You don't play that kind of music on the Sabbath! Don't you realize this is the Sabbath Day?' No music like that was played on Sundays, no fiddling dancing tunes, gracious no. He put us off that pretty quick. He was a great old dad, but he was pretty strict.

John Messer also laid down the law about liquor. Emma Treadwell recalled, "I used to hear him telling the boys, I used to hear him giving them a lecture once in a while. He said, 'I'm going to tell you right now, if you ever come home and have any of those drunks with you, throw them into the woodshed, just not into the house. I don't want them in my house. Nobody that boozes, I don't associate with them.' So, I guess they paid attention. He didn't care much for liquor, and I never saw the boys coming home full. I never saw them under the influence."

There was certainly liquor around, even though after May 1, 1917, it was illegal to sell liquor except for "scientific, medicinal, sacramental, and mechanical purposes." Prohibition had no effect on the flow of homebrew from the stills in the community. Donald himself was too young at the time to drink, but later he remembered how the performers at dances would take a good swig at the bottle after every dance. "It seemed to keep them going, gave them a bit of an uplift," he said. Hayes laughed when he recalled seeing a horse and wagon trotting past, the man still playing his fiddle as the animal took him home.

Tobacco was another matter. Donald started smoking as a ten-year-old and continued throughout his life, it seems with the tacit approval or at least the acquiescence of his father and mother.

The Messers escaped the Spanish Flu epidemic of 1918, but around that time, Margaret Messer began spending more and more time resting in bed. A once robust and pretty woman, she had delivered eleven children in twenty years. Their birthdates ran like clockwork, starting at nine months after her wedding day and continuing every twenty to twenty-six months: Jannie Maud (April 1889), Margaret "Belle" (June 1891), Norman Allwood (August 1893), Mary "Alice" Victoria (June 1895), John Andrew Moffat (February 1897), Roy "William" (February 1899), George Connell (October 1900), Harry "Leonard" (November 1902), Emma Elizabeth Ellen (January 1905), Doris Mildred Christina (August 1907), and Donald Charles Frederick (May 1909). Margaret was still having babies when Jannie, her eldest daughter, was having hers, and Donald had nieces and nephews his own age. Margaret's illness was thought to be "of the feminine

The Messer family in about 1911. Back row: Donald in the arms of
Margaret Messer, Emma, Harry "Leonard"; middle row: George,
Doris, Jannie Messer Clifford, Alice; front row: John Willis Clifford,
Millard Clifford on Jannie's lap. Courtesy: Dallas Davis.

organs," either cancer or some condition resulting from an injury
suffered during Donald's birth.

"Margaret got poorer and more poorly," said Lorraine Hickey, her
granddaughter. "Donald used to go into her bedroom when she lay
down, and he'd get her to whistle some tunes. She could whistle really
well, and he would learn new tunes that way." The young boy and his
mother spent many hours in this curious duet, the pale woman lying
on the bed, wrapped in quilts for warmth, whistling a Scottish tune,
the then eleven-year-old Donald seated at her bedside, playing by ear,
seeking the melody. Besides these new songs, he had accumulated
an extensive repertoire, having added the songs of his cousins and
neighbours to those that his mother had taught him, and he would
delight in playing for her.

In June 1921, Margaret was scheduled to undergo some medical
tests at the hospital in Saint John. She planned to go down a few days
before her appointment and rest up at the Harrison Street home of

her eldest daughter, Jannie, and her husband, Fred Clifford. George drove his parents to board the train in Harvey Station and then stopped to talk to the physician.

"Dr. Dougan," he said, "Mother won't be back alive, will she?"

Dr. Dougan was noncommittal. "He tried to keep it back, but he knew," said George's daughter, Muriel Martin. "She'd been ill since shortly after Donald was born."

The next time George saw his mother was when he met the train carrying her body back to Harvey Station a week later. She had died at Jannie's house on June 5, 1921, a few days after reaching Saint John. She never made it to the hospital, nor had the scheduled tests. The cause of her death is uncertain, and Muriel Martin said that several other women died with similar symptoms. "Uncle Bill's wife died and Ab Messer's wife. Jim Messer's wife died of the same thing." In each case, the extended families took in the children and raised them as their own, the makeup of the families shifting back and forth as widowers remarried and fathers once more felt able to take care of their offspring.

Donald had turned twelve just a month before his mother's death. He moved to Saint John to stay with his sister Jannie, to whom he remained close for the rest of his life. Perhaps his mother had arranged for Jannie to look out for her youngest in those days before her death. Doris and Emma, two and four years older than Donald, stayed home to assume their mother's domestic responsibilities: to pickle and can, make jam, do the wash, and prepare the meals. George and Leonard, still at home at twenty-one and nineteen years old, would help run the farm.

The duration of Donald's stay in Saint John is unclear, but before too long he returned home to Tweedside, perhaps to finish his schooling, perhaps to be near his sisters. He missed the farm — a place of open pastures and brooks emptying into the Oromocto Lake, of hardwood and softwood forests, of marshes and pools — a place where he could climb to the top of the hill behind the barn and see the fields of three neighbouring family farms in the valley below. He continued in school until he was fourteen and finished the fifth form, but he

The milk truck driving down the Messer farm lane in about 1929.
Donald's Uncle Bill's farmhouse can be seen at the far right of the
photo, his Uncle Walter's farmhouse at the far left.

Courtesy: Lorraine Hickey and Muriel Martin/Messer family.

did not go on to secondary school. His future seemed set; in time he
would follow in his brothers' footsteps, going out west in the summer
and then working in the woods in the winter, or, if he were lucky, he
might get a job with the railway as an engineer. His father thought
that was the wisest plan. "You could always make a living with a
shovel," he had said many times.

Emma, who had always hoped to go to normal school (the precur-
sor to teacher's college), stayed home instead to care for Donald,
Doris, George, and their father. Donald took on his share of the farm
duties. He was still small in stature, but nobody had called him "runt"
in years. It was a good home to grow up in and a good way of life.
There weren't many idle moments, and there were always jobs to do
around the barn. After dinner, when neighbours or family dropped by,
there was music and games, singing and storytelling. Five of Donald's
siblings had settled nearby, and others visited from time to time. On
the rare occasions when something momentous was happening in the
larger world, the boys would walk down the road to the McGowans'

Donald at age nine at the farm at Tweedside, New Brunswick.
From left: Edgar Coburn, Donald's brother Roy, Donald's
brother "Leonard", John Messer, and Fred Pollock.

Courtesy: Lorraine Hickey and Muriel Martin/Messer Family.

house. Mr. McGowan had a crystal radio set, and by turning some
dials, he could tune in to WBZ Radio in Boston to pick up a program
of recorded music and newscasts.

～

At some point, Donald managed to buy a better fiddle from Big Alec
Little, a tinker who made regular trips through the Harvey area.
He paid $12 for it, all his nickels and dimes and likely some of his
mother's precious savings, but its finer quality made him sound like
a real musician rather than like a child trying to copy one. He experi-
mented with his style and reached a level of playing that he had not
been able to achieve before.

With increasing frequency, Donald was asked to perform at weddings and dances. The invitations came from a wider area: not only
Tweedside, but the neighbouring communities of Brockway and
Hoyt, Harvey Station, Lake George and McAdam. At the age of
twelve, he would drive to his engagements in the family Model T

Ford, the headlights of which were powered by a magneto. He liked to drive fast, and the faster the car went, the brighter the headlights would glow. Finally they would pop from the high voltage generated by the magneto, and Donald would have to get out and hang a lantern over the hood of the car so he could see and be seen. Gas was cheap. "A $50-barrel of gasoline would last us a year," said Hayes Messer.

Donald teamed up with other fiddlers, including his Uncle Jim Messer and his brother-in-law Charlie Bell. They played for parties, weddings, barn dances, and other special occasions, and they began to make as much as $5 for an evening. The work was seasonal because getting around the countryside in the winter was just too difficult. The roads were ploughed by the farmers themselves with homemade ploughs and teams, and they did it only once a week so they could get to the store for provisions. Each trip to town took so long that "you pretty well ruined the day" by the time you got there and back, said Muriel Martin. Most people simply put their cars up on blocks and stored them until spring.

Like his brothers before him, Donald went west to work on the Saskatchewan wheat harvest. When he was fifteen, he boarded the train to Regina in early August and joined up with Andrew, who had remained working out there and who would eventually own a large farm. Harvesting was hard work, with long days followed by cold nights in an unheated caboose, where he slept with the rest of the farm labourers. He was appalled that the men working the harvest played cards on the Sabbath, something that he had never seen before. As difficult as the work and living conditions were, he stuck it out to the end of harvest, and then headed home for a stint working on the Woodstock to McAdam railway line. It looked even more certain that Donald would follow his brothers who had gained regular employment with the Canadian Pacific Railway.

There was a pivotal dance to play. On September 25, 1925, Ella Christina Swan married Harold Elmer Langley. Ella was the schoolteacher in Brockway. Harold worked on the railway and was the son of the lady Ella boarded with. Between them they knew just about everybody in the community, and close to three hundred guests attended their wedding. In a break with tradition, the wedding service was held on the house veranda, under an archway of maple leaves. Donald did not play during the service; Ida Little, a friend of the bride, played the piano for that. Donald did play for the wedding dance, and what a party it was. There was enough food for twice the number of guests. The items included 10 nut cakes, 3 fruit cakes, 6 Brede cakes, 7 chocolate cakes, 4 currant cakes, 8 Washington pies, 300 doughnuts, 286 peanut cookies, and 260 cream puffs. Donald played until the food was gone and the sun had risen. At the end of it, he knew he wanted to do this, to entertain people with his violin, and he believed that he could make a living at it.

"He did go into the woods that fall at winter freeze-up, but he didn't stay long," said Muriel Martin. "He took a notion. He had been in the woods, and he took a notion and said to his friend there that he thought he'd go to Boston. They thought he was foolish. But he said that he had a desire to go there and take a few lessons. Grandpa told him, 'You'll never make a living on the fiddle.'"

The Diner and the Five-and-Dime

Sixteen-year-old Donald Messer trudges despondently up Warren Street in the Roxbury district of Boston. He wears a pair of work pants and scuffed heavy shoes that would look out of place in a wealthier part of the city. But Roxbury is an area of immigrants — Scottish, Irish, and German, a few of them Jewish. Like him, they have come to America to escape poverty and bleak futures, and their garb is not unlike his.

Donald wonders if he has made the right decision. Boston is vastly different from Tweedside — a bustling city rather than a quiet farm community. Everyone moves fast, walking as if they know where they are heading, walking with the certainty that they will get there. Everybody, that is, except him. Today, for the second time in three weeks, he has been fired from his job, and he can't understand why.

He reviews his time at Walton's Restaurant. He has arrived early every morning, long before his shift started. He has spoken politely and worked hard, scrubbing pots and pans, running errands, and doing chores. Yet today, the manager told him that he would have to let him go. There wasn't a shortage of work to do: Donald kept busy from his arrival in the morning until he left at night, and he met the new boy, his replacement, when he was gathering his things and getting his final pay. He has to presume that somehow he has failed to live up to the expectations of his employer.

Obviously he is missing something, perhaps some etiquette of city employment. His previous job at Durant's, a restaurant very different from Walton's, also seemed to have been going well. Durant's was for the very wealthy, for people who dined on food that Donald had never eaten, couldn't even imagine eating, like a one-kilogram porterhouse steak, sautéed chicken livers, or oysters Rockefeller, and they ate seated in red leather booths.

Donald was too new to this level of society to recognize any of Durant's famous patrons, but the kitchen staff had pointed out actors and writers and wealthy businessmen seated at the tables. They told him gossip about these people that made him uncomfortable, even though they took it in stride. He doesn't think listening to gossip would warrant getting fired, though, and, as at Walton's, no one ever raised the slightest complaint against him. Tomorrow he will go back to the employment agency. He has no useful trade to offer in a city, but he is willing to work hard at even the most menial tasks.

⌒

Donald was luckier than many. His Aunt Mary owned a rooming house at 1935 Johnson Place, just a few blocks away, and he was well fed and well housed in an attic bedroom. He didn't have to compete for lodgings in this overcrowded city, but he still needed a job. His return to the agency the next morning met with success: he was offered a third chance to make good in the restaurant business. This time, the agency sent him out to Field's Corner, to a Famous Lunch Diner. Donald worked hard for the Greek owner. He was still doing dishes and general chores, but he seemed to be well liked, even appreciated, and he expected to be kept on. He looked out the kitchen one morning and saw the agency manager and the owner of the Famous Lunch in a heated discussion.

It turned out that the "employment" agency was fraudulent. The agent found jobs for men in return for a week's salary, saw to it that the men were fired, and provided the employer with a replacement, who in turn would soon be let go. Donald's boss refused to take part in the scam, and Donald remained at the restaurant for the next eighteen months. It was a menial job, but it came with a distinct advantage. The Famous Lunch was known then for its tiny eight-centimetre-long hot dogs and buns, chili, and rice pudding; it was a place where both families and businessmen liked to eat. One of the daily customers was the manager of the nearby Woolworth's. He noticed this quiet but efficient young man and offered him a position at the store.

As a receiving clerk, Donald earned a salary of $16 a week, with a potential raise of $1 per month if he performed well. More important to Donald's future, this job exposed him to sales and marketing. Woolworth's carried just about everything from hairnets to goldfish, and until 1932, the company sold everything in the store for one of only two prices — either $0.05 or $0.10. The store had a soda fountain and a lunch counter, where Donald could eat cheaply by buying reduced-price meal tickets in bulk. A favourite dish then — Boston baked beans and brown bread — remained a favourite dish throughout his life.

Donald did well at Woolworth's, often staying late to dress the windows for an additional $1 an evening. He was saving money, and indeed there was little for him to spend it on: a weekly trip to the Metropolitan Theater with his cousin to hear performers such as Rudy Vallee, after which they gorged on banana splits; an occasional evening of bowling; or a visit to radio station WBZ, the same station he had listened to on his neighbour's crystal set in Tweedside. He took on a part-time job as chauffeur and learned his way around the city. On evenings at home, he listened to the radio, learning Irish and Scottish tunes from shows like *The Irish Minstrels*, and he practiced his fiddle, adding these new tunes to his repertoire.

Perhaps it was serendipity that Donald lived with his Aunt Mary, or perhaps it was a calculated plan. He had come to Boston hoping to take some music lessons. Mary's large home had formerly been a conservatory of music, and her boarders were a mixed group. It took Donald some time to meet the other residents because he left earlier in the morning than most and often returned later at night. He might have had an opportunity to mingle with them in the evenings when he practised his violin, but his aunt would not let him play downstairs. Donald suspected that she did not wish to appear unsophisticated and countrified in front of her friends and tenants. Whatever the reason, he was once more relegated to playing in the attic.

One of the house residents was Professor Henry Davis, a teacher of violin and piano. He had taught at the conservatory formerly housed in this building, and he returned to live there when Donald's aunt and uncle bought it. One evening, Professor Davis heard Donald practising and asked if he had had many lessons. Donald said no, that he had never had the opportunity to study music but played entirely by ear. The professor was more than a little impressed, declaring Donald to "have extraordinary talent."

Donald didn't take him seriously, and Davis's remarks "went in one ear and out the other." Davis sensed this, and, perhaps fearful that Donald might let his talent go to waste, he offered to teach Donald himself, with help from Edith Hurter, another Boston musician. Regardless of how talented this young man was, Davis understood that Donald would need to know the mechanics of music if he wanted to reach his potential.

Years later, in an interview published in the *Atlantic Advocate*, Don Messer described this year of music theory lessons as an "Alice in Wonderland" experience. "They started me off on scales. I found them pretty monotonous after having played by ear so long. It was terrible to be cut down to nothing but scales the whole time. I had to learn whole notes, half notes, quarter notes, sixteenth notes, and then put them together in a certain time." He found no joy in playing this way and described the lessons as drab. Nevertheless, he recognized the value of what he was learning, and he persisted with the lessons for a year. All the while he continued to play by ear. He found it easy to memorize classical music scores, and he would perform with Professor Davis's string ensemble without any sheet music. At the same time, playing second or third violin forced him to concentrate on the timing of a piece rather than the melody. The skill he developed proved invaluable to him in his future role as bandleader.

Donald progressed steadily at Woolworth's, eventually achieving the post of assistant manager. He learned to select and manage staff, to develop copy for advertising, to order stock, and, most importantly, to manage a large budget. He was in line for a store of his own and a future in retail and business management when he received a letter from his sister Alice, a letter teeming with news of family and home. The Messers always kept in touch with each other through letters, most of them written in pencil on lined paper, but this one struck a poignant chord.

It seemed he was always working, and he had made few friends in Boston. As he rose up the ranks at Woolworth's, he had been advised to stay clear of any social entanglements with his clerks, or indeed with any of his staff. Sensible as the advice was, it made for a lonely existence for a young man used to the gaiety and warmth of life in his home community. Also, his visa was running out, and he would soon have to decide whether he would return to Canada or seek American citizenship. Boston had been good to him, but Donald wasn't ready or willing to cut his ties to Canada.

Exactly when Donald returned to Tweedside is unclear, but he may have seen early signs of the crumbling economy. He knew of wealthy people selling Cadillac cars for $100 cash, of line-ups at banks that did not open. He may have seen evidence of future hardship in his store, as sales clerks feared the loss of their jobs and unemployed maids and other servants came looking for any work he might offer. Perhaps he saw people in Woolworth's who would never have shopped in a five-and-dime store but found they could not afford to shop anywhere else. A man of Donald's determination and resourcefulness might have surmounted the isolation, the changing economic climate, and the expiry of his work visa if each of these difficulties had come singly. Converging as they did gave him strong incentive to move home. He had enjoyed his life in Boston and the benefit of his years there. He had learned music theory and an appreciation for the classical repertoire that would stay with him his whole life. The contacts he had made and the business experience he had acquired would prove their worth over and over again. Still, in early 1929, he was just happy to be heading home.

Donald, newly returned
from Boston, about 1929.

Courtesy: Messer Family.

The young man who returned to Tweedside was a different person from the boy who had boarded the train four years before. Gone was the ill-fitting suit, replaced with one of a more flattering cut that he had purchased in Boston to wear to the theatre. He had a quiet confidence about him now that radiated even from photographs, projecting the impression that his feet were securely planted on the ground; though still slight of build, he would not be easily swayed or dislodged. He had the same open gaze, but now his eyes assessed and took note. He was handsome, almost dapper in his white suit and hat, and he would not have looked out of place on any business street in North America.

There was no place for the suit at Donald's new workplace, so it lay folded in the chest of drawers in that attic bedroom where his school clothes once lay. Instead, he dressed in overalls when he went to work, lucky enough to have found employment with the CPR, lucky enough to have two brothers who were engineers and able to vouch for him at a time when so many men competed for so few jobs. It seemed that he would be a railway man after all.

Living in the CPR bunkhouse, he worked the line from Woodstock to St. Andrews. His experience with a large family stood him in good stead, as did his time working the harvest out west, but life in the bunkhouse took his ability to live communally to a whole new level. He also acquired new management skills. Railway workers generally received $1 a day. The men couldn't afford to squander it on meals in restaurants, so they bought groceries collectively and divided the bill amongst the crew. Donald and the others found ways to feed themselves for $0.19 a day, keeping $0.81 in their pockets for their families back home. Hard as life on the railway was, it reinforced for Donald the need to live frugally, to never assume that jobs or savings were secure.

On his days off, Donald was again in demand for dances and parties, partnering with different performers from the community and sharing the $1.50 the evening's work brought in. There was no demand for his classical repertoire, but Donald continued to play it for himself when he was home, spending an hour or two every day practicing the classical scores that he had learned from Professor Davis. He continued to do this all his life, though only in the privacy of his home or on the road when he was alone and believed no one could hear him. His education in music theory placed him in a select minority. He was no longer just a technician who played only what he heard; he was now a musician with a theoretical understanding of what his ear told him and the ability to read music, which very few musicians of his era could do.

Though they couldn't fully appreciate Donald's new technical skill, the dance patrons did recognize that his style and ability were superior to those of other community musicians. He sounded different, too. Playing more on the lower strings, he gave his music a rich tone and a New England style that he had learned in Boston. He also found a great demand for the Irish and Scottish tunes that he had learned from the Boston theatres and radio programs. He had assembled quite a collection of these pieces by the time he returned to Tweedside; his prodigious memory and faultless ear had allowed him to transcribe them from memory, and eventually he could recall several hundred tunes at will.

⌒

While Donald enjoyed the family get-togethers in Tweedside and loved being near Emma and Doris, whom he had missed so much, he knew he would have to leave again if he were going to succeed with his music. The job on the railway was a godsend, allowing him to contribute to the family rather than burdening them, but he knew that he did not want to spend the next forty-five years as a railway man.

He also recognized that community dances and weddings would not satisfy his hunger to bring his brand of music to a wider audience. His experiences at Woolworth's, at the Famous Lunch Diner, and even at Walton's and Durant's had shown him that he needed to develop a product that would stay in demand, that he could provide in consistently high quality, and that would be identified with him. Only then would he stand out among the many talented musicians in the province.

What he had to do if he wanted to make a career of old-time fiddling was market himself, and Donald Messer, lately of Woolworth's, knew marketing. He recognized that radio was the medium offering the widest exposure and took to spending more time at the home of his neighbours, the McGowans, where he could listen to WBZ in Boston and WGY in Schenectady, New York. He listened to the recorded music with a critical ear, wondering how he could make radio work for him. He had yet to record; he had no disc to send to a station for airplay. Donald was enterprising, and those hours of listening to radio combined with his experiences in Boston and his community frolics, enabled him to come up with an effective plan.

In 1929, Donald wrote to his sister Jannie in Saint John. It had been several years since he had lived with her, and he had matured from the heartbroken twelve-year-old he had been after his mother's death. He was still Jannie's baby brother, and when he asked her if he could stay with her again to give him a chance to pursue his plan, Jannie and Fred welcomed him into their home. They had five children of their own by then, with a sixth due the following May, and it must have felt a little bit like home at Tweedside, with a child around every corner. Donald was especially close to his nephew, Millard Clifford, who was his own age, and they became lifelong friends. Millard had just joined the Saint John Fire Department, which paid him $25 a week, a lofty sum when many of the firefighters and all of the salvage corpsmen were volunteers. He would rise to be captain one day.

As soon as Donald moved to Saint John, he went to CFBO, the recently opened, privately owned radio station. With no recordings, he would have to promote himself as a live performer. Although he had never performed live in a radio studio before, he knew he could play the violin, and he was content to let the violin speak for him. Family connections again paved the way. Fred Clifford, his brother-in-law, knew many business people in Saint John, working as he did as a railway conductor. One day, Fred suggested to a friend, the manager of Atlantic Fish Wholesalers, that it would be a fine idea for the store to sponsor a live performance of Don Messer on CFBO. Such a performance would be a novelty that would garner far more attention than the usual recorded music.

The station manager agreed to give it a try, and Donald then had to find someone to accompany him on the piano. His sister Emma was an excellent pianist despite her lack of training, and he had frequently relied on her at home concerts, but she was married and living in Brockway. He would have to find someone local, someone with talent and enough courage to play live on the radio. A girl named Cathy Orr seemed ideal, and together they practised a few numbers, enough to fill their allotted fifteen minutes. Donald carefully wrote down the tunes in his tiny script. There were seven, none longer than two minutes, and this careful timing left a full minute for the transitions between tunes. This was a practice that Donald kept to his entire life, believing that any tune running over two minutes ran the risk of boring people and potentially losing the audience.

Thoroughly prepared, Donald and Cathy presented themselves at the studio, which was located on the second floor of the Admiral Beatty Hotel on King's Square. The experience proved terrifying, and he still shuddered when he reminisced about it forty years later.

> We arrived at the station to find an old Victrola playing music over the air from a small studio. When the last record was played we had to dash in and attempt to tune up while the station announcements were made. Then the announcer came in, read off the seven numbers

we had written down, went out, and closed the door.
Well, we simply started playing the first tune, and when
that was finished we tackled the next one, and so on
until we reached the bottom of the list. Then the announcer returned and told us the program was over. It
was the longest fifteen minutes of my life.

Donald recognized immediately that he was onto something worth-
while; his conviction that live music would appeal to listeners was
sound. Feedback was good, and the innovation caught the attention
of a businessman, the owner of Kemp Jewellers. What was especially
gratifying was that Mr. Kemp approached Donald to inquire about
sponsoring future programs. Donald's product was now in demand.

Kemp offered to pay $3 per program, $1 each for a band of three.
That wasn't much money, but for a half-hour program instead of a
whole evening of playing at a barn dance or wedding it wasn't bad,
either. Donald took the concept a step further: if one business was
prepared to sponsor his music, perhaps two or three others would
also be interested. They were indeed: he managed to line up five
sponsors for his show.

Then he showed the initiative that would lead to financial success:
he bought a half-hour of radio time, filled it with music, and made
a healthy profit of $4 from sponsorship. Combining income from
playing on the radio with money he made performing for dances,
weddings, and parties looked promising, but the prospect raised a
new concern. To make it work, Donald would need to gather a group
of musicians he could rely on, individuals with both talent and a sense
of responsibility. He needed musicians who could play a number of
different instruments, who could deal with the stress of live radio performances as well as the long days and nights involved in performing
at dances and private parties. So much New Brunswick talent seemed
to have gravitated to Saint John that his biggest challenge would be
to choose the right people for the mix. As it turned out, that was a
knack that Donald had in spades.

Musicians and Troubadours

It is 1934, and Don (as he now calls himself) is in Jannie's parlour, listening to the *Hugh Trueman Show,* an amateur talent program broadcast from CFBO in Saint John, still the only New Brunswick radio station. Don has that look he gets when he listens carefully to someone playing an instrument or singing, attentive to the notes and the rhythm, sensing whether this person has talent or whether he can develop this melody for one of his own compositions. He leans forward, his ear tilted closer to the radio, and his right foot starts to tap. Don hears something in the music that excites him. He doesn't catch the name of the performer, nor do we know whether the fellow won that day, but Don has heard enough to know he wants to meet this young man who plays the harmonica so well.

The next time he meets Hugh Trueman on the street, Don asks him who was playing the harmonica on that show. "Frederick Lawrence Landry," says Hugh.

When Don finally meets Frederick, he talks with him briefly, congratulates him on his playing, and then gets to the heart of the matter he has been waiting to take up with the young man. "What's your father's name?"

"Ned Landry," replies Frederick, thinking they are about to play the Maritime greeting game of tracing family history, determining connections by birth or marriage. That is not what Don is up to. He has decided to hire Frederick, but he has to sort something out first.

The "first photo of the group taken in a radio station, 1929."
Maunsell O'Neil (aka Joe LeBlanc), Eldon Rathburn, Don Messer,
James McCausland, Roy Duplacey.

Nova Scotia Archives and Records Management, *Don Messer fonds*, 1998 – 132/047

"We'll call you Ned," says Don. "Do you want to play for my program?"

"Yes," Frederick answers, and becomes one in Don's band, the New Brunswick Lumberjacks. He is thirteen years old and will eventually be a multi-time winner of the Canadian Open Old Time Fiddlers' Contest and the recipient of both a Governor General's Award and the Order of Canada.

ᓚ

A sixteen-by-twenty-three-centimetre black and white glossy photograph, dated 1929 and captioned "the first photo of the group taken in a radio station," is taped inside the front cover of the first of Don Messer's four scrapbooks. The scrapbook may have been purchased specifically to record this event, the beginning of the next stage of Don's professional development as a musician.

The studio bears no resemblance to today's soundproof and highly technical broadcast studios. It was on the second floor of the Admiral Beatty Hotel in downtown Saint John, likely the same studio where Don and Cathy Orr played their duet. Rectangular in shape, it appears to measure about three by five metres, and the floor covering seems to be linoleum. The studio looks like a dining room minus the table and chairs, but it could just as easily have been a converted guest room. A heavily varnished door and a glass-fronted bureau break up two of the walls. The third wall is hung with heavy floor-length drapes to absorb sound and counteract the hard surfaces of the glass and wood. A square soundboard on a tripod and a microphone stand at the front of the group.

The five musicians in the photograph wear white shirts, suits, and ties. Their shoes are polished to a high sheen and their hair is neatly combed. On the left is fiddler Maunsell O'Neil. He stands at the microphone, the soundboard in front of him, his fiddle and bow at rest. A talented fiddler and performer, he was one of the first men Don hired. O'Neil played the roles of announcer, musician, and sound engineer, and the responsibilities appear to weigh heavily on him. In his persona "Joe LeBlanc, Acadian lumberman," he might open a show with, "Well, I'll be a son-of-a-gun. This is Joe LeBlanc from the Nort' Shore," or at a dance, he might kick off with, "Let 'er go dere, Don Messer, in the key of D." He specialized in corny jokes and tart one-liners. The group loved Maunsell because he worked as a salesman for the Smiles 'n Chuckles Chocolate Company. Even when the financial returns were low, the men got to eat a lot of chocolate.

Eldon Rathburn, only thirteen years old, is in the back left corner of the 1929 photo, seated at the grand piano. He played on and off with Don Messer for the next few years, until he took first place in the McGill University pianoforte competition. Eventually he became one of Canada's premier composers. Rathburn was a rarity: in rural New Brunswick, men played the violin and women played the piano, and he was the first male pianist to work with Don. At the rear, in

An enlarged version of the *New Brunswick Lumberjacks*, 1935,
which sometimes performed under the name Don Messer's Old
Time Orchestra. Duke Nielsen on bass at back right; Sammy Cohen
on clarinet in front of him; Maunsell O'Neil at the microphone;
Wally Walper in cowboy suit on guitar, Ned Landry on harmonica,
Don Messer on fiddle, seated next to Ned Landry.

Courtesy: John Clifford [L. M. Harrison].

the right corner of the photo, is James McCausland on drums. On the
right in front is Roy Duplacey on banjo. Don stands in the middle of
the room, holding his violin in his familiar pose, ready to strike a note.
He is twenty years old and looks impossibly young to be bandleader.

ے

A bandleader he was, though, and Don took to the role in earnest. He
knew what he wanted in performers, and he tried very hard to get the
right mix of musicians. It wasn't just their talent that was important;
they also had to get along as a group, had to pitch in and pull their
weight. Their ability to work well with Don and the others often
determined whether they stayed with the band or their tenure was
brief. Don was as much the Woolworth's manager as he was a fiddler,
and as bandleader, his managerial side dominated.

The *New Brunswick Lumberjacks* in 1935. Back Row: Don Messer,
Ned Landry, Charlie Chamberlain; front row: Duke Nielsen,
Ralph (Jiggy) Watson. Courtesy: John Clifford.

The members of Don's band received a flat rate for each performance, and Don had to divide up the money amongst the players. Thus
he had to keep the group small, but at the same time, he had to
create variety. In auditioning musicians, he seemed to have followed
no standard pattern. Instead, he relied on his keen ear for music and
his ability to recognize people who shared his willingness to work
and perform. There would be many changes to the group over the
years. Duplacey left to be replaced by Sammy Cohen on clarinet.
Wally Walper, who dressed as a cowboy complete with ten-gallon hat,
fringed leather vest, and chaps, joined as guitarist and vocalist, but
sometime in 1934 he left to pursue a successful career out west. Jiggy
Watson came and went, as did trumpeter Harold MacCrae, pianist
Ray Calder, and drummer Gerry McNeil.

The band played under different banners, depending on its size and purpose. When the group consisted of only Don and two others, it went by the name Backwoods Trio. Don often needed a bigger sound, and for that he pulled together a larger group and called it Don Messer's Old Time Band or sometimes Don Messer's Old Time Orchestra. After 1934, he usually performed under the name New Brunswick Lumberjacks, but even that name could mean three musicians or twelve. There was really no consistency.

Don's and the band's fortunes changed substantially in 1934. In that year, he introduced three new players who would take the band to a higher level of performance and set it on the road to fame. Ned Landry had come from a musical family: his uncles were fiddlers, his grandfather made fiddles, and his mother played the accordion. He was already a seasoned performer, playing regularly with the Robichauds at anniversaries and weddings. Life had not been easy for Ned, coming as he did from a poor family living in the slums of Saint John.

"I don't mind people knowing that," said Ned. "We were so poor we had tin tubs for bathtubs." Although the family had managed to pass on their love of music, Ned had not had the nurturing family life that Don had enjoyed. He played the harmonica or mouth organ, and he played it very well from a young age. Like his future boss, he, too, had been attracted to a fiddle, his uncle's, and he had taken it out of its case and tried to play it. The consequences had been dramatically different. While Donald's misdemeanour had resulted in gentle indulgence and encouragement, Ned had been harshly punished. The unfairness of that beating angered his Aunt Rose, and she gave Ned one of her husband's old fiddles. Another relative gave him a bow, and Ned began to teach himself to play. At age thirteen he was helping his family, for when he played at parties, the people gave him a lunch and $0.35, along with the leftover food to take home to his parents.

Two of the musicians who joined Messer in 1934 remained with him until death dissolved the partnership. Julius "Duke" Nielsen was the first of these, a multi-talented man who would eventually play the banjo, guitar, bass, piano, and, according to rumour, twelve other instruments. Duke was the son of Julius Wilhelm Nielsen, a Dane who had been playing cornet in a German circus band when John Philip Sousa heard him and brought him to America. While on tour in Canada, Julius Sr. met his future wife, who played alto horn in the Woodstock, New Brunswick, Salvation Army Band.

Duke picked up music at an early age: by seven, he was playing guitar with his father, and by the age of eight, he played cornet in a Salvation Army band. His father died when Duke was ten, and his mother, unable to support him and his sister, placed them in an orphanage. His sister's fate is not known, but Duke soon fled the orphanage and joined the navy as a boy bugler. The navy did not suit his creative spirit, and, perhaps remembering his father's tales of circus life, he left the navy and joined a circus as a roustabout. It became his chosen family, and he learned new skills to add to those musical gifts that he already possessed. Sleight of hand, sword swallowing, fire eating, and bear dancing were added to his resumé.

Duke was working in a lumber camp in Lepreau, New Brunswick, in the winter of 1934. Circus employment was seasonal and lumbering filled the off time from late autumn until spring breakup. He had ample opportunity to play his banjo and learn other tunes from his fellow loggers, for the evenings were long and cold and the cookstove enticed the men to gather round its welcome heat. Duke must have been a big hit with his music, his magic tricks, and his stories of life on the road under the big top.

When spring came and the woods were too wet to navigate, nineteen-year-old Duke did not go back to the circus. Instead, he took a job as a short-order cook on a hot dog concession cart in downtown Saint John. Late one night, Don and some of his musicians came along the street after performing at a dance. They were hungry and stopped to buy a hot dog. Duke seized the opportunity and told Don that he could play several instruments.

"Well, come on down for an audition," said Don.

"I did," said Duke in 1967, "and I have been with him ever since."

It was as simple as that. Duke never had any opportunity to flaunt his bear dancing talent, but Don frequently called upon his other abilities. With him on board, the New Brunswick Lumberjacks could, like other bands, incorporate vaudeville acts into their performances. Duke's routines gave the musicians a break, created a change of pace for the audience, and best of all, engaged the crowd. What better way to win over men, women, and children of all ages than to draw them in with magic tricks? Duke and his sleight of hand did exactly that for the next thirty-nine years. Even after the band dropped the magic act at break, Duke continued to entertain the members of the band with his tricks.

Charlie Chamberlain, too, fetched up in Saint John in 1934, but he had gone there hoping to find work at the city's port. He had held a variety of jobs since 1924, when his father, the chief of police in Bathurst, New Brunswick, had been killed in a car accident. Mrs. Chamberlain was determined that none of her six young children would ever see the inside of an orphanage. In the days before government social assistance, only one reasonable option remained: the children would have to go out to work. At the age of thirteen, Charlie headed to the woods to help support his family. At the very least, his absence meant that his mother had one less mouth to feed. With his guitar, Charlie soon became a fixture in the lumber camps, singing and playing the songs taught to him by the men of Irish and Scottish descent who worked in the woods, and he learned to step-dance on a platform improvised from barrel tops.

Most recently, he had been working in the woods in the winter and on a road crew in the summer. He was looking for something more permanent when he boarded the Ocean Limited in Bathurst heading for Saint John, where Lydia, his wife, was working. He had his guitar with him, as usual, and he entertained the other passengers by singing his Scottish and Irish tunes. Fortuitously, Lansdowne Belyea, an accountant and friend of Don's, was on the same train. He heard Charlie singing in the next car and went to speak with him. Their conversation was repeated in 1967 to an *Atlantic Advocate* reporter:

"What's your name?"
"Charlie."

"Would you like to sing with a band?"

"Sure would."

"Then I'll introduce you to Don Messer."

Belyea knew that Don needed a vocalist, one who suited the style of his music better than the cowboy Wally Walper. Belyea also recognized that Charlie had a remarkable voice and a gift for entertaining. As good as his word, Belyea arranged for them to meet at the Saint John music store where Charlie's audition would take place. It may have been his rendition of "Lonesome Valley Sally" that won Don over. That and his charm would have been hard to resist, and he was offered a spot with the New Brunswick Lumberjacks. Charlie accepted, but the decision was a risky one. Big and strong as he was, he would likely have been hired on at the port for more money. But Charlie was first and foremost a musician, and the thought of making a living doing what he loved best won him over.

Like Don and Duke, Charlie had been performing for an audience since the age of seven. He had a powerful voice, one which would have benefitted from professional training and learning how to read music. However, his first lesson proved to be his last. Charlie was not ready to have someone tell him how to hold his mouth when he sang, nor was he prepared to have someone criticize the way he breathed. For years afterwards, he would regale journalists with his rendition of that lesson, his eyes rolling as he mimicked poor Miss Agnes Forbes. "I went down there and the woman told me, 'You're not breathing right.' And I said, 'What do you mean? I breathe in and I breathe out.' And then she wanted me to go 'ooooo.' I told her I would be back in a while, but I never went back."

Don, Duke, and Charlie each had enormous talent and musicality, and even Don was, for the most part, self-taught. They were bound by yet another common thread: each had lost a parent at a young age. Don's mother died when he was twelve, Duke's and Charlie's fathers had died when their sons were nine or ten. Perhaps this experience brought them close; perhaps it forged a familial bond they weren't even conscious of. Whatever the reason, these three would work together until death separated them. They were more like brothers than bandleader and performers, and like brothers, on occasion each pushed the others to the limit but never quite hard enough to break the bond.

By 1934, five years after returning from Boston, Don believed he was on the right track. He had chosen his core group well: himself as fiddler and bandleader, Duke as bassist, banjo player, pianist, and vaudeville performer, and Charlie as guitarist, vocalist, and ebullient personality. Not only did they balance each other musically, they complemented one another's strengths and weaknesses. Don's reticence and quiet demeanour in public was hardly noticed due to the effervescence and zaniness of Duke and Charlie.

As well as signing on these stellar performers, Don made another change. The group was not yet making much money, but this was the Depression, and the fact that they could feed themselves was in itself an accomplishment. Regardless of the economy, or perhaps because of the pall it spread, there was new delight in dances and frolics, in opportunities to get together and forget financial woes in favour of joyful music. The band continued to perform for dances and parties, bringing in extra cash as they could, and on occasion they would play for the troops stationed on Partridge Island. Once a quarantine station for Irish and English immigrants, this tiny island in Saint John Harbour by then boasted a small fishing community and a military station manned by the Loyal Company of Artillery. It was by all accounts a dreary posting, and Don and his group were invited over to perform, travelling there and back via the army duty boat. They also brought in a steady income playing the thirty-minute intermission between films at the Franklin Theatres. In addition they took on odd jobs, anything that would pay the bills: Charlie worked for a farmer and Don sold coal and fish. They would not have to do so for much longer.

In the 1930s, the public paid a licensing fee of $1 per year to receive the radio signal. Don learned that there were already five hundred

Don, Duke, and Charlie, the original *New Brunswick Lumberjacks*
playing at CFCY (Charlottetown), 1934.

Courtesy: John Clifford [Craswell Portrait Studio].

thousand subscribers in Canada and knew he had been right to focus
his efforts on radio. With such a big audience, his group would become well known and more and more in demand for private parties.
On April 18, 1934, the then privately owned radio station CFBO
became a CBC affiliate and changed its call letters to CHSJ.

Heading up the station was J. Frank Willis, who called Don one
day with a request. Don had auditioned with him earlier and had been
advised to re-audition with a group rather than as a soloist. It was a
good thing he had. "Can you fill in with a fifteen-minute program
over at our new station?" asked Willis.

It is hard to understand how Don could possibly have made money
on this venture. The sheer magnitude of getting his players to the studio, setting up, playing for fifteen minutes, and then packing up and
travelling home again made a mockery of an hourly wage, but it was
the step that Don had been looking for in his quest for a more reliable
income. He called this first single program *Backwoods Breakdown*,

and it was a tremendous success. Charlie was largely responsible. His rendition of "Weyland's Fate," the story of a gallant lumberjack who drowned when the log-jam on which he was working broke up, brought in a flurry of appreciative phone calls before he had even finished the song. In fact, the audience response was so good that Willis engaged the band to play on a regular basis. Though it was only for fifteen minutes every other week at first, the show was scheduled during the two-hour national broadcast and reached an audience across Canada and into the eastern United States.

∾

Precisely when Don Messer started touring is difficult to establish. He had always travelled, performing in central and southwestern New Brunswick communities. Some weeks he would have a performance on Wednesday in Harvey Station, on Thursday in Woodstock, and on Friday in Hartland. Travelling on tour sounded exciting, but in fact it was exhausting, and the excitement was seldom desirable. Flat tires were a constant problem because of the poor condition of the roads. On one occasion, returning to Saint John from St. Stephen, a distance of 127 kilometres, they had eight flats. Each time they would stop, mend the tire, and carry on. By the time Don arrived home, he was driving on the rims.

In the early days, the men travelled in a Model T Ford, but then, in about 1935, Don's sister Doris loaned him the money to buy a Model A. With the help of the entire family, Doris had gone to normal school, and now she repaid the family by helping Don buy this very necessary vehicle. At first, the group carried their instruments in the car, as uncomfortable as that was, but that became unfeasible as their numbers increased. For some months, they had set up Duke's bass fiddle on the running board and tied it to a door handle. Of course, they reaped the predictable reward of this folly: one day the car was sideswiped by another vehicle and Duke's bass was sheared off. Duke had picked up what was left of the instrument and carried it home in a canvas bag.

Don kept detailed notes about these tours, recording everything from the price of gas to the mileage to the order of tunes at the performances. His first notebook shows that in June 1935, he put 1,531 miles on the car, using 51 gallons of gas at a cost of $15.30 and 8.5 quarts of oil at a cost of $3.20. In July he put a further 1,605 miles on the car, in August another 2,482 miles. On another page is a program, nine carefully laid out tunes starting with "Rag Time Band" and flowing through "Kid Steps," "Lullaby Boy," and "Old Time" to the final

Doris Messer, at the time of her graduation from normal school, 1926.
Courtesy: Dallas Davis and Lucille McCrae.

"Old Timer Finish." Here, too, are each player's earnings: Charlie Chamberlain, $2.00; Jim McCausland, $2.50; Eldon Rathburn, $2.50; Rae Simmons, $2.50; and $2.00 for the host. Admission was $0.25 but included "free smokes." They made good money that night because they had a sponsor, Eastern Bakeries, but when Don added up his expenses, the picture looked less rosy. It cost him $0.50 for his bed and $1.40 for meals ($0.70 each for lunch and dinner). He noted that he slept late and thus didn't have to pay for breakfast.

After the bass was destroyed, Don built a trailer to carry the instruments. He was mechanically adept and had enjoyed tinkering ever since, as a boy, he had made water wheels for the brook behind the house. He used this skill to convert the rear end and wheels of an old car into a trailer. Then he added a canvas cover to protect the instruments.

Even with the instruments safely lodged in the trailer, the Model A remained too small to hold all the musicians, so they took turns riding in the trailer. Duke, a member of the militia, had a warm army greatcoat, and whoever was relegated to the trailer also got to wear the coat. It was the only way to keep warm. On one occasion, young Ned Landry glumly climbed in and wedged himself as low as he could among the instruments, snuggling deep into the coat and pulling the collar up around his ears. They set off, behind schedule, and Don, always a fast driver and always fretting about being late, stepped on the gas. To his surprise, the car ran very well, and didn't lose any power going up hills, which seemed odd. He glanced in the rear-view mirror, rather pleased that the trailer was such a resounding success, and saw that there was in fact no trailer following behind.

Don slammed on the brakes and turned the car around. All the men were terribly worried; they couldn't afford to lose any more instruments. Any thought of Ned completely slipped their minds, so preoccupied were they with the scene that might greet them: an over-turned trailer with violins, drums, bass, and guitars strewn across the road, or worse, crushed beneath the trailer. Fortunately, the instruments were fine and so was Ned, though he was justly disgruntled that it took them so long to rescue him. He spent the rest of the trip lying across the laps of the back-seat passengers, with Charlie rubbing his feet to restore feeling to them.

Don and his troupe did suffer another financial setback on their return from a tour in the Kouchibouguac area. They had seen a farm-house on fire and had stopped to help put out the blaze but, unable to make much of an impact, they had set off with Don at the wheel. The others soon fell asleep. Sixty-four kilometres northeast of Moncton, Don felt heat on his neck and pulled over, only to see the trailer go up in flames with all their clothing, instruments, and equipment. The only instruments unharmed were the two violins in the car. The damage was estimated at $500, a loss that took months to recoup.

The New Brunswick Lumberjacks continued to earn a steady if small income from radio, but it was not sufficient to support them and their growing families; they had to keep performing in the communities. There is no question that the group loved the work. Don was happiest when playing his fiddle and entertaining people with his special brand of old-time music. Unlike other bands of the time, the New Brunswick Lumberjacks and Don Messer's Old Time Band performed a set program with very little downtime. On a Saturday night, they started at nine o'clock and continued until midnight, never playing past twelve because of the Sabbath. There would be one square dance of about fifteen minutes per hour, and in the middle of the evening they took a fifteen-minute break. They performed the rest of the time, and their audiences loved it.

A poster from the Old Time Harvest Dance at the Chapel Grove Country Club depicts the flavour of their shows: "Let the old timers come and show the young people how to dance the old time dances the way Mother used to do them. Gents 35 cents. Ladies 15 cents." Another announcement said, "Something out of the ordinary in entertainment is promised local citizens when Don Messer's radio orchestra visits Campbellton tomorrow evening. Messer's orchestra includes leading artists in their line, and those planning to attend the entertainment may expect an exceptionally fine program." This event included a buffet luncheon.

Touring served several purposes, keeping the band in the public eye and building an audience for the records that Don still planned to produce, even though RCA Victor Company had turned him down in 1934. Don was disappointed but undaunted; for him, building the business was vitally important, but he was keenly interested in the music itself, in hearing the jigs and reels and waltzes particular to a community or geographic area. Often at dances an old-timer would approach him and ask if he knew a certain song. If he didn't, he would ask the person to play it for him after the show, and Don would laboriously transcribe the tune. He not only kept the music he loved alive, he spread it around.

Unfortunately, this eagerness to share was not always reciprocated. In 1933, George Wade and His Cornhuskers, a well-known Toronto band, appeared in Saint John. They had been unable to perform a requested polka, and Don had been summoned to the stage from the audience. After the show, he had written to the band and requested a couple of their tunes. He was both surprised and hurt when he didn't receive a response.

The income from touring was minimal, but it was money at a time in the Depression when a man couldn't buy a job. The musicians would try to get home after their performances, but if that wasn't possible, they grabbed sleep whenever and wherever they could. They had money only for necessities. Charlie recalled, "We didn't have enough money one night to sleep in a rooming house, but we had this old pup tent with us, so we slept down on the beach. We woke at five in the morning, the tide was coming in, and our feet were getting wet." They slept on church pews and on dance hall floors, but most often they slept in the car. Don seldom let anyone else drive, so while he navigated the roads with the aid of headlights that were about as much use as a candle, they bundled themselves in their coats and dozed off.

Meals were irregular and often consisted of crackers and sardines, perhaps left over from the performance in Blacks Harbour when the sponsors, unable to meet their guarantee, had paid them off in cans of sardines. Even if the band played late, the men would try to get up early so they could take advantage of breakfast specials: baloney sandwiches, a plate of beans, and a cup of coffee. Charlie used to joke that they were so poor the mice used to walk across the floor with tears in their eyes. Don added, "I think not only the mice. I think we did the same thing."

There were no roadies then, and the men had to set up their own equipment, give their performance, mingle with the crowd and sign autographs, and then pack everything up and head home. Because they had no microphone, Don always tried to book a hall with good acoustics. "We played a lot of theatres because of that," said Ned. Some of the buildings they played in were appalling, and more than once they arrived to find that the piano onstage was not only out of tune but missing a few keys.

Those were the days of gumboots and plaid shirts. "We thought we were pretty hot," Don said later, but there was good reason for the functional attire. Many dance halls were on farm land or beside railway tracks, and the men often as not had to trek through mud to get to their venue — a venue that would be lit by kerosene and heated only by the warmth of the dancers. It came to be known as the Kerosene Circuit.

Don and his band didn't travel beyond the Maritimes in the thirties, but at that time, the Maritimes to all intents and purposes included Boston and the Eastern Seaboard. The route between the two was known as the Irish Corridor, so numerous were the immigrants from overseas who left the Maritimes for the more prosperous job opportunities in the United States. In the 1800s, this practice caused the New Brunswick legislature to lament that New Brunswick was left with the ne'er-do-wells, because all the immigrants with ambition took off for the States. As much as the United States had gained in workers from Canada in the past, musicians in Canada now reaped the benefits of close ties to Boston and New York.

The New Brunswick Lumberjacks gave a performance in Boston on New Year's Eve 1935, a performance the Saint John papers covered, including the details that "1936 appeared in the form of Miss Marnie Fournier in black shorts and black silk stockings, breaking through a paper screen which covered the door into the hall." Reassuringly, it was also noted that the "chaperones were Mrs. Nix, Smith, Morse and Coffyn."

Later in 1936 and again in 1937, Don took on the role of tourism tout for the Province of New Brunswick. For six weeks in 1936 and four in 1937, the New Brunswick Department of Natural Resources hired him and his New Brunswick Lumberjacks to travel to Boston for the New England Sportsmen's Show. The chance to perform in the United States brought several benefits to the men, including a base salary and an opportunity for exposure. Any Boston-area bookings were a bonus; the most important exposure resulted from the publicity that ensued back home. Maritime papers treated Boston as a very important city for the Maritimes, and local papers were far more likely to carry news from Boston than from their own community.

When the boys went to Boston in 1936, they did their gig at the show dressed as "real" lumberjacks, costumed in wool plaid shirts, breeches, and boots. The stage was set up in front of a log cabin which had been carefully shipped by the province and reconstructed below a huge map of New Brunswick. Government officials extolled "the sporting and scenic attractions of their native province" and sold "time" in the log cabin while the band presumably exemplified the warmth and charm of New Brunswick hunters and fishers. The effort was very specifically designed to promote New Brunswick as a fishing and hunting destination for the affluent families of the Eastern Seaboard. It was extraordinarily successful: fifteen thousand people visited the show twice daily, and the province arranged for the group to go down again in 1937.

To travel to Boston for just this show would not likely have been worth the cost and aggravation for Don. Union regulations required them to get permits six months in advance, but once he had the permits, if he could set up additional performances while they were there, he had a chance to turn a tidy profit and garner more exposure. In 1936, he did just that, booking them at spots as diverse as the Brookline Country Club, where they performed for the Roosevelts, and at radio station WHDH. Don's efforts paid off. When he and the New Brunswick Lumberjacks were invited to take a test at NBC, all the papers reported that "Don and the 'Jacks were the first Canadian band east of Montreal to pass." Success in the States was clear proof they had made it, that they were recognized outside New Brunswick. Few Canadians at the time could make such a claim, and nothing would increase the group's marketability more.

In 1937, when the New Brunswick Lumberjacks returned for a repeat appearance at the Sportsmen's Show, they achieved even greater success, but at the price of nearly losing Charlie. They were invited to perform on *Major Bowes Amateur Hour*, a very popular program heard over CBS radio. To be invited to appear on this show was without precedent; Major Bowes supposedly received fifteen hundred

letters a day from aspiring competitors. Charlie was the star of the
show, and he was invited back for future competition. At the end of
his run, he was offered a chance to perform at the Silver Slipper, a
New York nightclub with a clientele of businessmen and entertainers.
Jimmy Durante, the headline attraction the evening Charlie was to
perform, sat in the audience to listen to this young Canadian. So impressed with Charlie was he that he spoke to a Hollywood agent who
offered Chamberlain a contract. Luckily, Charlie was not interested.
He didn't want to leave Canada, and he didn't want to leave Don and
Duke. The three of them had become a tightly knit family.

Duke did leave briefly in 1937, joining a Montreal hotel's chamber
music quintet. During his time there he auditioned for and won a job
with the Benny Goodman Canadian Tour. Benny Goodman was the
undisputed King of Swing, but fortunately Duke left the band and
returned to Saint John at the end of the tour. Don needed him if he
was to take advantage of an opportunity coming their way.

Between 1934 and 1939, Don's connection with the CBC through
CHSJ had its ups and downs. *Backwoods Breakdown* enjoyed great
popularity with listeners, but in 1936, CBC management decided to
cut the proportion of music on the network from seventy per cent
to fifty per cent, and Don had to make sure that the New Brunswick
Lumberjacks didn't get lost amongst all the other musicians vying for
a piece of that reduced percentage. He achieved that by promoting
himself and his band, by constantly performing on the road, and by
showing up when he was scheduled to do so — an uncommon virtue
in the business.

At other times, such commitment wasn't enough. In 1936, Don
sent a letter to Frank Willis, the regional manager:

> I see by our evening paper here where Mr. Bert Anstice
> (and his Mountain Boys) is again starting a new ser-
> ies of programs this Saturday night at eight o'clock.
> I certainly can't see any justice in Mr. Anstice getting
> another program after his supposedly dirty work last
> fall with the Commission. I can't understand why he's

given preference to my outfit, after all this type of music
originated here in the Maritimes and why should we
have to listen to made-up stuff from Upper Canada? I
certainly have been made to wait for all that I have got
and I still think my music is superior to Mr. Anstice's.
Why not have our orchestras alternate week about if it
could be arranged, or give each fifteen minutes weekly.
After all, it would be fair play.

He then reported on the turnout for his band at the New England
Sportsmen's Show and their successful tryout at NBC, where they had
been invited to play a daily program and would likely have done so
had they not faced union problems. Finally, he launched into another
attempt to make Willis see reason: "Getting back to the Commission,
would it not be possible to give us a thirteen-minute or half-hour period weekly for the summer months? I am just asking for fair play in
regards to Mr. Anstice." He closed the letter, requesting a favourable
reply, and signed it "Yours truly, Don Messer."

Don also complained privately to his friend Roy Duplacey, by then
living in Kirkland Lake, Ontario. Roy replied, "So you found out just
what the Radio Commission is. You are right, that's all they are, a
political bunch."

Don's radio work did not dry up, as he had feared, and by 1938,
Backwoods Breakdown was receiving more fan mail than any other
show except the *Happy Gang*. They played five evenings a week for
fifteen minutes, with a wrap-up half-hour program on Saturday evening. That success seemed irrelevant to the CBC executives. With yet
another change in administration, all performers had to re-audition.
Though Don repeatedly asked to be included in the fall lineup of new
programs from the proposed CBC Halifax studio, he heard nothing
back until the following spring.

On March 6, 1939, Don finally received a response from George
Young, Regional Program Director, CBC Halifax. It was not what he
wanted to hear. Young's letter was brief and to the point: he couldn't
accept *Backwoods Breakdown* at the present time, but "you can rest

assured that I will be in touch with you later as I definitely have you in mind."

Being borne "in mind" would not pay any bills, nor was it definite enough to warrant staying put in Saint John. War was looming, and rent was expensive, so Don took his family home to Tweedside for the summer. Living on the farm would let him save some money, and he could help George with haying. He had missed his brothers and sisters, and he was keen to spend time with them and give them a chance to get to know his wife and his two young daughters. They had a lot of catching up to do. Don also needed time to consider his future.

While he was at Tweedside, he received a telephone call from Art McDonald, who was then program director at radio station CFCY, the CBC affiliate in Charlottetown. McDonald offered Don a position as music director and orchestra leader, a challenging job because the station served the whole Atlantic region, the Gaspé, and the Eastern Seaboard of the United States. He accepted, on one condition: that they hire Charlie Chamberlain also.

Family Life: The Early Years, 1932-1939

Don sits at the kitchen table in Tweedside in August 1932, composing a letter to Naomi Gray of Saint John. He has been at it a long time, is having difficulty finding the right words. The Sunday stretches out in front of him. Not much happens on Sundays on the Messer farm.

He stares at the paper and his loopy pencilled scrawl. The beginning is okay, he judges: he has told her he is thinking of her and hopes she is well. But the rest of the paragraph gives him pause; he has filled it with news of the hay crop, his brother's serious injuries after a near-fatal accident, and a description of the truck smashed to pieces.

He sits back, looks out the kitchen window, and then starts to write again. His next paragraph is a mixture of longing to buy his uncle's farm and realization that Naomi would not be happy living there. He worries that she will have another boyfriend by the time he gets back to the city.

Don is smitten with this young nursing student, whom he met when he visited his sister Jannie in the hospital. Naomi is beautiful, tall and willowy, with large brown eyes set in a heart-shaped face. He worries that she will get lonesome while he is away helping George with the haying and go home to Belledune, worries that she will not approve of his farmer's tan. He finishes the letter, addressing her as "old Sweetheart." He recognizes that this is not a very romantic letter and acknowledges, "I am no good at writing love." He closes it with "a big kiss and lots of hugs" and a drawing of a square with "Donnie and Nonnie" inside it.

A few days later, he writes another letter. This one assures her that even though he went to a dance, he left in less than an hour as he found no enjoyment without his "Nomas." Even though he and she have their spats, he says, he wouldn't give her up for any of the girls there. An update on the state of Uncle Jack's piles spoils the romantic mood somewhat, but he signs off with "oodles of love and kisses to his beloved goldfinch."

Seven days later, Don writes to Naomi from Saint John. He went out the previous night to see *Rider of Death Valley* at the movies, he tells her, and then he treated himself to a visit to the ice cream parlour, as he used to in Boston. He sends this letter to Belledune, where Naomi has gone despite Don's entreaties to stay in Saint John. He notes with relief that his brother-in-law Fred Clifford saw her off and reported that she was "all smiles." It seems that Naomi is not always an easy person to be with, that she has a way about her when she is not pleased. Don reminds her that she has promised to give up smoking, though they have quarrelled about that. Like the first letter, this one ends with an apology. "These are not much like love letters, but I still think an awful lot of my Nomas. Thousands and thousands of bushels, Don."

Don is making money with his music. On the previous Thursday, he played at a dance and made $1.75, an amount that satisfied him very well. On the past Saturday, he had performed at "Billies," and he has a private party booked for the following Wednesday. He is confident that he can make a go of it and suggests to Naomi that they get married. The proposal could hardly be less romantic, coming at the end of a letter, almost as an afterthought: "Well Nomi, I will close now as I have to get dinner for myself. This bachelor business is no good, so I guess I will have to get hitched. How about it?" He somewhat vindicates himself with "Huggs" and a stick drawing of them kissing. Naomi is not swept off her feet by this declaration, and it will be months before they marry.

~

Naomi Dorothy Belle Gray was born May 19, 1913, to a Protestant farming family in Hodgin Settlement, New Brunswick, the youngest of twelve children for Steven Hodgin Gray and Ellen Eliza Pike. She was not the least bit musical, said her nephew Jack Gray. None of the Grays were, "couldn't carry a tune if they put it in a bucket. And I don't think she ever liked the violin much, she was Don's greatest critic when it came to that."

Her family's story reads like a history of rural New Brunswick working life. Her eldest brother, Burt George, was killed in the woods by a bolt flying off a donkey engine. Her second brother, Myles Stephen, went down in quicksand while working on the harvest in California. "He surfaced a week later," Jack said. The third brother, Gleason Sanford, and a friend died on Gleason's birthday, driving over the ice bridge to Detroit from Windsor, Ontario. Their bodies were still in the car when a fishing boat snagged it in the spring. Ellen Eliza, Gleason's and Naomi's mother, went to claim his body for burial, even though the coroner had no way of identifying him other than by the car. "Take off his right boot," she had instructed. The old scar across his big toe told the tale. She knew it was Gleason, for he had injured his toe while splitting wood.

The fourth brother, Joseph Greenless, met a different end. He had had surgery for an ulcer and was on his way to the doctor for a check-up when he ran into Billie Killoran. There was no love lost between the Grays and the Killorans in those days, said Jack, and the two were arch enemies. They got into a fight, and Joseph died. None of these brothers had lived long enough to celebrate his thirtieth birthday.

Clarence Henry, the fifth brother, would grow up to become Jack's father. He and Naomi were very close, and she missed him terribly when, as a young man he spent six months in a sanatorium because of his tuberculosis. It would eventually kill him; the TB combined with the treatment resulted in sepsis, and he died at the age of forty-four. Only one brother fared well: Oswald lived into his nineties. All of

Naomi's sisters — Annie, Grace, Nellie, Drucella, and Bertha — lived out normal life spans.

The Gray farm was large. They grew just over 240 hectares of potatoes, sold pulpwood, and raised beef, pork, and vegetables. It must have been a sad house in many ways — the death of her first four children through mishap and the fifth by disease weighed heavily on Ellen Eliza. She had birthed each of them in the upstairs bedroom, the one the stovepipe ran through and kept warm, even in the depth of a New Brunswick winter. It is hard to imagine how she kept going, how she had the courage to invest love in the remaining seven children. Grace Smith, one of Ellen Eliza's granddaughters, remembered her as "distant," not as affectionate as her quiet husband, who was, said Grace, a wonderful, kind, low-key person.

Naomi was close to her father, sisters, and brother Clarence but not to her mother, and she left Belledune as a teenager to train as a nurse in Saint John. Her sister Nellie, whom she adored, was there already, and she would board with her. She didn't have time to miss the family. Nursing training was difficult and engrossing, and she had little time to fret or to socialize with anyone. When she met Don at the hospital while he was visiting Jannie, his quiet, soft-spoken manner reminded her of her father.

Don was instantly taken with her, and courted her by writing to her nearly every day and sometimes twice a day when he was travelling. They were extremely close, said Grace. "He idolized her. Naomi was the centre of everything for Don."

On her part, Naomi may not have thought much of the fiddle, but she did respect what Don was trying to do. She sold tickets at the door when he performed in events close to Saint John. He played quite often at the Crystal Palace in St. Stephen, and he and Naomi would take advantage of that opportunity to visit Tweedside. Don's family liked and admired Naomi and visits were always cordial. Naomi's parents, however, didn't approve of her choice. They had not yet met Don, but he was a musician, and that said more than enough for them.

John Messer with George's children at Tweedside, New Brunswick, 1940s. John Messer, Vaughan, Hayes, Eugene, Lorraine, and Muriel.

Courtesy: Lorraine Hickey and Muriel Martin/Messer Family.

Not surprisingly, none of Naomi's family were invited to her and Don's wedding but then, neither was Don's family. The reason became obvious years later, when Dawn, their oldest child, was helping her mother search for legal papers after Don's death. "Mom couldn't get the safe open," Dawn said. "She had never opened it before. I helped her, and right on top was their marriage certificate. Mum got really upset when she realized that I had seen it. I didn't know why, and then I noticed the date. She was several months pregnant with me when they got married. It suddenly made sense to me why they never celebrated their anniversary." The date on which they said they married, April 5, 1934, was not the real date. They never would have felt comfortable celebrating either the real date or the make-believe one.

What Naomi never knew was that one of Don's brothers had been curious (or nosy) about the coincidence that their first child appeared exactly nine months after their supposed wedding date, and he had gone to Saint John to look up the actual date of their marriage. The entire family was aware of the situation.

Jannie and Fred gave Don and Naomi the use of their cottage on Treadwell Lake for their honeymoon. It was freezing cold in the frame camp, and they didn't stay long, although they would continue visiting that cottage for many years. When the Cliffords built a big camp in front of the old frame cottage, a large group of family and friends and sometimes members of the band would gather there. At those times, there would always be music and step-dancing. Don carried a square board in the car for these occasions. He would put it down on the floor before he began to step-dance so that he wouldn't ruin the linoleum. Don knew from experience what damage foot-stomping could do: once he had played at a dance where the dancers punched the knots right out of the floorboards. There was lots of dancing, but, said John Clifford, Jannie's grandson, "I don't remember Don or Naomi ever going in the water when they visited. They didn't like to swim, but they would come and spend a few days." Sometimes they would pack a picnic basket and take a Saint John riverboat up to Gondola Point to have lunch there.

The newlyweds moved into a cold-water flat in Saint John. Naomi, her training finished, worked in a doctor's office, earning a steady if small income. Don received small paycheques from CHSJ for his then-regular radio show, *Backwoods Breakdown*, which was broadcast nationally. Performing at dances and other events was his financial mainstay, but this income was sporadic and he had to spend a lot of time away from home to earn it. The apartment was sparsely furnished

Vella Clifford, Don Messer, Naomi Messer, Rae Simmons,
Florence Clifford, and her husband Millard Clifford at the cottage
at Treadwell Lake, New Brunswick, date unknown. Courtesy: John Clifford.

with only a bed and a set of table and chairs built by Fred Clifford.
They lived on gruel made of potato and corn, and sometimes — when
the money went to pay other bills — only of potato.

Don's family continued to keep in close contact. His sister Alice
lived in Chapleau, Ontario. They listened to his program on the
radio, and she assured him that "fifteen minutes wasn't long enough,
but we sure look forward to the nights you're on. I seem so overjoyed
that I can't as yet realize it is you." The closeness of the Messers is
heart-warming. Alice went on to say, "I trust you make a good hit
with the public and that you'll be on more often. Suppose Andrew

hears you, too, it's wonderful isn't it? It almost seems like a family visit when I sit there and listen in." That same familial dedication to watching Don would repeat itself when he went on to television, with his extended family gathering chairs and "getting as close to the TV as we could. We certainly listened to him," said Alice. Her husband, Walter, for his part, would wish that the show ran for a couple of hours, because "fifteen minutes is not long enough. We just get nicely interested when you ring off. You boys can sure make her ring."

Don and Naomi settled into married life of a sort. He was often on the road, and he just made it back from Boston in time to be with Naomi when she went into labour with their first child. She was born on Valentine's Day 1935, nine months after their fictitious wedding date. They named her Dawn Penelope — Dawn for a new beginning and Penelope for the goddess of great patience. Ecstatic, they wrote letters to all their relatives telling them their wonderful news. Nine days later, Don received a letter from Boston, from his aunt with whom he had lodged. "I am glad your wife is all over her suffering and you are a Dad now . . . well Donald, I wish you all the luck that a Dad can have." The next night he was back on CHSJ radio, and his normal fifteen minutes had been increased to a half-hour. It must have seemed a good omen to him.

When Don performed at weddings, dances, and other functions in the thirties, he earned only a pittance, but he gave the appearance of wealth, for he drove a car and wore a suit. It was not unusual for someone to approach him and offer to sell him something of little — or, on occasion, great — value. A fellow might approach him after the performance, as the band loaded up their gear, or he might wait by the exit, calling out to Don, "I have something to show you that I might sell for a price." Then he would bring out from under his worn clothing a fiddle and a bow. If Don felt that the man needed the money to feed his children, he would buy whatever was proffered. He didn't need another violin, certainly not one of the calibre that was offered, but if there was any way possible, he would buy it and take it home to Naomi. Over time, he purchased fourteen violins this way.

Don always paid cash. Naomi was the one who bought a violin

on credit from a music store in Saint John. Don had seen it one day when they were courting and had told her about it, how he had been taken by its quality and the resonance of its sound. It was more than $100, and Don would not buy it on instalments. He was still the child of Tweedside: if he couldn't afford to pay cash, he couldn't afford the item. Naomi was working then, so she went in and negotiated with the store owner. For $5 a week, she could buy the violin. It took her almost six months to pay for it, but this French-made violin would always be Don's favourite. He played it for the rest of his life, and he left it to his family when he died.

Letters flew between Don and Naomi while the Lumberjacks were in Boston representing New Brunswick at the 1936 New England Sportsmen's Show, and these letters give an intimate picture of their lives. Naomi's were often addressed to "Dearest daddy," a role Don was always thrilled with, and signed "Naomi and Dawn, the two that love you the most." Naomi wrote of her sadness without him: "I was awfully lonesome after you left and still am. I don't know what to do with myself."

Naomi told him about Dawn's development: she was beginning to speak, and when Naomi mentioned his name, the little girl looked up at his photograph on the wall. Dawn seemed to have endless colds, but "I put raw eggs in her milk now, and I think it is helping her a lot." She treated her own cold by rubbing her chest with camphorated oil. The apartment building was bitterly cold. "Well daddy," Naomi wrote, "it has been terrible cold here since you left. I thought sure I would freeze my rear lighting the fire in the morning." In fact, it was so cold that Dawn slept in Naomi's bed fully clothed in leggings, wool coat, hat, wool socks, and mittens. Even Jannie's home on Harrison Street, lacking insulation but far better constructed than Naomi and Don's flat, was heated only by the kitchen stove, burning coal twenty-four hours a day.

Amid the news and love notes, questions arose that hinted of worry about the future and their financial well-being. After the New Brunswick Lumberjacks' NBC audition in 1936, Naomi asked, "Are you going to be on all the NBC networks or has that fallen through?" In another letter, she lamented, "I soon won't be able to write to you (no stamps). Down pretty far aren't we?" Her next letter was even more worried: "The baby also needs medicine, but don't get discouraged pap. You will be saying I'm still nagging. Don't worry about Dawn, she is on the mend."

These letters must certainly have worried Don, who was working so far away, but they candidly reveal how difficult life was for Naomi. They were broke, and, because of the baby, she wasn't able to take on a nursing job. Hospitals were leery of hiring married women, and in any case the shifts were far too long to accommodate the needs of an infant.

As discouraging and harping as Naomi could be — and she did acknowledge this bent when she wrote to Don, "if you would kick my rear when I get in a tantrum, maybe I wouldn't be so hard to get along with" — she could be wonderfully supportive of him. On February 12, 1936, two days before Dawn's first birthday, she wrote, "So glad you are at last getting a break. There have been some great write-ups in the paper." There was apparently a photograph, too, showing Maunsell O'Neil and Charlie Chamberlain. Naomi couldn't find Don in the picture, but "the background was blurred so perhaps you were back there." Indeed, that's where he was, standing in his usual spot at the back of the stage.

That letter included another worry. Not only was Naomi terribly lonesome and unable to settle down to anything, but, she complained, she was ill, she had been ill ever since he left. "You know what kind of sickness I mean. I am getting so weak and no sign of it stopping either. If things were otherwise, I would go to a Doctor, but what's the use?" Even so, she sent "Barrels of Love and Kisses." Everything seemed to indicate that Naomi was pregnant, but there is no mention of a child or pregnancy loss. While Naomi was ill, Don felt neglected, not having received as many letters from her as he expected. He reported that he was well and had taken in a hockey game, a sport for which he had a great passion. When he wondered if she listened to his show and whether she liked it, she replied enthusiastically that it "sounded real snappy."

Money remained an issue. Naomi had had to borrow money from Jannie to pay the oil bill, but, she reported, the coal was holding out well. Don managed to send her $8, enough to pay $4 on the grocery bill and $2 on the insurance, with $2 extra for the milkman and paper boy. This pleased Naomi, and she promised him that she'd be "in the mood for love" when he arrived home later that week. She also mentioned that there might be a bit of railway work for him through Fred Clifford.

Naomi had heard a segment about Don on *Radio Ramblings*, a report that he had secured a six-week contract with radio station WHDH, Boston. This wonderful news bode well for their future, she thought, but she feared she would go crazy if he didn't come home soon. (The opportunity came to naught because of music union restrictions.) Almost at the end of his stay in Boston, she asked Don if he had seen anything of "my royal family" — three of Naomi's sisters lived in the Boston area. (He had not. Apparently, her marriage still rankled with them, and none of them attended his shows.) Then she closed with, "I suppose if you are making any money, I will have to put up with Dee Dee and myself for awhile," and signed her letter, "Big hugs and Kisses, from Mum and Dawn."

These letters were a lifeline to Don, who missed his family as he worked so far from home to build a future for them. More than thirty years later, he spoke of his realization about how difficult it was for Naomi and Dawn home alone in Saint John. "I was just as lonesome for them as they were for me, but I just couldn't bring myself to give up the violin; it had become part of me."

When Don was at home, sitting on the front step, relaxing and watching the neighbourhood remained one of his favourite pastimes. Dawn's first memory of her dad is of sitting with him on the door-step at her Aunt Jannie's house on Harrison Street, Saint John, just enjoying the afternoon together. Perhaps her mother was busy with the new baby, born a few months earlier on January 30, 1938. This second daughter was called Lorna Naomi, a combination of Lorna from the romantic heroine Lorna Doone and Naomi's own name. Dawn's second memory is of the day in May 1939, when King George V and Queen Elizabeth visited Saint John: her father lifted her to his shoulders so she could see the royal couple over the huge crowd. Only a few months later, Don's big break came. The family would leave Saint John and move to Charlottetown with the promise of a secure job and a chance to set down roots.

The Road Well Travelled

Canada declared war on Germany on September 10, 1939, and thirty-year-old Don left for Charlottetown soon after. He bundled Naomi and the two girls and Charlie, Lydia, and their four children into the car and then filled their laps with containers of clothing, housewares, and sheets. Boxes of pickles and preserves were tied to the fender, furniture to the roof. They looked like a Gypsy caravan.

Don was excited about this new opportunity. Keith Rogers, who owned radio station CFCY in Charlottetown, had received his first commercial radio licence in 1925 and had promptly set up a studio in his house. By 1935, he was ready to expand his operation from his sole Prince Edward Island station and liaise with private broadcasters across the country. Unable to manage the radio station and the expansion by himself, he had hired L. A. "Art" McDonald to manage the operations. That was the clincher for Don — he knew and respected Art from his time in Boston, and he looked forward to working with him.

The salary was less than Don had been earning at CHSJ, but the $12.50 a week he was offered came with a contract and a title: "musical director and orchestra leader." He saw a future here, a chance to turn his music into a secure and well-paying job with some permanency. The fact that the job came with an office and a studio felt like a commitment, and he was tired of operating on a hope and a prayer. He would initially do a program of old-time music once a

The boys relaxing on Prince Edward Island, about 1940. Back row: Duke Nielsen, Ned Landry, Don Messer; front row: Rae Simmons, Charlie Chamberlain.

Courtesy: Chamberlain Family.

week, but he expected that if he could make this program successful, it would expand into something much bigger.

McDonald had to fill the position of music director because, at that time, radio stations (and, later, the pioneering television stations) needed house bands to play interludes and introductions to programs. George Chappelle and His Merry Islanders were regulars on CFCY, and Chappelle likely expected to be awarded that job. McDonald and Chappelle did not always work well together, and, as it became clear that Canada would go to war, several of Chappelle's regular players had enlisted in the Armed Forces. Their personality conflict and Chappelle's having lost his key players worked in McDonald's favour, and he brought in Don Messer.

Charlie Chamberlain came to the Island with Don, and Ned Landry followed soon after. Duke Nielsen hesitated at first, but he, too, eventually moved over. However, Don needed more musicians for a stable, regular house orchestra. In short order three of Chappelle's musicians switched to Don's band, either fortuitously or because Don poached them. Rae Simmons played the clarinet and saxophone. Like Duke, he had received his training in a Salvation Army band. "He had learned to play clarinet at school but would race home every day at noon so that he could practice on one of the instruments that he had

Don Messer and His Islanders, circa 1940. Back row: Rae Simmons, Duke Nielsen, Bill LeBlanc, Charlie Chamberlain; front row: Don Messer, Jackie Doyle. Courtesy: John Clifford [Craswell Portrait Studio].

borrowed from the band," said his wife Shirley. "He played the clarinet and saxophone equally well but preferred the sax." Bill LeBlanc became Don's new drummer, and Jackie Doyle became his pianist. Together they became known as Don Messer and His Islanders.

The first program ran on November 11, 1939, about a month after Don had arrived in town. Art McDonald acted as MC, a role later taken by Rae Simmons, and the first tune was Don's own composition, "Operator's Reel." The program was an immediate success and Don kept his fingers crossed that he would get more time on air. While he waited for that to happen, he scraped tanks at the Irving Oil refinery to make ends meet. Charlie made extra money Simonizing cars.

In short order, Don got his wish: *Don Messer and His Islanders* went to air twice and then three times a week at three p.m. Don knew then that the move had been a good one for both the group and the family. Keith Rogers was on the leading edge of broadcasting, and Don had confidence that he would prosper under his tutelage. The appreciative Charlottetown audience frequently packed the station's viewing gallery three deep to watch the show, and that bode well for attendance at dances. The station shamelessly plugged the band's appearances on the *Outports* program daily, so wherever they appeared they were greeted by a large and receptive audience. The Islanders were, in effect, the station house band and enjoyed all the benefits of that relationship.

Don more than lived up to his part of the bargain. He would go in early every morning, often arriving during the morning religious broadcasts and thus came to know most of the clergy. Then he would go home for lunch with Naomi and the girls and return afterwards to the studio. "We used to watch him leaving the house at one o'clock on Mondays, Wednesdays, and Fridays for rehearsals," said his neighbour. "You could set your clock by him. He hated being late."

Now that Don and his band were no longer independent but obliged to play on the radio three times a week, they had less freedom and time for road trips. Because of the war, concerts and dances would focus more on the war effort than on Don's personal appearances. Any revenue in excess of the guarantee now went to the military's mess funds. The rules that accompanied these new responsibilities were even stricter than Don's own.

Keith Rogers was a military man by training and by nature. His rules were clear. Band members received fees of $25 or $35 or one-sixth of the income after necessary deductions for travelling, with the understanding that if bad weather or other unforeseen circumstances should interfere with a performance, the amount might be reduced by Mr. Messer. They must practice complete sobriety at all times, and if they failed to do so, Mr. Messer must discharge them without consulting the station. Bickering or arguing over payments and fraternizing with members of the Armed Forces were forbidden, and attempting to steal the girlfriends of civilians or soldiers would be met with instant discharge. Mr. Messer was expected to report on the behaviour of his men every two weeks.

Don Messer and his musicians on tour at Sunny Brae, Pictou County, Nova Scotia, 1940. Back row: Bill LeBlanc, Duke Nielsen, Don Messer, Tex Cochrane, Jackie Doyle, Charlie Chamberlain; front row: Ralph Watson, Rae Simmons, Jim Morrison.

Courtesy: John Clifford.

The war years were good years for Don, keeping him closer to home on a day-to-day basis and allowing him more time with his family. Don Messer and His Islanders played for many dances at the Armouries in Charlottetown, which gave the wives of the band members a chance to attend. Partly out of patriotism, they played for hundreds of servicemen at the RCAF station in Summerside, Prince Edward Island. Initially these young men didn't appreciate Don's type of music, couldn't understand the attraction of square-dancing. Before long, he converted them and, not incidentally, developed a faithful audience that, after the war, would disperse to all corners of Canada.

In 1940, the Islanders started to take longer trips, leaving Charlottetown for weeks at a time and travelling to all three Maritime provinces and into Quebec. Don called his Pontiac his eight-manpower car because it took eight men to push it up every hill in Nova Scotia and along the Gaspé coast. Frequent trips on the ferry to Nova Scotia to perform at the military messes in that province gave Don opportunities to strike up conversations with other fiddlers, compare notes, and try to track down more and more elusive tunes. Eventually, the band chartered a seven-passenger Gipsy Moth aircraft to make the passage across the Northumberland Strait from Charlottetown to engagements in Truro and Halifax. The *Dartmouth Free Press* reporter Helen Hogan voiced the feeling of many: "We sure appreciated the *Islanders*. . . . Give them a call and they would fly over for about $25."

In 1944, Norm Ripley was a soldier in the Irish Regiment waiting to be posted overseas, and he saw Don and the band perform in Mulgrave, Nova Scotia. "Some talked between sets to use up time so that they could play less; his attitude was different," he said. Don was there to provide good value for money. Later he would charge $0.50 for the concert and then have an intermission. After the intermission, audience members could buy tickets for the dance that followed for an additional $0.25. Most patrons paid the $0.75.

Don's structure of offering a stage show and a dance as part of the same program was new, and other groups did not copy it. As late as 1946, the Glace Bay newspaper noted that "somewhat of an innovation was introduced last night — a concert prior to the dance." Don continued his policy of asking for a set fee, and once this guarantee was met, the fundraising body that booked him kept the rest of the gate. The Kinsmen sponsored the dance in Glace Bay, and others were held under the auspices of such diverse groups as the Freemasons, community hockey rinks, the Muscular Dystrophy Association, the Women's Missionary Society, and Fredericton Little League.

Still other dances were booked by farmers who staged a barn dance every year and paid a guarantee, keeping the rest of the revenue. Patricia Ross of Truro remembers Don Messer coming to her brother's farm before the hay was put in and while the cows were still out to pasture. The dance was held in the hayloft, but she was never allowed to attend because she was too young.

Halford Hall in Harvey Station, New Brunswick, was a frequent stop on tours. It was, after all, close to Tweedside and Don's family, but it had other advantages. The acoustics were tremendous: the lay-out of the hall, with the stage in the middle of a long wall, meant that the sound was good anywhere people stood. Best of all for the dancers, the floor was springy. Hayes Messer, Don's nephew, remem-bered Halford Hall well. It was the scene of his one and only "guest appearance" with his uncle's band.

> They quite often arrived up home at the farm in the afternoon before the performance, and most of the band would be with him for a visit, and sometimes they would stay for supper. Uncle Don asked me if I would take part in his show that night.
>
> 'No, I will not,' I said.
>
> 'Now look,' he said, 'you don't have to do anything. I want you to help Duke Nielsen with something.' Duke did magic tricks on stage.
>
> 'No, no, I don't want to do it.'
>
> 'Look,' he said. 'Duke will just start his show there at the break in the music. All you have to do — when they ask for someone to come out of the crowd, you get a seat in the front and you just jump up there and come on up.' Well, Lordy, I didn't want to do that. I was fourteen or fifteen. 'You don't have to say a word. You just help him.'
>
> 'So what do I have to do?'
>
> 'Well,' he said, 'I'll tell Duke that you're going to do this.' And he turned and said to Duke, 'He's going to help you with your act tonight.'

That evening Hayes went to Halford Hall, paid his admission at the door, and made his way to the front row, as directed. The hall was not fancy, with benches around the perimeter and rows of chairs with boards laid across them to provide seating for the stage show. The audience members were dressed in their best, the men often smoking pipes, even while they were dancing.

Hayes sat quietly, getting more and more nervous as the set wore on. He had no idea what Duke had planned for him. He had seen his ribbon act, in which Duke kept up his patter to disarm the audience and then, all of a sudden, pulled ribbons out of his mouth and hung them on a hanger. There would be more than a dozen of them by the time he finished, all of different colours and each almost a metre long. Hayes hoped he wasn't expected to do that.

When the time came for Duke's performance at intermission, he called for a volunteer from the audience. Hayes was chosen, and up he went on the stage.

> Duke tied a necktie onto me, and then he cut that necktie into a dozen pieces with a pair of scissors and put them into this paper bag. Then I had to repeat after him these magic words. I just about went through the floor. The whole time, Uncle Don was standing over in front of the piano with a big grin on his face. I pretty near choked. Anyway, Duke had this magic wand, and he circled that over the bag. Then I don't know what all he said, and then he turned around two or three times and he said, 'So what do you think of me cutting your necktie all to pieces?'
>
> I said, 'I didn't like it. You'll have to replace it.'
>
> Duke said, 'We'll see what we can do.'
>
> He put his hand in the bag, and he pulled the necktie out the way he took it off me, all in one piece. Everybody in that hall, well they hollered and whooped. There was hardly a person in that hall that didn't ask me, how did he do that? And I said, 'I don't know.'
>
> Well, Uncle Don, he laughed over that.

In 1942, drummer Warren MacCrae came on board. He had been playing drums since age ten, had been a member of both his school band and a Salvation Army band, and by the age of twelve had been playing with dance bands. He was a surprising candidate for Don Messer and His Islanders, having more education than the rest of them put together. By 1942, he had a Bachelor of Arts and a Bachelor of Education, but for unknown reasons, his teaching practicum had not been successful. He was planning to enter law school when the chance to play with Don Messer presented itself. Warren had so much fun that he abandoned law school forever.

Don Messer and His Islanders had become so popular that the show was moved from its regional daytime slot to seven p.m., a prime spot, three days a week on the CBC Trans-Canada network. Then, in 1945, the government chose the Islanders to boost the spirit of Canadians in the services, and the program *Friendly Voice of the Maritimes* was heard in special wartime broadcasts co-produced by the BBC.

"We used to listen to the Monday, Wednesday, and Friday show at the supper hour," said George Breckenridge, whose father once worked with Charlie Chamberlain in the woods. "We had the old battery radios, and you could only turn them on when the battery came back up, so we turned them on to hear *Gabriel Heater* from New York, to get the war news, and *Don Messer*."

Nineteen-forty-seven was a watershed year for the Islanders: Don hired Marg Osburne, the only woman who ever became a full-time band member. Don included many female guest performers, some of whom performed frequently, but Marg was the only real Islander. She was born on December 29, 1926, and, like Charlie's family, hers was made up of singers rather than instrumentalists; her maternal grandfather had a huge repertoire of folk songs. Most of the family members had a piano or organ in the house, and family get-togethers revolved around music. They sang a lot of hymns — Marg later told journalist John Braddock that she learned to sing harmony by singing hymns with her brother.

Marg had no plan to make a living from music, but when she was sixteen, a cousin bet her $5 that she wouldn't enter a competition sponsored by radio station CKCW in Moncton. The prize was a job singing on a weekly broadcast of Western songs, likely a forerunner of today's country and western material. Marg had sung in choirs since childhood and was comfortable in front of an audience, but she had never performed in a studio, nor had she ever sung with a microphone. She quavered her way through the audition. To her great surprise she won the job, and for the next two years, billed as "the girl from the singing hills," she went into the studio once a week to sing old-time Western songs.

An announcer at the station made a recording of Marg and sent it to Don for consideration. Although Don saw no role for Marg at that time, he said he was prepared to contact her if he had need of another vocalist. Before long, that need arose: Charlie Chamberlain had been badly injured in a car accident. Would Marg consider joining the group until Charlie had recovered? She jumped at the chance. Marg had blossomed from a nervous amateur to a professional performer in those intervening years. Having dropped out of school to pursue a musical career, she was eager for the opportunity that working with Don Messer would provide.

The choice of Marg was remarkable, given that the rest of the band was male and in their twenties and thirties. Likely, Don was thinking mainly of her radio experience; he would hardly have considered it suitable for Marg to join his all-male band on tour. Her job interview was unlike any other that Don had conducted. Her father, Jarvis Osburne, accompanied Marg to Charlottetown to meet this potential employer and ensure that his daughter would be well cared for. The interview may have gone well, but Mr. Osburne nevertheless insisted on escorting his daughter to all rehearsals and meals over the next three days. He returned to Moncton only after he felt certain that he had found her a suitable boarding situation and the men in Don's group would behave in a gentlemanly fashion toward her.

When Charlie recovered, said Marg, "They couldn't get rid of me. We became fixtures on the show, there was no separating us."

Don Messer and His Islanders with Marg Osburne, 1947.

Courtesy: John Clifford [Tweel].

In 1949, Don felt that he was ready to branch out, thanks to the fan base his radio program had built outside the Maritimes. His first annual summer tour took him to Ontario where square-dancing had become something of a new craze. The response to his brand of old-time music was remarkable. In June that year, five thousand people attended the Islanders' performance at Toronto's Mutual Street Arena. Billed as a square dance, the tickets went for $1.25 each, which brought $3,125 into the group's coffers. Marg Osburne recalled the scene in 1967; it remained as vivid to her then as it had been eighteen years before. "There were tiers of people standing on the floor before the stage. No one was dancing — just standing. And they remained there all night, watching and listening, and they continued to stay until the very last song." More interesting was the impact that Don Messer and His Islanders (and some of the other bands) were having on Canadian cultural awareness. The Ontario Department of Agriculture had begun sponsoring square dances to "foster rural community spirit," and the Department of Education regularly held square dances in elementary schools to "acquaint city schoolchildren with the pioneer culture of their ancestors."

From Toronto, under the auspices of the 4-H clubs, the Islanders went on to tour Guelph, Smiths Falls and Kingston, Pembroke and Renfrew, Cornwall, Cobden, and Arnprior. They headed to Kirkland Lake, where Roy Duplacey had moved when he left the group in the early thirties. He was thriving in this northern mining community, performing as the Hobo Banjoist, and Don had continued to keep in touch with him, though he had resisted Duplacey's repeated entreaties for him to move to Kirkland Lake and form a partnership.

The tour was hugely successful and made a great deal of money for the host organization. Don had asked for a guarantee of only $500 for each performance, vastly underestimating the popularity of his music and the enthusiasm for it. The band members signed thousands of autographs, recognizing with some satisfaction that the demand attested to their growing popularity.

Two other long-term players joined Don Messer and His Islanders in the early 1950s. First, guitarist-fiddler Cecil (Cec) McEachern came on permanently in 1951, although he had played with Don previously, going on the 1949 tour. Then, in 1952, when Jackie Doyle left, Waldo Munro came to Charlottetown for an interview. Don had invited him to the house on Belmont Street to try out on the family piano. Grace Smith, Naomi's niece, was visiting her aunt and remembers a man coming to the house for an audition. Grace had heard that he was a left-handed pitcher famous in Pictou County, Nova Scotia, for having pitched a no-hit game. She didn't know much else about him.

Like so many of the others, Waldo had fallen in love with music as a young child; he had started teaching himself to play the piano when he was nine. At the age of fifteen, he had taken a few theory lessons, and his improved talent got him a job first with a country music group, the Peerless Entertainers, and then later with a jazz band, the Royal Swingsters. Somewhere along the line, he learned to play the trombone, too, but it was the piano that Don heard him play. He was amazing, even to the young Grace, who sat enthralled in the living room listening to him play in the Harlem stride style of Fats Waller. Don hired him on the spot.

At first, Don Messer and His Islanders — all those men and Marg

Don Messer and the Islanders on tour in 1949, Guelph, Ontario.
Back row: unknown, Duke Nielsen, Charlie Chamberlain;
middle row: Warren MacCrae, Jackie Doyle, Marg Osburne,
Rae Simmons; front row: Cecil McEachern, Harold MacCrae,
Don Messer. Glenna M. Wilson.

— travelled by car when they toured. The trips were rough, for while the cities and towns had paved roads, Messer ventured far afield. In 1952, they pressed further west. From Fort William, Ontario, to Winnipeg, Manitoba, they drove at times on roads that were simply poles laid crosswise in the mud. Mud was everywhere. "It built up like putty," Don said, "all over your boots, all over the scrapers, and then all over the bedroom floor. You had to undress on the bed." Between small prairie towns, most of the roads were gravelled at best, and Don's impression was that "from ten miles outside of Regina, one could point the car for the city and take off," so flat and treeless was the landscape. They took to carrying along cans of gas in each car because the service stations were so far apart. Beyond the Prairies, they moved on to British Columbia, to the Okanagan Valley (the prettiest place in the world, according to Don), Nelson, Penticton, Kelowna, and Revelstoke. Everywhere, thousands of fans turned out. That surprised Don because the fiddling tradition was different out West. Fiddlers there played in the Metis tradition with more of a swing, and he had not been sure how well his brand of playing, with its strong rhythm or beat, would be received. He needn't have worried.

The Islanders headed back through the Prairies with the same tumultuous response, but their pace began to wear on them. The travelling was as exhausting as the schedule. In one forty-eight-hour period they drove about twenty-four hundred kilometres and performed two shows, with no time to sleep. They couldn't keep that up. They were playing more than paid performances: they gave free concerts in sanatoriums, at the Saskatoon Penitentiary, and at hospitals for the mentally ill. At every location they built a fan base, not just for their music, but also for their professionalism. They were always on time, they did what they said they would do, and they raised a great deal of money for community endeavours. In the 1940s and 1950s, the Islanders toured Canada seven times by car and station wagon on roads that often were barely passable. It was said there wasn't a back road or concession line in the entire nation they hadn't travelled at one time or another. Through it all, Don cemented his deep and abiding love of his country.

What of the downside to touring? Don toured because he believed it was the best way to market what he did, but on a personal level, it was hard for him. A fastidious man, he liked his own toilet and his own bath; he hated using public washrooms. He missed his family and especially Naomi. At times trying to keep order in the group made his job a misery. On top of everything, as well as performing and leading the band, Don single-handedly took care of programming, payroll, contracts, schedules, transportation, and the playlist. Especially in the early years, Don may not even have made much money. In fact, despite his careful planning, the cost of travel, food, hotel rooms, and all the extras such as laundry and dry cleaning may have eaten up a lot of the anticipated profit. Occasionally, he actually went in the hole, paying his bandsmen's share out of his own pocket.

In 1953, the group went to Newfoundland, but the turnout in St. John's was so dismal that he turned around and went back home. He blamed the poor attendance on lack of publicity, but his brand of music never did catch on there. They learned a valuable lesson and made certain that in the future there were advance press releases heralding their arrival. So the band wouldn't be entirely dependent on ticket sales for revenue, they continued to sell autographed photos of themselves to fans, and eventually they developed souvenir trays and programs to sell. In the thirties, such sales had often paid for the gas to get to the next gig.

In 1955, Don's situation changed radically. He suffered a heart attack and had to delay joining the tour. The others went on ahead without him, but it soon became obvious that the tight control Don exerted on the group, as annoying as it was to them, served a purpose. Also apparent was that Don would have to accept help — he could no longer carry the entire load by himself.

Family Life: The Middle Years, 1939-1955

Don is about as content as he has ever been. The move to Prince Edward Island has been good for his family and his career, giving him the financial security he has longed for. He has a full-time job at CFCY and a band that has come together well, playing to packed houses when they tour and to an appreciative radio audience when they are home in Charlottetown.

He and Naomi have bought a house, something he thought might not be possible as little as two years ago. They have moved out of the duplex on Chestnut Street and into the small one-and-a-half-storey frame house on Belmont Street, up by the racetrack. It is not an elegant address, situated on the wrong side of the tracks, but it is a decent address, and the house has a large garden, perfect for his growing family.

The Messer's house on Belmont Street, Charlottetown, Prince Edward Island. Johanna Bertin.

Naomi, Dawn (front), Lorna, and Don in Charlottetown, Prince Edward Island, about 1940. Courtesy: Lucy McRae and Dallas Davis/Messer Family [Craswell Portrait Studio].

Don feels blessed by the birth of a third daughter, Brenda Gail, in September 1943. She was premature and weighed only a few kilograms, but she has done well and is now a thriving eighteen-month-old. She is a cheerful child, enjoying the attention of a protective mother and two doting older sisters, by then eight and five. Don and his youngest have a special relationship, perhaps because he missed so much of Dawn's and Lorna's early life. When they were little, he was constantly on the road, establishing himself and his band as worthy of notice.

He goes into Brenda's bedroom for the nightly ritual. As soon as she sees him, she grasps the rail of her crib with her pudgy hands and pulls herself up so that she is standing, her face almost level with his. She bends her knees and then straightens them, bends them again and begins to bounce in anticipation of a rhythm that she knows well. On her face is a look of adoration, and she giggles. Don takes a deep breath and comes close to expelling it, almost overcome with the contagion of her laughter. He gathers himself and launches into the song that she loves so well, "Pistol Packing Mama." Brenda giggles, she gurgles, she shrieks with unadulterated joy. He finishes the song and starts over again, unwilling to end the moment even though he knows Naomi will be annoyed with him, will tell him off for exciting Brenda when she should be settling for sleep. When he has finished, he kisses the little girl on her forehead and she lies down, a smile curving her cheek. It is as if she and he have a conspiracy to protect their special time together.

∾

Life was good as Don and his band gained a reputation and a following. *Don Messer and His Islanders*, his weekly radio program on CFCY, Charlottetown, had been increased to two and then three broadcasts a week. Then the program moved from the afternoon to the seven p.m. prime spot on CBC's Trans-Canada network. He and the station manager, Art McDonald, developed an excellent working relationship based on mutual trust and respect, and at last Don had had a chance to record some of his own compositions using the radio station studio. Long over RCA Victor Company's 1934 rejection, he now had a contract with the Compo Recording Company of Lachine, Quebec. To date the band had recorded "Operator's Reel," "Belfast Jig," "Cock of the North," and "Ploughboy's Reel" on the Apex label, and soon he would start receiving the royalties at the rate of $0.03 per radio play, not for the traditional tunes, but for his own compositions. Three cents was not a lot of money, certainly, but it came without extra work, and every penny counted. No longer would his family's security depend on his public performances. A National Film Board movie about him and his music called *NFB Shoots East*, made in 1943, gave him national exposure and brought in requests from across the country for the Islanders to perform at fairs and arenas. Don didn't yet feel ready to branch out beyond the East Coast. For now he was happy staying in the Maritimes.

Then everything changed. The girls had been coughing a lot lately, didn't seem to be able to get over their colds, and Don came home from the studio one day in March 1944, to find that Lorna and

Brenda had both been diagnosed with whooping cough. In the days before antibiotics, this was frightening news. The family existed with little sleep. Don would rock the girls at night, giving Naomi a rest, trying to comfort the girls when they couldn't sleep for the paroxysms of coughing that would overtake them. The Board of Health tacked up a sign on the door cautioning others to keep away, but strangely they allowed Dawn to continue attending school. She alone had escaped the whooping cough; perhaps her resistance stemmed from an unrecognized bout among all the colds she had suffered as a baby in Saint John.

Within a few weeks, both Lorna and Brenda seemed to be recovering, and Don and Naomi allowed themselves to relax. Brenda still seemed a little fevered, so Naomi arranged for the doctor to make a house call. Don looked forward to getting a better sleep that night. Instead, he got a phone call that tore his world apart. Naomi, hysterical, begged him to come home from the studio. He left immediately and drove the short distance home to find the physician, Naomi, and their neighbour, Kaye McInnis, in a state of turmoil.

Naomi had put Brenda down for a nap after bathing her. Knowing the doctor was on his way, she had gone to change her own dress, wanting to be presentable when he arrived. Lorna was having an afternoon nap, and Naomi, not hearing Brenda, thought gratefully that she had been able to fall asleep. When Naomi entered her daughter's bedroom to check on her, she detected a quality of stillness not normal in a sleeping infant. Brenda was not asleep, she was dead. They learned later that the whooping cough had developed into pneumonia.

Don and Naomi, in shock at the sudden death of their youngest, had an immediate problem. Lorna was still asleep, but Dawn was due home from school soon. Don set out from the house to intercept his eldest daughter. Dawn remembers that day as if it were last week. "I came down the road from school. I was nine and in grade three. Our house was next to the railroad tracks, and I saw Dad walking back and forth along the tracks. He was never home at that time of day and he never walked there, and I knew right away that something was wrong, terribly wrong. He was looking at me, just kept looking at me as I walked towards him. Then he told me about Brenda."

Brenda's death signalled the beginning of a very dark time for the Messer family. They held her wake at the house and then carried her casket to the church for the service. Somehow they got through the funeral with the help of the band members, all of them coming to the house afterwards for cake and tea and drinks while Lorna and Dawn stayed in their bedroom. Don returned to work the next day, but his friends and neighbours remember him suffering terribly. Naomi sank into a deep depression.

Not only had she suffered the loss of her youngest child, but, because of her status as the wife of a popular musician, their tragedy was public. She received letters from strangers, one of which suggested that, as sad as her baby's death was, at least "there must be consolation in knowing that she died in peace and in the presence of those who loved her — not killed by bombs, machine guns, or in a concentration camp as so many other babies do in other lands." As inappropriate as the letter was, it must have meant something to Don, for he placed it in his scrapbook. Naomi remained unwell. Her weakness and lethargy grew worse until Don needed to hire a woman to help with the children. Naomi then took to her bed, too weak and ill to leave it. The doctor prescribed another pregnancy, the only thing he believed to be successful in bringing women out of the profound grief that Naomi was suffering. Within a month, Naomi indeed became pregnant, but her health did not improve as expected, and eventually her doctor ordered tests.

Naomi was diagnosed with tuberculosis, like her brother before her and later her niece and her mother. Her pregnancy was very difficult; her disease exacerbated her exhaustion and depression. To ease the loss of Brenda, she and Don planned a memorial for their baby, eventually settling on the idea of donating a furnished room for the Sunday school at Zion Presbyterian Church, at the corner of Grafton and Prince streets in Charlottetown. The brass plaque states only that the room was furnished by Mr. and Mrs. Don Messer; it makes no mention of their loss of Brenda.

❧

Janis Veda was born January 4, 1945. Don chose her name as he had the names of the other girls, calling her after Janus, the god who looks ahead and behind, perhaps to recognize the loss of Brenda and the hope of a new beginning with this little girl. He was very close to this child and remained protective of her throughout his life. Naomi was distant at first. "I don't think Mum was really keen and she would often say she hadn't wanted another. I think that might have sunk in with Janis," said Dawn.

The birth of this baby was a personal joy to Don, and there were celebrations at work, too, for that year the Islanders reached a milestone: their 425th consecutive radio broadcast. Don's music continued to reach the United States, where it had been broadcast since 1934, entertaining hundreds of former Canadians and attracting new American fans, who would write to Don and ask him where Prince Edward Island was. In his self-appointed role as tourism promoter, he would walk to the service station, purchase maps of the Island, and send them to the inquiring fans. It was typical of Don to respond to such requests from his audience. He was a generous man, and it seemed only fair to share his good fortune.

The Messers weren't rich, but they were considerably better off than their neighbours and friends. One of these neighbours, Jeannie Miller, was (and remains) Lorna's close friend. Her father kept five hundred chickens in their back garden on Easton Street and sold eggs and poultry to the market. They still had an outhouse, as did many of the other neighbours, whereas the Messers had indoor plumbing, complete with a bathtub and a flush toilet. Details like this let Jeannie and others know that Don was doing well at a time when the war limited the availability of many items.

Naomi did her laundry with a wringer washing machine every Monday, She didn't have a sophisticated washing machine like the circular Bendix that the Nielsens had, a piece of equipment that provided great entertainment for Lorna and her friend Jeannie, who would happily spend an afternoon watching the laundry go round and round. Gradually Naomi began to recover from her tuberculosis and depression, taking a greater part in the everyday care of the children, making their meals again and getting them dressed. It was a good thing, too, because by the summer of 1945, Don was on the road again on his summer tour of the Maritimes.

First, he drove Naomi and the girls to Belledune for the summer. Her family had grown to like Don and enjoyed his visits to the farmhouse. He would always have his fiddle packed in the car trunk, and they would entreat him to get it out and play. "His fiddle playing was different than anybody else's," said Naomi's nephew, Jack Gray. "The music just sort of flowed out of his fiddle." Jack's father, Naomi's brother Clarence, was a big fan. Jack recalled that when Clarence was home with tuberculosis, he would listen to the program on the radio three times a week. "When that fifteen minutes was on, we could not move. Fifteen minutes is a long time for a child to have to sit still."

Jack's sister remembers Naomi from that time. "Compared to the other aunts that came into the house, she was not as affectionate. The other aunts and uncles would come in and go around and give each of the children a hug, or at least pay attention to us. Naomi would come in and say hello, but then she had other things to do."

Jack recalled no mention of Brenda. In fact, years later he named one of his own children Brenda, having no idea that Don and Naomi had lost a child by that name. Even if she kept her pain to herself, this lifeline to her family became increasingly significant to Naomi and the children. When Don started his cross-Canada tours, she and the girls would often head north for a time. If she were going to join Don in mid-tour, she would first take the girls home to her mother, and then she and Don would arrive together after the tour to take them home to Charlottetown.

～

Don and Naomi were always an integral part of their neighbourhood. It was Naomi who had cared for Jeannie Miller's younger sister Olive after she was mortally burned when she fell into a bonfire. Then, when Jeannie was twelve or thirteen, her parents separated and she was sent to Ontario to live with her married sister. It was not a good situation and she ran away. Despite her mother's entreaties, she would not go back. Instead, Jeannie returned to Charlottetown and moved in with the Messers. She stayed for the school year, though, as she recalled, "I practically lived there anyway. I was there every day growing up." Years later, Jeannie would take her boyfriends over to meet Naomi, who never liked any of them, except finally, the man who became Jeannie's future husband. "She didn't hesitate to tell me so, either," said Jeannie.

Back then, Jeannie recalled, she used to irritate Naomi with her constant chatter. "She'd tell me to sit down and shut my mouth." Jeannie also remembered an occasion when Naomi was very angry with Dawn. Though Jeannie was Lorna's age, she had skipped a year of school and ended up in the same class as Dawn. "I was sick one time," Jeannie said, "and Dawn wouldn't give me my homework. Well, Naomi tore more than a strip off her."

Tearing a strip off someone would land Naomi in trouble. In fact, in 1949, it landed her in court. The Messers were very close friends with their neighbours, Eddie and Kaye McInnis. The children were always in each others' homes, the three Messer girls back and forth with the McInnis boys. There were no fences between the yards, and the children had free rein. One day Naomi had had enough. Janis was sleeping, and one of the McInnis boys was making too much noise. Naomi told him to be quiet, and it may be that he ignored her or perhaps even sassed her. Naomi was shaking out the mop at the time, and she walloped him with it. Despite the long friendship, Eddie and Kaye called the police, and Naomi had to appear in court, where she was found guilty of assault. Don apparently felt terrible at the time, but eventually he would tease Naomi about it. "Do you think they'll feed you in jail, Naomi?" he'd say, or, "Maybe I'll come visit you when you're in jail."

"Naomi had a short fuse. She was fun but she could be sharp," said Jack. Naomi herself recognized that and also recognized that Don acted as a buffer between her and the girls. "When the kids were small," she told Lloyd Sellick, Don's first biographer, "I would be on the point of punishing them, but Don would just then decide to take them for a drive. By the time they got back, things had cooled off." She must have found her situation frustrating: she was a single parent while he

Lorna, Naomi, Janis, Don, and Dawn about 1950. Courtesy: Dallas Davis [Craswell Portrait Studio].

spent so much time on the road, and when he was home, he undermined her authority by being the easy parent they all adored. At the same time, she understood his need to make up for his frequent and long absences.

When the McInnis family moved out soon after the mop incident, Don bought the house and sold it to Ruby and Cleaver MacLean. According to Dawn, he chose them as neighbours. He knew them to be decent people, and he judged that they would be a good support to Naomi when he was away. That summer he had made his first national tour, and he expected to do the same the following years. The MacLeans were younger than the Messers and would have five boys eventually, but the two families became very close and remained friends the rest of their lives.

Before they took possession of the house in October, 1949, the MacLeans installed a big Iron Duke range that had belonged to Cleaver's mother. The day they moved in, Don got up early to light their stove so that the house would be warm on their arrival. After dances, the couples often took turns hosting each other, Ruby said. "They'd come over here and have lunch, or we would go over there and have lunch. My sister lived down the street, and she used to love potato and salt herring. She'd have a big pot of that on, and we'd go into this pot of potatoes and salt herring at midnight, and Don just loved that. He would always eat raw onion with it."

In 1949, Naomi took up driving. She had been determined to learn for some time, and certainly it would be convenient if she could drive, especially when Don was away. Neighbours were always willing to help, but neither Don nor Naomi liked to be dependent on others. So, with some trepidation, he bought her a Vanguard, a big solid car reminiscent of the British checker cabs. Naomi enjoyed her new-found independence, but she always seemed to encounter formidable difficulties: poor drivers on the road, trees where there should have been none, turns where before the road had been straight. In truth, she was a terrible driver, and it was not long before she drove the car into the ditch, somehow missing the turn into the driveway of their house. Naomi climbed out of the car, announced that she would never drive again, and she kept that vow, except when she had no alternative.

༄

Don travelled so regularly and missed the family so acutely that he tried to spend special time with each of them when he was home. Dawn has fond memories of her closeness with her father, of his protectiveness. She remembers how he picked her up and carried her after she crashed her bike on Passmore Street in Charlottetown. She doesn't recall whether he took her to the hospital, but she does remember feeling safe and secure when he held her. Movies were a special time, too. She and her father would go to the Capitol Theatre to see Westerns, with stars like Roy Rogers and Gene Autry. "Oh, he loved those shows," said Dawn. "And when he couldn't take me, I would go into the living room and say to him, 'Dig in your pocket and pass out the dough, I am going to the show, you know.' And he'd laugh and give me a dime or a quarter." They would sometimes go fishing with a couple of his friends, and when Dawn went to camp, he would always try to drive her there and pick her up again.

Don drove his children to school every day when he was home, and if other children needed a ride, he would take them, too. Jeannie

Miller remembers him going far out of his way to drop her at her school before she transferred to the same school his own children attended. As far as school concerts, graduations, and other ceremonies went, the children have no memory of him being there — he was either working or travelling. Christmas concerts fell at the height of the busy party season, and by the time school graduations were held, Don was on the road touring.

Don spent less time with Lorna than with Dawn, but Lorna was very much her mother's child. Even so, when he was home, he was always in the house, a quiet presence

Janis Messer on the lawn at Belmont Street, circa 1952.
Jeannie Miller.

practicing on the violin or sitting at his desk in the hallway next to the kitchen, writing music amid the family noise. Jeannie Miller loved the tune "Red Hot Canary," and when she begged him to play it for her, he always did. "He took the time to do those things," she said, "and I just loved listening to him."

Janis had an adventurous spirit, and Don loved to take her skating. One afternoon, he had taken her to a pond just across the railway track and down the road from the Messers' house. She became chilled, so he began to remove her double-runner skates to take her home. "Janis just would not sit still," Dawn said, "so Dad finally gave her a swat on the bum. She had such a look of shock on her face that he never raised a hand to any of the children again."

Janis, an escape artist, did give him pause. Dawn said, "Dad was always going with a ladder because she was a climber and a faller. She would climb up on a roof, and he'd get a call and he would say, 'I've got to go again.' And he'd go and bring her down from some roof. And then in the spring, she was forever falling in the brook behind the house." This fearlessness once nearly ended in disaster. Janis often went next door to the Arsenaults' house for the afternoon to play with her friend. Mrs. Arsenault didn't worry that Janis might fall into the basement they had dug the previous fall; she knew it was there and had never shown the slightest interest in it. That spring the foundation was full of water, and it drew Janis like a magnet. When Mrs. Arsenault looked out her kitchen window to check on the children, all she could see of Janis was the back of her snowsuit floating on the murky water. She ran out, grabbed the suit by the hood, and scooped Janis out.

Other families made a big fuss at special times of the year, but the Messers did things differently. The Christmas tree went up Christmas Eve and came down right after New Year's. Don did play the Christmas concert at church, but he didn't give a lot of presents. Everybody got gifts, certainly, but not big ones. Dawn remembers with special affection the year she wanted an expensive doll; she had seen it in the store and had come home and raved about it. She knew it cost too much, but she wanted it badly. Don managed to buy it for her. He wouldn't deny his daughters anything he could afford to give them — or almost afford.

"Dad celebrated New Year's more than Christmas, but he loved to have the family home," Dawn said. "He was usually performing on New Year's Eve, so it would just be people coming over on New Year's Day." Truth be told, Don, worked every New Year's Eve from 1929 until 1971, a fact so remarkable that in January 1972, the newspapers reported he had just spent his second New Year's Eve ever with his family.

Meals at the Messer home were much like the meals at Tweedside, with everyone gathered around a formally set table. Naomi wasn't a great cook, but Don's tastes were simple. He loved a boiled dinner of beef with onions, potatoes, and turnip in a clear broth, not in gravy thickened with flour, and he wanted a dumpling on top. He also liked hot peppers, and he liked steak. Having lived through the Depression, he was frugal with food. "If Mum fried potatoes," Dawn said, "he knew how many potatoes there were and how many each of us could have. And he cleared his plate. I mean, he never left a scrap of food on his plate." Breakfasts were fried baloney or brown bread and beans, and Sunday dinners were always roast chicken or roast beef. There were foods that Don would not eat, not because he didn't like them, but because of the risk they posed to his livelihood. He would never eat clams or oysters or lobster because he couldn't take the chance of injuring his hands.

The Messer children spent summer days at the beach if they were in Charlottetown, swimming at an area known as the Butts from Victoria Day until Thanksgiving. The water was often cold, but in the 1940s and 1950s the beach was good, and it was only a short walk from the house. Don would never go into the water when he joined them, but he happily sat on the beach for a short time. Sometimes other members of the Islanders and their families joined them, and they would build an open-pit fire and roast hot dogs. Having fun at the beach didn't interfere with work: Don and his band still had their daily rehearsal, and then at seven o'clock, they were on the air.

Jannie Clifford, Don, and Naomi at Tweedside, New Brunswick, around 1952. Courtesy: Lorraine Hickey/Messer Family.

Don avoided discomfort, perhaps because he endured too much of it on the road. He didn't like to camp, and he didn't like cottages. On one occasion, Lorna convinced her parents to rent a cottage at Rosebank, Prince Edward Island. Don appeared to enjoy himself, but he preferred to be home when he wasn't on the road; he liked to stay put for as long as he could.

Even so, he made time to go to Tweedside every summer. Hayes Messer remembered those times vividly. "When Uncle Don [and the family] would come up, we'd sometimes all get in the car and go down and visit Emma. He'd get on the violin and she'd be on the piano. I remember we were down there one night and she said to Don, 'Have you heard this one?' Boy, could she play those fiddle tunes on that piano. She'd sit there with her head back and her eyes shut. She taught him a few of his fiddle tunes. And my dad, George, he was a great step dancer, and he'd hit the floor — he couldn't keep his feet still." After a family gathering like this, there would be so many people in the house that some of them slept on buffalo robes on the floor. They called it a "shakedown."

Don loved musical evenings with his family, when everyone and anyone might play. When he was performing, though, he was all business. He would sometimes invite community people up on the stage to play with the Islanders, but first he wanted to ascertain that they could play well. In 1952, Harold Cleghorn, one of his grandnephews found that out the hard way when he attended a dance in St. Andrews, New Brunswick. He had gone to the dance at the invitation of his next-door neighbour. Harold played the fiddle a bit, and she apparently thought that it would be a fine idea to introduce him to his great-uncle and ask if he could perform on stage. Don said no.

"I didn't expect him to let me play," said Harold. "I didn't want her to even ask. It was embarrassing. But if I had been at his home I know it would have been different." That was it in a nutshell: when Don was performing, he was a perfectionist. It was not the time to encourage beginner players. Musicians who approached him quietly before the show and proved they were good enough might be given some time on the stage.

Naomi never complained about Don's frequent travelling. She seemed to understand that was what he did, and she knew it provided for their security. Nonetheless, the family missed its peacemaker and life was not easy, especially when he was away for many weeks on his national tours.

At sixteen, Dawn had developed an independent spirit. She no longer wanted to share a room with her sisters. Instead, she moved into the finished attic where Don stored his music. It was a large space, with a ceiling that sloped so steeply she could stand only in a narrow strip down the centre of the room, but it gave her privacy and distance from Naomi. Dawn and her mother had always had a stormy relationship. Naomi was hard on all the girls, but Dawn was strong-willed and would not back down. During her teen years, she left home on several occasions, staying with friends until Don phoned to tell her that he had sorted things out with Naomi. Twice, in 1950 and 1951, Dawn went on tour with the band. "My mother wanted to get rid of me for the summer," she said. Dawn had a wonderful time, seeing the country, sharing a room with Marg, and spending time with her dad, whom she adored.

Dawn was always daring and had more than her share of attitude. When Don sent the other girls to the corner store with a grocery list, they

Lorna and Dawn at Belmont Street, Charlottetown, Prince Edward Island, about 1952.

Jeannie Miller.

would buy only what was on the list. Dawn would add pop and candies to her father's account. She was safe if he got the bill, but woe betide her if Naomi caught on. Usually she got away with her mischief with Don, until the day she put more than $1,000 worth of clothes on his account at S. A. MacDonald. He didn't make her return her purchases, but he did cancel his account at that store.

Her dating was another cause of concern. Don had advised her when she was fourteen, "there's enough in your own faith, be sure to pick someone in your own faith." A frequent churchgoer, he held conservative religious views. He neither understood faiths other than Presbyterianism nor wanted to, thanks to his youth in Tweedside, where the religious communities tended not to mix.

Lorna, too, seemed to now disregard her father's wishes. She had been told not to play with Marion, the girl across the road, but she continued to do so. One weekend when Lorna was nine or ten, she, Jeannie, and Marion decided that they would attend a meeting of the "Holy Rollers," the name they gave to the Pentecostal group having a revival meeting in a field at the end of Eaton Street. Despite specific instructions not to go to the tent, they decided to go anyway. They were going to be saved, not because they had any strong religious inclination to do so, but because the Pentecostals had a radio program on Saturday mornings, *Bringing in the Sheaves*. The girls wanted to get on the radio to sing, and they had to be saved to do that.

"That's how bright we were," said Jeannie. "Here we are, going out Saturday morning to sing, and who walks in the studio but Don. There's a big glass viewing window in the studio, and we were in there singing our lungs out. Don walks right up to the window and just crooks his finger at us, beckoning us, and out we go. We were so stupid. We knew Don went to the radio studio every Saturday morning, but we so badly wanted to get on the radio."

Naomi blamed Dawn, who said, "I really think she thought I was a bad influence on Lorna, that somehow she had to protect her from me." Despite her Pentecostal adventure, Lorna, like the other Messer children, disliked going to church. "It was the worst part of the weekend," said Dawn, in part because it was her job to make sure that Lorna did go. "No one knew stubborn like Lorna. If she didn't want to go, Mum would be yelling at her from the back porch, telling her she would be late. I would be yelling at her because she had decided to sit down and wasn't going to move. It was awful, just terrible." There was some validity to Naomi's concern about Dawn's influence. She had learned to drive when she was eleven, about the same time she started smoking. By fifteen she was "borrowing" her mother's car, thinking Naomi would never find out. She ended up in a ditch and had to get a farmer to haul the car out with a horse. "Mothers always find out everything."

ↄ

When Janis was still a baby, Naomi became pregnant again. She had recovered from her depression after Brenda's death and had regained her strength, but she miscarried a baby boy at twenty weeks' gestation. She was devastated by this loss. Her and Don's grief goes some way to explaining the entry in 1952 of a new child into the family.

Mystery surrounds the story of Gray LeBlanc, and the question of whether the Messers ever legally adopted him remains unanswered. One thing is certain: they took him in with the best of intentions. Gray was the infant son of Lottie LeBlanc, Naomi's niece, one of Jack Gray's sisters; thus, he was Naomi's great-nephew. Lottie and her husband Clarence (Kite) LeBlanc had a child, a daughter called Karen, and when Lottie was seven months pregnant with Gray, Clarence died in a car accident in Moncton. Lottie and seventeen-month-old Karen moved back to the family farm in Belledune, and on October 18, 1952, Lottie delivered Gray in the same bedroom in which Naomi herself had been born.

Lottie needed a skill to survive as a single mother with two babies, and she decided to take a hairdressing course in Charlottetown. A sister went with her to help with the little ones, but it is apparent that Naomi and Don spent a lot of time with her and took a shine to the

Gray LeBlanc,
Belmont Street,
Charlottetown,
Prince Edward island,
circa 1953-1954.

Jeannie Miller.

baby boy. They missed Gray dreadfully when, after completing her course, Lottie moved to Toronto with her two children to stay with her Aunt Grace until she had a job.

Lottie became very ill in Toronto and was unable to work, so it was decided that she and the children would move back to Belledune, where Ellen Eliza would be able to help Lottie look after her children. By this time, Ellen Eliza, struggling with tuberculosis, was no longer up to the task, especially caring for an infant, so she wrote to Naomi asking her if she and Don would take Gray until Lottie regained her health. Karen would stay in Belledune with her mother and grandmother.

Don and Naomi had both grown up in a culture in which families took in children of relatives at times of illness, so the decision was easy. They drove to Belledune to pick up Gray. In truth, they were delighted. They adored the little boy, and his entry into their family after the loss of their own son must have seemed like divine intervention.

It had not been easy for Lottie to give Gray up. Perhaps she thought it would be for only a short time; however, Don and Naomi were reluctant to return him to his mother when her health improved. "They didn't want to give him back," said Grace Smith, Lottie and Jack's sister. "I can remember Lottie and us talking this whole thing out and thinking, well, she's married to Don Messer, they have a lot of money, and maybe this might be the best for Gray. I mean, his children were always well dressed, and he had two cars."

Don was certainly in a better financial position than Lottie to raise Gray. He had a steady income from his radio show, additional income from performances in the community and on the road, and royalties from his recordings. Home life was peaceful: Dawn soon left for nursing studies in Halifax, Lorna was a well-behaved sixteen-year-old, and Janis was an easy-going homebound nine-year-old.

Gray was doted on. Naomi easily shifted back into baby-care mode and Don seemed delighted with his son, bringing him cowboy outfits from tours out west. Gray began to appear in magazine articles, which referred to him variously as Don's son and Don's adopted son. He developed such a close friendship with Ruby and Cleaver's son Allison, who was the same age, that when young Allison was angry with his mother one day and decided to leave home, he packed a little box with underwear, a toothbrush, and a photograph of Gray.

೪

One day in June 1955, during a live performance on CFCY, the station manager noticed that Don seemed to be in great pain. Indeed, Don later described the sensation, "like a lamp bulb lighting up inside of me." True to his nature, he completed the last bars of "Till We Meet Again" before collapsing on the floor. At the age of only forty-six, he had had a heart attack. Difficult as it is to believe today, he did not go to hospital; instead, he was taken to his home and directed to take ten weeks of bed rest, the common treatment of the day. One of his first visitors was Charlie Chamberlain. When Naomi answered the door, she told Charlie that Don was to have no company. His bedroom was on the main floor, so Charlie simply went around to Don's window. "He thought the world of Dad," Dawn said. He was so upset he was crying.

Don's heart attack must have been a terrible shock to everyone. To make matters worse, the summer tour was about to begin, and it would be over before Don had finished his prescribed ten weeks of rest. Yet, for financial reasons if for no others, the commitments had to be honoured. The show must go on.

"And What a Band it Was"

Don is in the studio at CBC Halifax, in the middle of a rehearsal of *Don Messer's Jubilee*. He stands as he always does, upright, his violin held close to his left side, at the ready. He doesn't look much different in 1964 than he did in the scrapbook photograph of the group in 1929. Perhaps he has lost some hair, but he has not aged in any remarkable way nor gained any weight.

He looks around him. Anyone could be forgiven for not really knowing what year this is — the players in the band have not changed since 1952. Two of them have been with him since 1934. Thirty years is a long time to maintain a musical partnership, but the bond that holds these people together is greater than a business arrangement.

Don finds it hard to believe that they are still on the air after five years. The show has been very popular with the audience, gaining top spot two years in a row, even beating out *Hockey Night in Canada* and the *Ed Sullivan Show*, but Don takes nothing for granted. Life and the CBC have dealt him some harsh blows in the past, and he knows that diligence and popularity do not guarantee security. He will not deny that the CBC has given him opportunities otherwise unavailable, given him a chance to perform to an audience of millions of Canadians. It is a hard master though, offering no long-term security, no contract beyond a season, and no pension. He ponders how long he can keep going from contract to contract, wonders how long people will continue to like his sort of music.

Don Messer, 1939.

Courtesy: John Clifford [Craswell Portrait Studio].

Don looks over at producer Bill Langstroth. He senses that Bill is ready to resume the taping of the instrumental, and brings his violin up to his shoulder, paying close attention, waiting for the cue that will set the band in action. It comes, and Don launches into his rendition of "Rippling Water Jig."

All of a sudden, he isn't in the viewfinder. "He wasn't on camera," said Langstroth, "and I couldn't find him anywhere." He pans left and right. No Don. So he steps out from behind the camera to get a better look, to see where Don has got to. "He'd wandered over to pick up a dime lying on the floor of the studio," he said in delight. "Then he smiled at Don Tremaine, and with his funny little laugh said, 'every little bit counts' and put it in his vest pocket." That was Don in a nutshell.

Don's relationship with the CBC had already lasted more than twenty years. It dated back to 1934, when radio station CFBO, the first Saint John station, affiliated with the two-year-old Canadian Radio Broadcast Commission and became CHSJ. It was Frank Willis, the CRBC regional director, who had asked Don to audition with a group. The New Brunswick Lumberjacks were that group, and *New Brunswick Breakdown* was their show. One benefit of that auspicious beginning was the cachet that CRBC connection provided. Hector Charlesworth, chairman of the CRBC, recommended the

New Brunswick Lumberjacks to their government as ambassadors for the province at the 1936 New England Sportsmen's Show in Boston. That opportunity had led to many others.

When the CBC came into being in 1936, the proportion of broadcast time devoted to music decreased to fifty per cent. Don had to scramble once again. Finally, it had been a noncommittal response to Don's pleas about the further 1939 cutbacks that had driven him to accept the music director's position with CFCY, in Charlottetown. After climbing to even greater heights of broadcast success and popularity, Don once more had to suffer the vagaries of CBC network management.

Don Messer and His Islanders, launched in 1939 and broadcast on the *Outports* show featuring traditional music, continued to be enormously popular, and record crowds turned out to Islanders shows on their summer tours. Despite this, in 1953, the CBC decided to stop broadcasting the radio program nationally and return it to its Maritimes-only audience. Hundreds of protest letters came in, many from Ontario and places west, and the matter was raised in Parliament. The outcry caused the CBC to reinstate the national program in November, but they refused to restore its three-times-per-week time slot. Instead, it played only once a week for thirty minutes. Don found such apparent arbitrariness unfathomable. His hard work and success seemed to have little impact on programming. To a man who planned everything carefully and made choices based on expected outcomes, the CBC's decisions were incomprehensible.

While he was frustrated with the seeming lack of logic of CBC programming decisions, Don was also fretting about a choice he would soon have to make: whether he would take his program onto television. In 1953, ten per cent of Prince Edward Island households had television sets. Although Don enjoyed watching, he didn't see himself as a television performer. But Keith Rogers, the owner of CFCY, wanted to move in that direction, so, in preparation for that day, he had trained the men on the new technology. Rogers's death in 1954 temporarily put the plan on hold, but Don knew that he would have to face that choice again in the future.

Although his heart attack in June 1955 had delayed his attendance on the Islanders' summer tour, it did not keep him at home for long. At first, he had obeyed his doctor's orders, sending the band off without him. It soon became apparent though that the Islanders did not function well without their bandleader's firm guiding hand, and Don was forced to join up with the band in order to salvage the tour. He got the group back in good form in time for the August booking of the Islanders at the Lunenburg Fisheries Exhibition.

On the way there, they stopped in at CBHT, the CBC-TV studio in Halifax. Don had been invited for an interview and a chance to perform a few selections on a program called *Gazette*, hosted by Max Ferguson and produced by Bill Langstroth. After the Islanders played, the switchboard lit up with calls from enthusiastic listeners, and Bill Langstroth recognized that he had discovered the makings of a potential hit. The next morning, he approached his boss with the idea of a new TV show featuring Messer.

Before Langstroth received a response, CFCY-TV on Prince Edward Island began broadcasting from the newly built station on Strathgartney Hill, the highest elevation on the Island. Don Messer and the Islanders launched their television show in 1956 and Keith Rogers's vision came to fruition. The location did present some difficulties for the band. During inclement weather, when the cars couldn't make headway up the steep slope, the men had to hike up on foot, dragging the bass behind them.

Then on November 4, 1956, CBC Halifax issued a press release saying, "On Nov. 16, 1956, at seven thirty p.m., the friendly face of Rae Simmons will lean towards a television camera and announce that this is . . . Don Messer and His Islanders. In so doing Rae will usher in the first of a series of twenty-six weekly half-hour television programs." The show would be called *The Don Messer Show* and would initially be broadcast only in Halifax. Within a few weeks, the show reached all the CBC affiliate stations in Sydney, Saint John, Moncton, and Charlottetown through the new CBC Maritime network. Though Don feared that he wouldn't transfer well to television, he believed his old-time music would. It certainly did. The station switchboard received six hundred calls voicing approval of the show.

The show brought with it additional income for the men. As bandleader, Don received $100 per show. Rae as MC received $65, and Charlie was paid $60. The sidemen each got $50.75. Strangely, there is no record of Marg's salary. They were still doing their weekly nationally broadcast radio show on CFCY, performing at weddings and banquets, recording on vinyl disc, and planning their next summer tour. In addition, by 1957, Don and His Islanders were making regular guest appearances on CBC radio and television in Halifax. He was pleased by what he viewed as a significant indication of success, but he was becoming exhausted from so much travelling back and forth. He made the decision to move to Halifax, where he felt his future lay. It was a difficult decision for him and his family, for they loved living in Charlottetown, and he was still contracted for the weekly radio program on CFCY.

Don moved to Halifax in 1958, but other members of the band delayed until they were certain the move would be a good one. They, too, enjoyed living on the Island, and they had been able to maintain part-time jobs while doing the CFCY radio and TV shows because of the proximity of the station to so much else. Charlie worked at a service station close to the radio studios, and he often ran over in overalls, performed, and then ran back to work. All of these factors would have to be considered in a move.

ᶜᵔᵔ

On September 26, 1959, the Islanders broadcast their last regularly scheduled CFCY radio show. The public clamoured, not simply to have the show reinstated, but to have it broadcast on the national network, rather than only regionally. For the second time, Don Messer's name was raised in Parliament, when the Honourable George Nowlan, then Minister of National Revenue, promised to do everything he could to ensure that people across Canada could tune into the show.

Don Messer and His Islanders about 1952.

Provincial Archives New Brunswick, Paul Chamberlain Photo: P533.2.

The show's cancellation was, in fact, a relief for Don and those of his group who had moved to Nova Scotia, for they simply could not sustain the travel required to produce a show in two provinces.

A month earlier, in August 1959, *The Don Messer Show* had been tested as a summer replacement for *Country Hoedown*, seen on Friday nights on the national CBC-TV network. So positive was the public's response that *Don Messer's Jubilee* was launched on September 28, 1959, as a regular weekly offering. For the first time, "Goin' to the Barn Dance Tonight," the show's theme song, rang out into Canadian homes from coast to coast. It would become one of the most recognized tunes in the country.

The first national telecast was nerve-wracking. "It was like starting radio all over again," said Marg Osburne. Her nervousness was somewhat reduced because the CBC had hired a professional MC. Marg had had no difficulty working with Rae, but Don Tremaine had a more polished manner, a dignity and sophistication that fit with the CBC's self-image.

Cast of the *Don Messer Show*, 1959.

Nova Scotia Archives and Records Management Don Messer Collection, 1998 – 132/072/330.

Bill Langstroth said of that first broadcast, "Don Tremaine was master of ceremonies for the first time, and I was brand new to national television. I had laid it on so there would be three commercial spots. Well, the first commercial rolled a little early, and Don Tremaine wasn't through his announcements. So I stuck with Tremaine and then cut into the commercial, the beginning of which had already gone." The wall beside him suddenly shook. "Then a little man burst through the door and yelled, 'You've got it all wrong! All wrong! All wrong!' "He was very upset," said Langstroth. "He was the agent for the sponsor."

That the program made it to air at all was quite an achievement; Toronto executives had initially been aghast at the idea of televising the show. "You can't be serious! Put that on the network? You're out of your mind," was their first reaction. "Certainly the show was a musical anachronism, a nostalgic connection to the audience's lives," said Tremaine. While the public response was good, not everybody was enamoured of the show. Ron Poulton of the *Toronto Telegram* sneered, "As a production piece, Messer's show makes me wince every time I look at it. It takes such studious care not to relax. Its props are museum pieces. Its bandstand looks like a refugee from a jitney dance." The *Globe and Mail* TV critic objected to being "force-fed corn by the CBC." *Time Magazine* labelled the show a "Hillbilly Hit." That moniker offended Don. His show was a presentation of music that was hundreds of years old and an important link with Canada's heritage.

Don Tremaine plus the *Jubilee* cast was a winning combination. A poll conducted on June 10, 1960, by the Bureau of Broadcast Measurement showed *Don Messer's Jubilee* in the number one spot, reaching 1,706,900 households. Hot on this success, CBC radio, perhaps yielding to George Nowlan's promised pressure, launched a new radio show to begin October 3, 1960. They used the tried and true *The Don Messer Show* and broadcast three times a week from Halifax on CBC's Trans-Canada network. Sponsored by Canada Packers, it was a huge success: surveys showed that one home in every three tuned into the show.

Those shows were a nightmare for Waldo Munro, the pianist. "Don Messer used to tell me to leave a couple of the numbers out while we were recording for Trans-Canada radio programs because the piano was so bad and out of tune. I used to shake before live radio solos, knowing the difficulty I'd run into with the piano."

Don Messer's Jubilee would be a huge amount of work for Don, but it would be worth it. By 1963, ninety per cent of Canadian households had a television. He took his responsibility to his audience very seriously and spent close to a week preparing each show, choosing the music, selecting the guests, and writing the arrangements. He would meet with Bill Langstroth on Monday and they would look at an overview of the show. On Wednesday, the entire cast rehearsed from seven p.m. until ten p.m. and often taped the music and singing. They rehearsed again on Thursday from four p.m. until they were satisfied. And then they videotaped. As Don had done on Prince Edward Island, he submitted an initial draft of his program a month in advance. Don did not like surprises. Everything was carefully scripted,

Cast of *Don Messer's Jubilee*, 1963. Back row: Marg Osburne, Don Tremaine, Don Messer, Charlie Chamberlain; front row: Lynne Sheehan, Maurice Belair, Ernst Grundke, Karen Todd, Janice Blue, Don King, Art Fabean, Mary Wile. CBC Still Photo Collection.

even the casual conversations. Everything was timed to fit the thirty minutes allotted, every word considered in the schedule.

Matilda Murdock, nearly eighty-nine years of age and still playing jam sessions at Miramichi, New Brunswick, pubs on Saturday nights, described being on the show in 1964. She had taught herself to play the fiddle as a nine-year-old by listening and playing along with the wax cylinders of an old phonograph. Her father felt that Matilda had real talent, and when Don Messer came through Loggieville, New Brunswick, in the 1950s, he encouraged his daughter to audition with him. At the time, Matilda didn't realize the importance of the opportunity — she would far rather be outside — but she did play for Don, and whatever he heard in her led to a lifelong correspondence about music and a guest appearance on *Don Messer's Jubilee* fifteen years later. That was an entirely new experience for her.

"I was a little backward at the time and didn't want to foul it up and ruin the whole thing. I knew the importance of the show," she said, still thrilled at being invited to be on *Don Messer's Jubilee*. "It was a very big honour, and such a pleasure because of their hospitality. It was hard for me, bringing up six children in the country, and I wasn't playing or practicing as often. But they told me, 'You can do this, don't be nervous,' and I had a script."

Don and, by extension, his band's courtesy was almost a byword. Pianist Bill Guest recalled:

> As long as you did your job, he didn't complain. If you were doing something he didn't like, he would say, "I think it would work better like this." Very quiet, like. I was a guest on the show, and during rehearsals I was getting ready to play together with Don. They had me standing behind him, and he stopped the rehearsal.
>
> Langstroth said, "What's wrong?"
>
> Don says, "We're not doing it this way with Bill Guest."
>
> Langstroth replies, "I want him standing there."
>
> Don quietly says, "No, this man is a guest on my show. He's the featured guest and he'll stand in front." And he insisted.

That tale could have been told nineteen years earlier by Norm Ripley, who remains an active fiddler into his mid-eighties. Norm had first met Don in 1942 when he was in Mulgrave, Nova Scotia, with the Irish Regiment. In 1952, they met again. By this time Norm was a professional square-dance caller, and Don called him up on stage at a performance when he was on tour. "'What tune do you want?' he asked me. "I replied, 'It doesn't matter as long as it's in 6/8 time.' Now here is a guy who tried to make his guests sound as good as he could," Norm explained. "He stood in the back and always ran his

"I hope you'll enjoy 'Baking for the love of it' as much as I've enjoyed being 'chief taster'!"

Don as "chief taster" for Pillsbury Bakeries, 1961.

Credit: General Mills [Leo Burnett Company Ltd].

orchestra from behind. I likened him to a horse driver." Standing in the back suited Don well. He didn't like to be in the forefront on-stage, didn't like the cameras panning in on his face for a close-up.

Something else Don didn't like was being asked to act. "They always tried to make him do commercials," said Jeannie Miller, smiling at the memory. "In one of them he pulled a tea bag out of his pocket. It just wasn't him." He did it because that's what he needed to do to bring in the sponsors. Over time, he would allow himself to be photographed in a chef's hat for a recipe book put out by Pillsbury, with the catch phrase, "I hope you'll enjoy baking for the love of it as much as I've enjoyed being 'chief taster.'" He and the other members of the band would be expected to meet executives and dealers from Massey Ferguson and attend their awards banquet, where it was said that Duke Nielsen dazzled them all by opening oysters with his car keys. They obviously impressed everybody, including some of the dealers, who could hardly believe they were really shaking hands with Don Messer and His Islanders.

Don had a lot of fun with *Don Messer's Jubilee*, in his own quiet way, and he loved the reaction he got. At the same time, "He was very professional," said singer Catherine McKinnon, a frequent and popular guest on the show. "Everything that was chosen came from Mr. Messer. He was the boss, it was his baby. There was respect and distance because he was a very contained man, not demonstrative at all. He was definitely the man in charge, he was the visionary, he was the one who put it together, and he was the one who chose all the tunes. It was as simple as that. He was the boss."

The shows had a set pattern. After the familiar theme, "Goin' to the Barn Dance Tonight," the band would play a few tunes. Then the guest artists would perform — instrumentalists, singers, step dancers — or the Buchta troupe of dancers that would be added in 1959. A duet by Marg and Charlie might come next, followed by "Quiet Time." The cast gave "Quiet Time" another name: the God Song. "In the studio it was, 'What are we going to do this week for the God song?'" McKinnon recalled. The announcement of the first show on August 7, 1959, read: "Music and dancing, country style, with Don Messer and his Islanders will be featured. Featured singers are Charlie Chamberlain and Marg Osburne. The guests on the first show are dancer Marlene Weatherbee and singer George Longrad. The host on the show is Don Tremaine."

Catherine McKinnon always felt blessed to have worked with the band, which she described as "so loved and so acknowledged and so welcomed into the homes of this country." Her sentiment is a common one. Don Tremaine called Don "a lovely man to work with." He had simply been assigned to the show to take over the MC duties that Rae Simmons had performed on radio and in live shows, and it was a lucky break that he fit in so well. Even luckier, the brass in Toronto held the same opinion.

"The funny thing was," Tremaine reminisced, "many years back before then, probably around 1936, my mother heard Don Messer on the air, and she said to me, 'Oh, that man is a tremendous fiddler, he's just great.' I was a little boy about seven or eight years old, and here I am, years later, fronting the band." And what a band it was.

"It was the most remarkable bunch of individuals, and I say individuals because although they were a team, they were individuals," said Tremaine, with some wonder at Don's ability to manage them. "My God, you have never met a more diverse group. Warren MacCrae had two degrees, Charlie had two grades, I think. Duke was a renegade, Charlie was a renegade. But they all knew who the boss was, and they knew their livelihood depended on him. He was a very serious family man trying to make a buck and keep the family eating."

Perhaps that focus on the job and the music rather than on the thrill of fame is part of what kept Don open to individuals and receptive to new talent. In 1963, for instance, he listened to an enterprising young Scotsman who became a featured guest on *Don Messer's Jubilee* from 1964 until 1972. That was unusual in itself for Don was a staunch supporter of Canadian talent, believing that Canadian musicians had few opportunities elsewhere, and he insisted that *Don Messer's Jubilee* use only Canadian musicians.

Johnny Forrest was living in Edmonton when Don came through on his 1963 summer tour. Determined to audition, he had gone early to the hockey arena to slip in before security was tightened. He knew that the band would give two shows, and he counted on finding an opportunity to meet with Don. He had to be careful. Ken Reynolds, who had become Don's tour manager, had seen Johnny sneak into the building and was looking for him. Johnny had approached Reynolds when he first arrived at the arena and had asked for a chance to meet with Mr. Messer, but Reynolds had told him, "Mr. Messer is going to be too busy." Johnny was not about to be turned away. He knew the promoter, Benny Benjamin, who offered to help. "I'll get his attention and distract him, and you run like hell," he'd told Johnny.

Eluding Reynolds while carrying an accordion wasn't easy, but Johnny managed to sneak into a locker room and sit there in the dark, waiting hours for the performers to arrive. By pure luck, Don and Charlie went into the locker room across the hall to prepare for the show. "I listened to the first show, and then when the intermission came on, I said to myself, Johnny, this is your chance." Grabbing his accordion, he darted across the dark locker room like a mole, crossed to Don and Charlie's room, and knocked on the door. "All they could see was this guy with an accordion. They didn't know who I was, so I introduced myself quickly and said, 'Mr. Messer, I've always wanted to meet you. Would you give a wee listen to me?' And I belted out my favourite song. I was with him ever since."

~

In June 1964, Don marked thirty years of broadcasting by recreating one of his earlier radio shows on television, using props, costumes, sets, and original recordings from the 1930s. That same year, he suffered a second heart attack. In an attempt to slow down a bit, he stopped do- ing the radio show. Fans complained, as did some of the band members who were accustomed to the extra money those shows brought in; however, Don's health would not allow him to sustain the workload, and Naomi was insistent that he take better care of himself.

He continued with *Don Messer's Jubilee* and the cross-country tours of the same name. For the most part, the relationship with the CBC worked, giving him a platform for the music he loved and tre- mendous marketing opportunities to gather an increasingly large fan base. The Islanders now attracted huge crowds everywhere because so many people wanted to catch a live performance of the band they watched faithfully every Monday night.

The high ratings continued through 1965 and 1966. When he was asked by the *Calgary Herald* why he thought that was so, Don replied with some bemusement, "I can't really say why the show is so popu- lar. It amazes me every time I look at the ratings. I know it can't go on. Maybe next week we'll be at the bottom."

That comment did not surprise Don Tremaine. "I don't think he ever came to terms with his fame. The kind of fame he had absolutely dazzled him." Tremaine has a plaque at his cottage commemorating the 1964 ratings: *Don Messer's Jubilee* was the most watched tele- vision program in Canada. "Don could never believe that," he said. "He was an extremely modest guy who never really came to terms with the fact that he was becoming a bit of an icon. It never occurred to him that he could be that important."

Don Messer was made an honorary member of the Stoney Tribe
and named Chief Big Eagle, Banff, Alberta, 1965. At right is Chief
Walking Buffalo. Courtesy: John Clifford [Jim Santa Lucia, Banff].

At the height of the show's popularity, *Don Messer's Jubilee*
reached fifty per cent of all farm homes and twenty-five per cent of
city homes. In deference to this mixed audience, Don decided that
the 1966-1967 season should reflect Canada's cultural diversity. To
mark Centennial Year, he dedicated each show to a province or terri-
tory and to the cultures that resided there. He composed new tunes,
among them "Banks of Newfoundland," "Fraser River Breakdown,"
"Mouth of the Tobique," "Joys of Quebec," "Red River Reel," "Prince
Albert Hornpipe," "Cowboy Jock from Skye," and "My Home in
Saskatoon." In 1965, he had composed "Stoney Reel" to honour
Chief Walking Buffalo, who had inducted Don as Chief Big Eagle, an
honorary blood brother of the Stoney Tribe of Alberta. Don had been
very touched by that tribute and by the gift of a headdress.

Halfway through the year, the CBC began to broadcast *Don Messer's Jubilee* in colour, which gave the show a boost, but Don was disappointed that they refused to send a photographer with the band on the Centennial Tour in the summer. Don felt that they missed out on a great opportunity to capture some historical events on film. The Canada Council had also turned him down, though it is unclear what help he had requested from them.

At the end of the Centennial Tour, ever conscious of the need to keep his program front and centre, Don and tour promoter Ken Reynolds sent centennial souvenir booklets to Cabinet ministers with a Christmas message summing up the success of the tour. "My personal wish is to have the show televised in other countries. Perhaps through this media we could share our expression of the Canadian family, musical variety which has continued to be so well received. I hope we can count on your support to this end as well as a continuation of our weekly visits to your home."

It was an odd letter, somehow self-deprecating, and it didn't highlight Don's popularity: a 1967 CBC poll showed that *Don Messer's Jubilee* still ranked third among Canadian programs, after *Hockey Night in Canada* and *Flashback*, and eighth overall, including American programs. Nor did it reflect the fact that his show commanded unprecedented audience loyalty. It didn't mention that the Centennial Tour had been judged the most successful of the Festival Canada Attractions with the highest number of shows and the largest audiences. For some reason, it didn't even list the invitations he had received to take the show to Germany, Cyprus, and England.

In 1968, *Don Messer's Jubilee* ranked fourth among Canadian television programs and ninth overall, and its audience was estimated at 2,750,000. Perhaps tempted by good news, the CBC mandarins decided to mess with a winning formula. They moved the show from Monday to Sunday, anathema to Don, who still respected the Sabbath as a day of rest. They then moved the show to Friday. Don was unhappy, believing that his audience would not tune in that night; they would be out shopping or with the children. Nevertheless, he signed a contract for eleven shows for the 1969 season.

Troubled Waters

Halfway through the evening, Don looks uneasy. He has never been animated in public performances, but tonight there is tension in his stance, a look of annoyance on his face. He glances to the left at Cec McEachern and then farther along the stage to Rae Simmons and Charlie Chamberlain. None of them will meet his gaze. He looks over at Bill Guest, sitting in at the piano for Waldo Munro, who is not well. Bill smiles back, a little hesitantly. Warren MacCrae on drums studies his instruments with uncharacteristic intensity. The only one who is acting halfway normal is the fiddler, Graham Townsend, the guest artist. There is something going on among the members of the band, but they have not made Bill and Graham privy to what ails them. The tension is palpable, like a violin string tightened almost to its breaking point.

When the set finishes, Don leaves the stage and goes into a room designated for the performers. Nobody joins him, but that is not unusual. Don likes his quiet time, does not always feel up to mingling with the crowds. People have thought him shy. In truth, he finds three or four voices distracting. One-on-one conversation is the only kind he is comfortable with.

The sponsors of the show come out and remove the benches and chairs for the dance. Tonight's setup is typical: a performance and then a dance. Don has done away with offering magic tricks at the intermission because they don't seem to be the crowd pleaser they once were. Instead, he has introduced guest performers — step dancers and musicians and vocalists — into the main program.

The room is ready for the dance to begin, but Don does not come out on stage. Graham and Bill go in search of him, worried that he is not well, that he is tired from their gruelling schedule.

"Don, you're just not up to be doing this dance, are you?" they ask.

"I'm not feeling the greatest," Don responds. But neither illness nor exhaustion is the problem. The band is annoyed at Don for something he has done, some decision he has made, and they have been paying him back the only way they know how: by sabotaging his performance. When he played, they have sped up or slowed down at their own volition. They've created an impossible situation, and Don has removed himself from the scene of torment.

"We'll go out and do the dance for you," say Bill and Graham.

Don never told his guest artists what the issue had been. Not only was he not given to confiding in members of his group, he didn't encourage them to address him as anything other than Mr. Messer. He kept a tight rein on them, had a strict and disciplined approach. "They all recognized that he was the king, he was the authority," said Don Tremaine. If the men wanted to stay with him, they needed to toe the line. As much as they hated the restrictions, though, they tolerated them; they knew that Don had provided them with years of employment when such opportunities for musicians were hard to come by.

Whatever the positive side of being the king, it also meant that Don suffered more than the ordinary stress inherent in this business. His personality was partly responsible. "He was pretty much a perfectionist," said Waldo in a 1984 interview with the *Atlantic Advocate*. "Don just got the best out of you without telling you so. You just naturally did your best." Don himself, in a moment of reflection, said, "I don't like to have castles fall down around me. I would prefer to take longer and be sure that things are correct."

Don had suffered his first heart attack in 1955 during a live radio show in Charlottetown, and his ten-week recovery period overlapped entirely with the schedule of the Islanders' summer tour. The band would have to travel without him if they were to honour their commitments and earn any money. When Charlie Chamberlain had wept at Don's bedroom window, he had feared for his friend's life, but he had also worried about whether the band could do the tour without Don along to manage it. Don handled the publicity, bookings, contracts, travel arrangements, and hotel accommodations by himself, as well as organizing the programs.

After considering the matter in his thorough way, Don decided that the Islanders would head west and fulfill their engagements. The bookings were all in place, and none of them could afford to take the summer off. Rae Simmons was put in charge; he would do triple duty as manager, MC, and performer. The tour would take them as far north as Flin Flon, Manitoba, and as far west as Edmonton, Alberta, and they would travel in two vehicles, with a trailer for their instruments.

They made it to Guelph, Ontario, without incident and performed to a sell-out crowd at the Guelph Memorial Gardens. They continued west, but it became apparent that while the men chafed under Don's control, they seemed to need it to function smoothly. Their performances did not go as well as they wished, and sponsors became anxious. Eventually, Rae contacted Naomi and asked her if Don could come out west to join them. If he couldn't, it looked as if they would have to cancel the rest of the tour.

That conversation must have been lively. Naomi was very protective of Don, and it is unlikely that she supported the idea. Don must have agreed, determined to save the tour and thus the reputation of the Islanders. Together, he and Naomi prepared for their trip west.

Naomi was not a good driver at the best of times, so the Messers' neighbours and good friends, Cleaver and Ruby MacLean, stepped into the breach. Cleaver agreed to drive Don and Naomi to Regina, Saskatchewan, taking leave from his railway job and leaving his pregnant wife behind. Dawn was at nursing school in Halifax; Lorna would look after Janis and Gray. The plan was that Don would rest on the trip, recuperate for a few days at his brother Andrew's farm at Grand Coulee, Saskatchewan, and then meet up with the band in Athabasca, Alberta, north of Edmonton.

Don's beloved 1951 Hudson Hornet, which he drove
on three national tours. Courtesy: Lorraine Hickey/Messer family.

Cleaver loved to drive, and operating Don's Hudson Hornet must
have been a real adventure for him. They made it to Saint John the
first day and then to Rumford, Maine, the next. Each night they
stayed in a hotel so Don could have a good sleep. In the beginning,
Don spent most of the time resting full-length across the back seat,
but soon he moved to the front seat to take on the role of navigator.
When they arrived in Regina, they stopped first at the train station so
that Cleaver could ride the train home, and then, with Naomi at the
wheel, they drove out to Andrew's farm, twenty-four kilometres outside Regina. That night, lightning struck the house, leaving a gaping
hole around the entrance box and electrical meter and blowing all
the fuses.

It is unclear how long Don stayed at Andrew's farm, for almost
immediately, it seems, they were on their way to Athabasca to meet
the band. Don and Naomi took turns at the wheel for the 805 kilometres, and Don must have found the straight roads, clear visibility,
and sparse traffic reassuring. They reached their destination safely,

and Don was able to resume his position as bandleader and saw the tour through its originally planned schedule.

~

Don stopped handling every aspect of touring by himself after his heart attack. It is astonishing that he managed to do it for as long as he did — twenty-six years, starting with his first forays into band management in 1929. But the heart attack frightened him and his family. He took to reading and collecting articles on heart attacks, and it was not lost on him that stress and cardiac illness were connected. He agreed to delegate the responsibility.

Ken Reynolds came to his attention. He was certainly capable: a federal civil servant by day, an industrious and ambitious tour promoter by night. Ken was already handling country singer Wilf Carter and, by all accounts, was doing a good job of it. Don contacted him, and they began a correspondence that would last several years before Don hired him in 1961 to manage his national tours. The Maritime tours Don would continue to handle on his own with the help of Warren MacCrae.

Don and Ken Reynolds grew close, for they had a lot in common. Beyond two business people working together, they were a business partnership. From Ken's point of view, they had a special relationship. "Don relied on me implicitly for everything and he never questioned anything. He socialized with me in the evenings when we were on tour. We never talked about the show, we just had a nice chat, a relaxing time. We alternated between his room and my room, and we might talk about what was coming up the next day or the next week, but it was more a chance to get away."

Getting away from the band did not mean that Don did not know what they were up to. He had maintained full managerial control, and he did not hesitate to discipline them if he felt it was warranted. "Ken and Don were on their own having a wee dram together," Johnny Forrest recalled. They didn't socialize with the members of the band, would prefer to go off to their rooms by themselves and lock the door. Johnny, Warren, Cec, Waldo, and Duke decided to have a beer. It was early still by their standards, and they went down to the bar to catch the entertainment. At intermission, Waldo went to the piano and Duke went with him, and they started to entertain the lounge crowd. "Wee Donald showed up. He got my eye and waved at me with his finger. I got up and said, 'What is it?'"

"You tell the boys to stop right now and tell them I sent you," said Don, and then he turned and walked back to his room.

Don did not raise his voice, but Johnny knew that Don was angry. He went over to Duke and Waldo and said, "Hey Duke, you better stop. Don saw you and he tells you to stop."

"The next day on the bus," Johnny said, "when we all got paid hard cash for the night before, there was no pay for Waldo and no pay for Duke. No pay, I'm telling you. They were not supposed to entertain in the lounge. You do your entertainment on the stage where you are supposed to, to be paid." Decades later, Johnny remained a little in awe of his all-seeing, all-knowing mentor.

On this point Don was a stickler. He told biographer Lloyd Sellick, "If a performer doesn't produce, he must understand that cancellation of pay is automatic. There's nothing personal about it, and down through the years the boys came to know just where I stand. I expect good performance and good conduct from all members. The show must be good; the people must receive value."

Johnny discovered that the same theory didn't necessarily apply in reverse. Charlie had disappeared into the rum in Whitehorse, he said, and he was standing in for him, belting out "The Green, Green Grass of Home" and "Your Cheating Heart." "I could do all these numbers, but I am no Charlie Chamberlain." He was also filling in for Marg, who had stayed in Fort St. John, British Columbia, afraid to fly to Whitehorse in the tiny airplane after too many close calls. "I said to myself, I am in for a real good paycheque. But we came out of Whitehorse and it was the same money as always."

Don did have certain rules, and to breach them brought suspension. The first of these was that his band members had to be sober when they were performing. One time in Harvey Station, New Brunswick, when the show was about to begin, Charlie came into the room "with a big smile on his face. He obviously had a load on," said Vaughan Messer, Hayes Messer's brother. "Don took one look at him and beat it across the room and took Charlie into a side room. When they came out again, Charlie was stone sober, his face as pale as a ghost." Hayes doesn't know what Don said to Charlie, but the effect was truly remarkable, and Charlie performed to his usual high standard.

Alcohol consumption might have been a problem for a number of the men, but for the most part they managed to limit their drinking to after the performances. All of them enjoyed their alcohol, but Don indulged his love of a glass of Scotch in

Poster for National Film Board film *Cross Canada Cavalcade: Don Messer His Land and His Music*, 1971

Nova Scotia Records and Management Don Messer fonds, 1998 – 132/049/004.

private or with friends and family. Alcohol was freely available, even during Prohibition, and sometimes in the early days, when a sponsoring group had more good will than cash, the musicians were paid in drinks. Charlie's reputation as a good-natured drunkard springs largely from stories told about those times. Unfortunately Charlie often fuelled this reputation, telling self-deprecating stories for their immediate effect without foreseeing that they would stick with him long afterwards. For example, in the 1971 National Film Board movie *Don Messer, His Land and His Music,* Charlie boasted that he "had probably wiped more liquor off my chin" than the young men of the Chamber of Commerce had drunk. The comment may have made

Don Messer and His Islanders postcard sold at dances, 1948.
Duke Nielsen on grey horse; Harold MacCrae on brown horse;
Back row of buggy: Warren MacCrae, Don Messer, Ralph Watson;
front row: Rae Simmons, Marg Osburne, Charlie Chamberlain.

Courtesy: John Clifford.

him "one of the boys," but by the time it had been telecast repeatedly, Charlie's image as a boisterous drinker was so set that he couldn't have changed it if he had wanted to.

The members of the band covered for each other. There were no cliques or animosity; although nerves and tempers could fray under the delays and frustrations attendant on long-distance travel. Duke Nielsen was a tease and could irritate Charlie until one of the others would have to intercede. When the musicians couldn't bear to be in each other's company, they found constructive ways to escape. Waldo would go off somewhere and play his piano or find a pool hall and have a game with Marg's husband. Rae and Cec would take a walk. Marg would find a seniors home and, with Don's blessing, give an impromptu concert.

The musicians struggled somewhat to get proper credit for what they did. Cec McEachern, an indisputably excellent musician able to stand in for Don himself, warranted far more than his sideman status. Finding and keeping very talented musicians was part of Don's genius. While Cec always claimed that Don treated him fairly and gave him his due, others remain less satisfied, or perhaps they felt that Don received credit that properly belonged to the whole group.

Ruth Munro, Waldo's wife, is one of them. "Life was very hard for them," she said. "These men would travel halfway across the Island to make maybe $1.50 for a dance that night. The devotion they showed to Don Messer — yes, he was a great fiddle player, but he was only as good as the rest of the band with him." Waldo was hurt that he

Cecil McEachern, Rae Simmons, Duke Nielsen, Don Messer, 1960.

Nova Scotia Records and Archives Management. Don Messer fonds, 1998 – 132 – 071/287 [Maurice Crosby].

was never recognized as a soloist, only as a sideman. "He was a fabulous piano player, and he was Don Messer's pianist. He wasn't Don Messer's piano player."

She is right. Many will say that without Don Messer, the other musicians would not have achieved what they did, but that without them, he himself would have amounted to far less. Ned Landry who, in his mid-eighties, remains one of Canada's finest fiddlers, felt that he had something to offer, perhaps more than Don himself. Three-quarters of a century after Don first hired him, the fact that Don changed his name rankled: "I still don't know what was wrong with Frederick Lawrence," he said. "Don Messer was a banker," he added flatly, "not exactly like a performer. When I was with him in the thirties, I used to play the mouth organ, fiddle, and guitar, and I could step-dance at the same time, and imitate Donald Duck." He went on, his resentment building, "I sang, too, and I am a composer, too. I was a performer, Don wasn't." He was not through, "He was the boss, oh God yes. We used to get a few dollars, but he handled everything. He had the name and he had the CBC," he finished in a rush of emotion.

Bill Langstroth concurred, though his interpretation differs. "He was the keeper. He made it work and he got the credit for it, as well he might. He was a specialist himself, and he handed over the job of announcer/clarinet player to Rae Simmons. He handed over the lovable clown/step dancer/singer to Charlie. He handed over the female vocalist to Marg. He had great respect for their ability to pull it off." He also expected the same kind of respect from them.

Money and salaries were always issues, too. In 1934, when Don, Charlie, and Duke played on radio station CHSJ, the Saint John CBC affiliate, they were paid $25 a week. That was a lot of money then, far more than they earned when they went to CFCY in Charlottetown in 1939. There, although their salary dropped to $12.50 a week, it came with a contract and a sense of security. When Waldo Munro played the national live radio show in 1944, he said, he earned $19 and had a dollar taken out for tax. In the early 1960s, the CBC paid him $123.50 for each of the *Don Messer's Jubilee* performances, a fee that included rehearsal time. Even at the end, in 1969, the CBC paid him the princely sum of $191 a show.

As the bandleader, Don received more than the others, and Dorothy Nielsen, for one, felt this keenly. "They worked so hard for so many years. Don Messer had a good group because they were really loyal to him. If he'd had another group, he would have had to pay them a lot more." Again, Langstroth viewed the situation somewhat differently. "Don was very careful to make sure that he had his share, and his proportional share, of whatever the band was paid to do what they did. I understand that and I have no quarrel with that. He made it work, and he kept it glued together." The 1967 contract, one of the few to have been found, indicates that Don was paid $550 per show for thirteen shows. The members of his band may have been paid as little as $61.64 for two two-hour rehearsals, plus two hours overtime and an additional broadcast fee, supposing Don paid them according to the American Federation of Musicians pay scale. It is hard to tell, because there is no record of his arrangements with the sidemen. Ruth Munro, fiercely loyal to Waldo, felt that whatever they were paid, it wasn't enough for what they did. "They [the CBC] exploited them," she said.

Sometimes disagreement arose because of the amount Don charged sponsors of live performances as a guarantee. He had always asked for a flat fee, and sponsors kept whatever money they raised above that amount, often thousands of dollars. This money would go towards a project such as the building of a hockey rink or an addition to a hospital, or it would provide funds for the myriad charities so necessary in the time before government social security programs. When Ken Reynolds came on board, however, he and Don changed the system. They would offer sponsors two options: a set fee of $1,800 or sixty per cent of the gross, whichever was greater, or a fee of $2,500 or fifty per cent of the gross, whichever was greater.

The band had started to make some real money; in 1966, in one month on the road, they brought in approximately $65,000. (The extra benefit wasn't just financial, of course; as Waldo Munro told the *Atlantic Advocate*, "I'd sooner play in front of twenty thousand people than a camera any day.") The men — and especially their wives — sometimes found it hard to understand the distribution of that money. Sometimes they would play in a fancy hall, other times in an arena. In the early days, before they took a percentage of the gate, they would have $50 in their pockets after the show, but in the 1960s they earned far more on tour than their television salaries, even after paying for their expenses. Though Warren MacCrae, the drummer, was paid the least of them all, he nevertheless made enough money during the 1964 summer tour to pay off his entire mortgage.

The reality was that they were all more or less self-employed, without health benefits or pensions. They had no guarantee that any of it — the television show, the radio appearances, or the tours — would continue.

⌇

In 1964, Don had his second brush with death. This time he was at his home in Halifax. He was shaving, preparing for church, when he felt a sensation of numbness and lost consciousness. Even then, nine years after his first attack, it was not customary to take people who had had heart attacks to hospital. Instead the doctor and cardiac specialist came to his house. Despite both physicians' insistence that he rest, Don went to the TV studio the next day and appeared on *Don Messer's Jubilee* to allay rumours that he was unwell. Shortly thereafter he took some time off in Prince Edward Island, where he went into hiding, according to Jeannie Miller. "He wanted to be someplace where CBC producer Bill Langstroth couldn't contact him," she said, still protective of Don after all these years. "We had a house out in East Royalty, so we moved to the summer cottage and they moved into our house." Cec McEachern took his place until he recovered. The reason for the subterfuge was that only days after his heart attack, Don had been called to go to Camp Hill, where the CBC was staging a veteran's show. "They couldn't get the timing right," said Dawn, "and Dad was called in. He had to go in a wheelchair. It wasn't fair." Don got the band set with the timing, went home, and called the Millers. He felt he had to be unreachable if he was to get a chance to recover.

Now Don recognized the harsh facts of his insecure employment more forcefully than ever. At this time, he told his minister, the Reverend Allison MacLean, that he would like to break up the band and take life easy, move back to Tweedside, and perhaps build a cottage on the shore of Oromocto Lake, close to the family homestead. He worried about his band members, fearing that some of them would not survive the dissolution of the group.

"There is no question about it," Langstroth said. "Don felt he was the fulcrum, the father figure." As the father, it was his responsibility to make sure that he provided for those who depended on him. "He never gave himself a minute to relax," said Don Tremaine. "He never felt secure that it was going to last."

So he didn't disband the group. Instead, he set bigger and bigger goals for them and for his music. It was always the music: that was his focus. Really, the show had not changed much from the original format established so many years ago. "We're still barnstorming today. That's what these one-night stands are. The only difference is that in those days we played for dances and now we've turned the show into a concert," said Don in an interview circa 1965. Through all those years, Don had learned that there was no need to make things more difficult than they had to be. The program remained the same for each of the performances on tour, and once the band had learned it, they simply played it by rote every evening.

The musicians' wives sometimes came with them, now that their children were older, and that helped ease the loneliness that they all struggled with. Lydia Chamberlain, Shirley MacCrae, and Ruth Munro each travelled on at least one tour. Naomi usually flew to Winnipeg and travelled back east with them. Her presence changed the dynamics of the group. Nobody gave Don a hard time when Naomi was on the bus. She was the boss's wife, and she had no compunction about putting any of them in their place if she felt their behaviour warranted it. No one got past Naomi.

Touring at their level of success had its benefits, but it was still an exhausting endeavour. No longer did they sleep in train stations, saving money while they waited for the ferry to Prince Edward Island, or travel jam-packed in an old car to face an uncertain crowd. Now they travelled by tour bus, slept in hotels, and often as not were greeted on their arrival by a crowd of fans who had come hundreds of miles to hear them in person. Well-heeled sponsors recognized their marketability and sought them out for the benefit of being associated with the show. Of course, these very successes brought with them higher expectations. Sponsors expected to meet their idols, whom they had paid well. They anticipated that the players would attend their expensive post-performance receptions. Don had less freedom to just go off to his room and rest, but he needed the sponsors and couldn't afford to alienate them.

He and Massey Ferguson had worked together for years to their mutual advantage. Back in 1961, Don Tremaine had been granted leave from CBC to go on the western tour as MC, on the condition that Don paid his salary. They had played to sellout crowds for ten days in a row, and they were treated like visiting royalty. "Wherever we went," Tremaine said, "we filled the rinks; people were hanging from the rafters. It was absolutely amazing and exceptional fun." Massey Ferguson was thrilled with the results. "They sold tractors like they never sold before when they sponsored the Islanders."

Don was not, however, prepared to go out to the airport in February 1965, to meet the Massey Ferguson special aircraft on its way to Mexico, even though the request from the CBC brass pointed out that this was "the type of gesture which I hope will sustain interest in the show for some time to come." He sent some of the band in his stead.

⌒

Don decided that, for Canada's Centennial in 1967, he would compose a number of tunes to honour different regions of Canada. He then decided to publish folios for the year, and each week *Don Messer's Jubilee* would have a special focus, a special show that would be unique to a region or a culture of Canada. Still not satisfied with his plans to celebrate the centenary, he planned to mount a huge Centennial Tour.

He and Ken (who took a leave of absence from his federal job) set about organizing this Centennial Tour. Don had always had a deep love of his country, and he was excited about crossing it again and sharing it with Naomi. He enjoyed seeing different communities and was eager to meet other musicians who would help him in his quest to locate more scores. Unwilling to speak publicly, he nevertheless composed a personal message to Canadians and included it in the special Centennial Tour program, which came complete with photographs and biographies of the band members and a map showing the breadth of the tour. His curiously stilted message speaks of his gratitude to the people of Canada for their support over the years, thanks the sponsors, and asks that "each of us learn to get along with each other in this great country of ours and where possible, lead the way towards showing brotherly love in distant lands." Always conscious of an opportunity to expand his business, he ends with the hope to "be able to continue presenting our type of family entertainment and perhaps someday our show may visit other countries through television and personal appearances, where I am sure it will be well received." The Centennial Tour souvenir program widely dispersed his message, and sales brought in a lot of revenue.

The tour was immense in its scope. Despite turning down many requests, the band performed more than seventy times in sixty locations, from Wabush, Labrador, to Port Alberni, British Columbia. In eleven weeks, the schedule allowed the performers only seven days off, which meant that Don himself would have only seven days of rest. As it turned out, extra performances cut their rest days to three. It was a risky venture for a man with a history of heart attacks, and indeed he suffered a third attack, or at least a "cardiac episode," during the tour.

They were in Sault Ste. Marie, heading back east. Sault Ste. Marie had always been very good to Don, with large crowds, and he was looking forward to a successful show, even though he was exhausted.

This was day sixty-six of the tour, and they had arisen early in Dryden and then spent nine hours on the bus. Don never found living out of a suitcase easy. He didn't sleep well in hotel rooms, and the irregularity of meals bothered him more now than it used to. He had not yet been diagnosed with diabetes, but the symptoms were beginning to show: the fatigue and the thirst, the loss of weight, and the slow healing from injury. Weeks earlier, he had got a splinter in his thumb; the small wound had festered, and it was still bothering him.

Don decided to lie down for a while before heading to the restaurant, so he and Naomi rode the elevator up to their floor. When the doors opened, Naomi stepped out and started down the hall toward their room. She had only gone a few paces when she realized that Don was no longer with her, and she rushed back to the elevator to find him leaning against the wall, trying to reach the vial of nitroglycerin in his vest pocket. They managed to make it to their room, and Naomi, recognizing the symptoms of a heart attack, called the house doctor, who persuaded the town cardiologist to attend to Don. He felt Don's problem was overtiredness, so, despite the numbness in his legs, Don continued with his plans for the evening's performance.

What Don was selling on the 1967 Centennial Tour was national unity. In a message in the souvenir program, John Fisher, the Centennial Commissioner, made it clear that the aim was to "make Canada conscious of its cultures, the talents of its artists and the reason why we should preserve and develop the resources we have. . . . In spreading the Maritime Message throughout Canada we feel that a deeper, more meaningful interpretation is being encouraged for our easternmost provinces. For a country continually striving toward unity, this is reason enough to wish the Islanders every success." Don had become a willing instrument of nationalism; however, that didn't mean he received the financial support he deserved. Festival Canada, while subsidizing fifty per cent of the expenses of the New York Philharmonic Orchestra, gave Don's Centennial Tour next to nothing.

Family Life: The Late Years, 1956-1970

Don and Naomi sit on the couch in their Charlottetown living room, shell-shocked. It is May 1956, and their world has just collapsed around them, the certainty with which they faced each day destroyed. Lorna is pregnant. Naomi has been suspicious for a few weeks, has been watching her second-born with concern. Lorna is her favourite, and she knows her moods well, can tell if she is worried or unhappy or ill. In the last few weeks, Lorna has seemed to be all of those things, and that, together with the unopened box of sanitary products, has led Naomi to confront her eighteen-year-old. Lorna burst into tears, a conclusive answer that Naomi was dreading.

Another shock was in store, and Naomi has waited for Don to get home from the studio before allowing herself to absorb its impact. Lorna has admitted that she is not only pregnant, but also she is married to Don Hill. It is so unlike Lorna, so totally unexpected for this child to be untruthful, to have kept secrets from her parents. They haven't even properly met this man who she says is her husband. Naomi knows, or thought she knew, that he was part of Dawn's crowd, not Lorna's. She knows he attends Prince of Wales College, had heard that one night at a dance, some of the boys had shaved his hair off for some infraction of teenage rules. He is from New Glasgow and has brothers. All in all, it's not a lot of information about a son-in-law.

Naomi and Don talk by themselves, without Lorna, who has stayed in her bedroom, tearful and frightened and embarrassed. They don't understand any of this: why Lorna got married, why they haven't met her husband, why she hasn't told them, why he and she both continue to live with their parents. They suspect that his parents are as ignorant of the marriage as are they, and while that saves face, it is little consolation.

~

If Lorna hadn't been pregnant, it seems likely that the Messers would have tried to have the marriage annulled, said Jeannie Miller, Lorna's childhood friend. "It would be something that Naomi would do without hesitation. That marriage was so out of character for Lorna; she didn't push the envelope at all." Lorna was a very beautiful young woman, gentle and timid by nature, not one to do something as rebellious as elope. She had gone to summer camp once, but returned home the next day, too homesick to remain. Even on tour with her father, she had lasted only two days before flying home. Those close to Lorna came to believe that the marriage was Hill's idea, his way of gaining attention and sharing the Messer fame. He and Lorna had married at the Baptist church, the one he attended. "God knows what kind of story they told," said Dawn.

Lorna may also have been mesmerized by this young man. "I think she was really thrilled about being involved with Don Hill," said Jeannie. "He was a little bit older, he was good looking, and his family was not poor. He had older brothers that were very nice guys, and they were nice to Lorna." Still, she certainly kept their relationship a secret, even from her best friend. Jeannie had moved to Cape Breton, and Lorna had visited her there; Jeannie eventually realized that Lorna must have been already married during that visit. "She never said a thing about it. But she well knew that I didn't like him. He was a fly-by-nighter, always knew he was going to make a million."

It must have been a terrible strain for Lorna to keep such a secret. She hadn't been able to tell anyone, with Jeannie in Cape Breton and Janis, at eleven, too young to confide in. Dawn would have helped her any way she could, but she was overseas, and Lorna didn't even know how to reach her.

Lorna was still in high school, in grade eleven, and in those days, girls in grade eleven did not attend school if they were pregnant. Now that her parents knew, she could relax about that, and to her relief they seemed to accept Don as a son-in-law. At least her father did. Naomi was not as sure. "She accepted him, but with reservations," said Dawn. "He was very charismatic, very ambitious, and very smart." Naomi might have been hard on her girls, but she was fiercely protective of them if she sensed they were in any danger, and Naomi did not trust Don Hill. It could have been the secrecy of the marriage, it could have been the pregnancy; whatever the cause, Naomi withheld her approval of this unexpected son-in-law.

Lorna and her husband set up their own home in an apartment at the top of St. Peter's Road. They seemed to be doing well enough, and on Christmas Day, 1956, Lorna gave birth to her son, Daniel Charles. Two years later, on October 15, 1958, she would have a second son, Donald "Todd." Don must have felt his family history repeating itself. Here they were with three daughters — twenty-three-year-old Dawn, twenty-year-old Lorna, thirteen-year-old Janis, and six-year-old son, Gray — and their daughter Lorna had two children of her own, not much younger than Gray.

They would have little time to spend with Lorna and the babies, for Don and Naomi were getting ready to move to Halifax. Don was finding it more and more difficult to travel back and forth between the Island and Halifax for the taping of *The Don Messer Show*, and he felt that his professional future was in Halifax, not Charlottetown. It would be wrenching to depart from the Island, especially leaving Lorna and the grandchildren behind. Don knew that he could no longer sustain the pace; he needed to concentrate his energies on television and cut back on radio and community performances during the taping season. He was sufficiently worried about Lorna, though, that he asked Jim and Jeannie Miller to look out for her. They had moved back to Charlottetown recently, and that gave him some peace of mind.

In the late fall of 1958, Don, Naomi, Janis, and Gray moved to Halifax, to the Kearney Lake Road. For Janis, it was not a happy move. She was not comfortable in her new school; she didn't know anyone her age. Miserable, she asked her parents if she could return to Charlottetown to live with their old neighbours, Ruby and Cleaver MacLean, so that she could finish high school there. The MacLeans were like second parents to her, and in later years she continued to visit them every summer, eventually taking her own children with her. Living in Charlottetown also allowed her to keep in contact with Lorna and her two young nephews.

It's hard to discern how much Janis knew. Perhaps she picked up on the tension in Lorna's household, noticed that Don Hill did not encourage visitors. Jeannie said, "Don would sometimes try and prevent our friendship. We just never allowed it. I didn't drive, but Jim would take me over there to spend an evening." Jeannie had young children similar in age to Lorna's, and the two old friends would take their children to the park when the weather was good. In hindsight, Jeannie wonders whether Lorna might have confided in her if she didn't know already how Jeannie felt about Don.

Then one night, in the midst of a storm, Lorna called Jim. Could he come and get her? Jim immediately got in the car and drove to the apartment, where he found Lorna in bad shape. She had miscarried, and Don had left, taking the children to his mother's. Jim bundled Lorna into his car and took her home to Jeannie.

Jim and Jeannie were in a quandary. They wanted to phone Don and Naomi. They also wanted to put Lorna on a flight to Halifax. Lorna would not let them do either. They consulted with a lawyer, who advised them that if Lorna left, Don Hill would be awarded custody of the two boys. Lorna was terrified of losing her children. So she returned to her husband. "It was a heartbreak when Lorna went back to him," said Jeannie.

Just when Don and Naomi learned what was going on is equally difficult to know. Jeannie hadn't thought that they were aware, had always felt guilty that she hadn't gone against Lorna's wishes and told her parents. Years later, Don expressed anger to her, asking why they hadn't sent Lorna to him and Naomi in Halifax; although, he seemed to recognize the futility of his anger and thanked them for being with Lorna in their stead. "We never had good feelings about the whole thing," he said.

Canada in the 1950s was not enlightened in protecting victims of abuse, but Don found his own way of taking care of those he loved. He bought the house next door to his own and invited Lorna and her husband to come and live there. Don Hill was interested in a career in radio, and his father-in-law offered to show him around, to introduce him to people in the business. It was an offer that Hill was not willing to pass up. He and Lorna moved to Halifax and would have two more children while they lived there — a daughter, Brenda Anne, on January 1, 1960, and another son, Jeffrey Scott, on May 28, 1963.

〜

In their Halifax home, the older Messers seemed in many ways a typical Canadian family. They often went to the movies, and they watched television together, favouring the westerns *Gunsmoke* and *Bonanza*. Don always watched hockey and tried to take in games on the road if he could. "He was a big hockey fan," said Dawn. "He really enjoyed the game, and he'd have a drink of Scotch and so would my mother." Dawn was working as a nurse in Halifax for a short stint and would often get home at midnight or later. Don would say to her, "How about going into the KFC?' I'd have to drive back to town and get him a snack and he loved that. We would think that he would get sick of take-out food living on the road as he did, but he also got used to it," said Dawn.

Don always attended church when he was home, sitting in the back row as he did when he was a child. "He'd be at church early," said Eva MacLean, the wife of Reverend Allison MacLean, "and he would get in the back row, or one or two from the back, and he was the first one to leave. He would shake hands with my husband and leave. He wouldn't say hello to anybody, he didn't want any fanfare at all."

The Messers' domestic life was not without its worries, however. Having Lorna and her children under their watch next door could hardly have eased their minds completely about that situation, and then they began to have difficulty with Gray. Once he came to live with Don and Naomi in Charlottetown, there were fewer trips to Belledune, perhaps because of the awkwardness of the situation. Lottie didn't write to Gray for fear of interfering with Naomi and Don's parenting, but her sister Grace sent him birthday and Christmas cards.

It's uncertain when Gray learned that he was adopted, or rather that he was a child in limbo, neither living with his birth parents nor adopted by those who were raising him. Naomi and Don were not the ones to tell him. Dawn thinks it was his sister Karen who shared his life story with him during a visit to Belledune. She is not certain that he was told the identity of his mother, only that Naomi and Don were not his birth parents. This was devastating news to the little boy, and he began to try to discover the identity of his real mother. For a long time, Jack Gray says, he thought his Aunt Grace was his mother because she was the one who had written to him all that time.

Gray's behaviour became increasingly difficult. While they still lived in Charlottetown, Ruby MacLean said, "He was a nice little fellow, but he just didn't seem to want to mind Naomi. She'd get mad at him, but it wouldn't matter. Sometimes he was hard to control." Others felt that Gray was spoiled, perhaps because he was the only boy. In Halifax, while Don and Naomi were becoming re-involved in the lives of their grandchildren, Gray grew more and more troubled. "He was always getting into hot water," said Jeannie. She felt part of it had to do with Naomi's age. She was forty-nine the year Gray turned ten, and she struggled to deal with him. He was never in trouble with the police, never caused damage, but he would go out on the ice on the lakes, for instance, and stay out late. The Messers found it difficult to communicate with him, and he became an isolated little boy, living in the household but never seeming able to feel part of the family.

Seated left to right: Janis, Lorna with Scott on her lap, Naomi and
Don; in front, Danny, Brenda and Todd. The photograph appeared
with a 1964 *Chatelaine* article about children of TV stars.

Chatelaine.

It became very important for him to find his mother and to live with
her, Jeannie said. "He wanted very much to be with her, and because
of that, I don't think Naomi felt bad about letting him go. I think Don
missed him, he was his boy." Gray was no longer happy living with the
Messers, so they set in place a plan to return him to Lottie.

Charlie would be part of that plan, driving Gray to Belledune to
his grandmother's house. From there, his uncle Glen would drive him
to Mississauga, where his mother, sister, and stepfather were staying

with his Aunt Grace. It would be an awkward reunion; then twelve, Gray had not seen his mother since he was eighteen months old.

Gray stayed with his mother and moved with her to Orleans, Ontario, but he never seemed to find contentment. He began to get in trouble with the law and eventually moved out west. He did attend Don's funeral in 1973, disappearing again almost immediately after the service. Few in the family have had any contact with him since, though they did learn that he had called his first daughter Lottie, after his mother.

⁓

Don's second heart attack occurred in 1964, at around the time that Gray moved back with his mother. It was a horrible time for the family. They were losing Gray after twelve years, and Lorna and her children were moving to Burlington, Ontario. "It was really hard for Mum," says Lorna's daughter Brenda Hill Hudson. "When my father was transferred, it was like ripping her heart out. She loved her mum and dad without measure." Don did what he could to ensure her comfort and that of the children. He paid for the house in Burlington, and the car that carried them there. "Anything we had as a family . . . we were six steps ahead because of Nana and Grampie," said Brenda. Don and Naomi, with Janis in tow, fled to Prince Edward Island and the comfort of the Miller's East Royalty home. It must have seemed a haven to them. The CBC didn't know where he was and couldn't contact him, and they were spared the sight of Lorna's house, no longer a shelter to her and the children.

When they returned in the fall, Janis worked for her father as a secretary, putting to good use her training in secretarial school and bringing some kind of order to his office. She helped him answer his fan mail, organized his music, and doted on him. Always very protective of her since birth, he enjoyed having her work with him. He was pleased, too, that she had a boyfriend whom he and Naomi liked. He was worried about Dawn now.

Dawn readily admits that she never wanted to be a nurse and only went into nursing to please her mother. It was not a good career choice for her. Once in 1954, during her training, she had gone AWOL from the Victoria General Hospital and driven to Lunenburg, where her father was performing, to talk with him about leaving nursing. He had convinced her to stay, to refrain from disappointing her mother. She went back to Halifax to face a disciplinary hearing; the school officials had found out she had left. The ensuing reprimand did nothing to increase her affinity for the profession, but she stuck it out. Don couldn't attend her graduation, but he did send her a very expensive set of luggage. She believes he knew even then that his independent daughter would not be staying in one place very long.

After graduation Dawn worked for a very short time at a hospital, but, bored and unhappy, she left to accept a job as a nurse with Maritime Central Airways, which had been awarded a Canadian government contract to bring refugees to Canada. For two years Dawn flew back and forth between Canada and Europe as a flight nurse accompanying refugees from Hungary or flying polio vaccine to Russia. In 1957, she actually spent more time in Europe than she did in Canada. Dawn had always been the adventurous one in the family, the one who marched to her own drumbeat, the one the other girls envied for her glamour, and this job suited her very well.

Don was proud of her. He and she had always been close, always talked to each other as equals even when she was very young. When she left that job after two years and started nursing at the Moncton Sanatorium, he was relieved that she was no longer flying. Then she upset him by starting to date Myron (Mickey) Attis. Mickey was a real estate developer, a businessman with a finger in a lot of pies. That was fine with Don — he could relate to that. What he couldn't relate to were the facts that Mickey was Jewish and a professional high-stakes gambler.

Don, who was so conservative in his religious beliefs that he had advised his daughters to date only Presbyterians, was disappointed once again. Lorna had married a Baptist, and now Dawn was dating a Jew. Don knew nothing about the Jewish faith. He might have felt better had he known that Mickey's parents were as concerned as he was; in fact they had sent Mickey out of the country to give him time and distance to get over Dawn. But Mickey and Dawn were very much in love, and neither Don's disapproval nor the Attises' concern was going to keep them apart.

Dawn changed jobs again. She had returned to the airline for another stint, but then she left nursing altogether and went to work for Clairol, a manufacturer of hair care products, as a consultant. The job paid far better than nursing and came with perks. Dawn was a natural at it, with her flair, her beauty, and her business acumen.

Whenever she was on the Island, she would visit Ruby, and they had some good times together. "I'll never forget, one time after she got the Clairol job, Dawn said to me, 'Ruby, you want to get your hair tinted?'" Ruby wasn't sure of the wisdom of this but went along with it for fun. "So we started about six p.m., and we never finished until about midnight. After she was finished, I nearly died." Ruby had been transformed from a dark brunette to a blonde. "We had more fun that night," she recalled with nostalgia.

Dawn had bought a racehorse that she kept at Sackville Downs racetrack, and she frequently borrowed money from her father because she liked to bet at the track. "He was my banker," she said "but I always paid him back." When she was younger, she had bartered a car out of him. "I told him that I wasn't going to get married, and he wouldn't have to pay for a wedding, but I would like to have a car," she said with a laugh. "I always had to bargain. I bargained and I bargained, and I think he got a big kick out of it. So he'd said, 'Well, I'll see what I can do,' and he bought me a Volkswagen Beetle. It didn't even have a gas gauge or anything."

Lorna's marriage to a Baptist had caused Don and Naomi considerable distress, and Dawn's continuing relationship with her Jewish boyfriend made them very uncomfortable. Janis would earn the same disapproval. First, she broke up with her boyfriend of seven years, a man they liked and approved of and had always hoped she'd marry. Then she stopped working as Don's secretary and took a job in the business office of the *Halifax Chronicle Herald*. There she met David LeBlanc, a fluently bilingual sales representative who was a Catholic. Within months they were engaged. This upset her entire family, and not just because of his religion; they felt that she had jumped into this new relationship too quickly. Her niece, Brenda Hill Hudson recalled, "David was very charming, very enigmatic, and Janis just ate it up."

"She should never have married him, I begged her not to marry him," Dawn said. "I remember driving up Quinpool Road saying, 'Oh, Janis, go live with him. Don't commit.'" Dawn worried that Janis was marrying David on the rebound, still heartbroken after her breakup with her long-time boyfriend. Brenda seconds this. "I remember the whole family taking a step back and saying, who is this guy? He was just so not her type. The wedding was rushed, and I remember flying down and getting my hair done, and seeing Janis in her wedding dress and thinking, this just isn't right, there's something just not right. We're going through the motions."

Janis married David on November 8, 1968. It was a small wedding, with only the immediate family and clergy present. Don got his wish and the wedding was held in the Presbyterian Church; the officiant was Reverend Allison MacLean. In the beginning, Janis and David lived next door to Don and Naomi in the house that Lorna and Don Hill had lived in. It was convenient for everybody because Janis had returned to working for her father and David travelled a good deal. Despite living next door, Janis was afraid to stay in the house by herself and would move back into her childhood bedroom in her parent's home whenever David was away. David's absences were frequent, and, more troubling, he was spending a great deal of money. Don had always been generous with his girls, providing them with homes and cars, but David was spending their money on boats, knowing full well that Janis was afraid of the water.

❧

In the late summer of 1970, Dawn sat down with her father and told him she intended to marry Mickey. He reacted with dismay. "How can you marry someone that doesn't believe in God?" he asked.

Dawn responded, "We . . . they believe in God," and she gave him the book, which she recalled being titled *Who Is My God?* "He read it and seemed to be more peaceful with it," she said. She also realized that, in saying "we," she had let slip the fact that she had converted to Judaism. The idea was so far from Don's reality that he never picked up on her slip of the tongue, and Dawn never told him.

Naomi was more vocal about the wedding plans. "How could you do this to your father?" she would wail. Dawn, in a fit of pique and hurt, told her mother that if her father was that concerned about losing her chihuahuas when she moved out, he could keep them. "I always said Dad was more concerned about losing the chihuahuas than me," she said, still hurt by their lack of acceptance of Mickey. Don did keep Champagne and Impy, and neither he nor Naomi attended Dawn and Mickey's wedding on September 12, 1970. They did go to the reception, which was held at Mickey's (and Dawn's) home just around the corner from Don and Naomi's. Dawn had to beseech them to do so. "Please come," she had begged. "The deed is done. You don't have to stay, just come and meet a few people." It wasn't as if Dawn and Mickey weren't aware of what they were doing. They had known each other for fourteen years when they finally married at the age of thirty-five.

"Her marriage to Mickey did not sit well with Don and Naomi," said Jeannie. "They were both very vocal about it. Don very much believed in Protestants marrying Protestants." In his view, marrying outside one's faith just wasn't done. "Mickey's parents were far more accepting," Dawn said. "I became their daughter the day I married Mickey."

Dawn, who had always been able to negotiate with her dad, was never able to gain his acceptance of Mickey, despite Mickey's obvious generosity and acceptance of him and Naomi. In a twist of irony, the photograph that has pride of place in her living room is a poster-size print of a radiant Dawn and her handsome Mickey standing beside the Volkswagen Beetle she had bargained with her father for in lieu of a wedding ceremony.

Hardship and Heartbreak

Don sits in the CBC Halifax studio in February 1969, studying the journalist from the *Dartmouth Free Press*. She has come to do an article on *Don Messer's Jubilee,* and he hopes she will write a positive story. She is young, sophisticated, and intellectual — a combination that does not bode well for a review of him and his show. The intellectuals love to make fun of *Don Messer's Jubilee*, to call it corny and homespun. He has fought that prejudice for years and is prepared to continue fighting, but he has grown weary of the battle.

The journalist's name is Nancy White. He is relieved that she has at least some knowledge of music, some appreciation for the skill with which it is performed. She asks intelligent questions and has done her research. Don notices that she has relaxed since she came in and seems to be enjoying the meeting, perhaps in spite of herself, and he smiles. The collegial atmosphere in the studio has seduced her as it has many others before her. He knows now that her article will be positive.

He continues to watch her and listen to her questions about the format in which the show is taped. She is amused at the lip-synching, at the performers mouthing "most convincingly to the soundtrack of their own voices as the musicians play silently." That is how it will appear in Thursday's edition of the paper. The show has been pre-recorded for years now because pre-recording produces a far better quality of sound, but few people are aware of that.

The journalist has gone into the control booth now with Bill Langstroth, the producer of the show. Don continues to watch her as she listens intently to Langstroth and Penny Longley, his script assistant, and then asks to see the two-column script, with song lyrics and dialogue on one side and camera cues on the other. She seems to be following along, glancing up now and then as Langstroth gives instructions through a microphone to Milton Isnor, who in turn relays those instructions to the cast. Don watches her, wishes he could hear what is being said. He is no longer sure he can trust Langstroth.

When the article appeared on Thursday, February 13, 1969, it was indeed positive and even upbeat. Nancy White wrote that she "came away thinking that the show was the greatest invention since zippers, and that even if it's not your kind of music, you have to admit that it's well done." Don was pleased but could not shake the nagging worry that had been with him since the phone call from Sid Adilman of the *Toronto Telegram*.

Adilman was a writer on the entertainment beat with one of the biggest newspapers in the country. He had phoned Messer to tell him that he had looked at the CBC fall lineup and did not see *Don Messer's Jubilee* listed. Would Don care to comment on that?

Don couldn't respond, for he knew nothing about any planned changes. He had asked Langstroth about it, but Langstroth denied knowing anything. Whereas that might once have reassured Don, it no longer did. The two of them had worked well together for thirteen years, but last year things had started to sour between them.

Bill Langstroth had suggested that they might make some changes to the program, perhaps introduce some songs that were more current than the old tried-and-true numbers that they had been playing since the program's inception. Don disagreed with him. The show was about old-time music, and that's what he would deliver. He was okay with the occasional guest like Catherine McKinnon singing songs like "We'll Sing in the Sunshine," but his own band would stick to the songs that were requested by their fans, songs like "Put your Shoes On, Lucy (don't you know you're in the city)." Don knew what they liked and he wasn't about to tamper with it. He had no problem getting sponsors for the show, he was still getting copious fan mail, and he had always done well by listening to the fans. They, not Bill Langstroth, would determine what he played. All the CBC surveys in the world wouldn't make him change.

The CBC research survey was in fact a sore point. Published in June 1967, it was a scathing indictment of the show. Its very first sentence showed its bias. "Among those people who ever watch Don Messer, the most highly praised members of the cast are the Buchta Dancers, host Don Tremaine, and Don Messer and his music, each being enjoyed to the same extent. Next in line within the same viewing group, comes Marg Osburne and Johnny Forrest with Marg Osburne the slightly more enjoyed of the two. Finally there is Charlie Chamberlain, this year as last, the least enjoyed of the regular performers." Don didn't agree with the results, and he didn't agree with the methodology of the study.

Fortunately for the atmosphere of the show, he and Don Tremaine still worked very well together. "Don was very gracious and decent to me," said Tremaine. "He was a complex kind of character, didn't have any wild ambition, and I think he was continually dazzled by the fact that he was such a Canadian icon. We got along extremely well. He was very modest and had a bit of a sense of humour, too."

He would need that humour, for the CBC moved his program from Monday night to Friday night. They had offered him Sunday, a day that would likely have guaranteed success, but he wouldn't stand for that, didn't feel it was appropriate to have square-dancing on a Sunday. Friday was not his choice. He knew his audience would be out on Friday evenings, and thus his viewing numbers would decline.

He and Langstroth continued to meet to talk about the programs, the music, and the guests. The meetings were always cordial and productive. They seemed to have moved past the difficulty of the previous summer, when Don had taken the rather surprising action of requesting that Langstroth be removed as producer of the show. This issue had arisen after Don had tried to fire Vic Mullen, who had played the banjo and mandolin as a featured guest on the show for six years, and Langstroth had objected. Don had no quarrel with Vic's music; it was his attitude he didn't like.

Bill Langstroth recalled the incident. "Don indicated that he wanted Vic in the first place, to give a different dimension to the sound, but I think he had a personality problem with him. It was just a clash of different personality styles. Vic had unctuousness, that smiling American salesman smile. It grated on Don, it wasn't Canadian."

Mullen's own explanation for the bad blood is probably more on the mark. He recalled an incident during a rehearsal when things weren't going very smoothly and Langstroth asked for his input. He gave it and was horrified to hear Langstroth say through the microphone, "Vic and I have decided this is how we are going to do this song."

"I was a featured musician, it was not my place to tell the band what they were going to do," said Vic, still cringing at the memory years later. "I was wrong and Bill was, too. If that had happened to me as bandleader, I would have gone through the glass."

Vic believes that Don felt there was a conspiracy between him and Langstroth, but there wouldn't have been that animosity if Don's personality had been a little different. Although Vic saw in Don "a great deal of talent and a great deal of 'stick-to-it-ness,'" he said, "Don would bow to some of the things Langstroth wanted him to do, even if he thought they were wrong. Then he would fret about it to himself, and that put a lot of stress and strain on him. You could tell when he was not very happy with the way things were going with the band, or with the CBC, because he would be a little down, and if something went wrong, he might kick his toe against the mike stand and say a little gol' dang. But he never elaborated, he just made these reactions, and everybody shaped up and listened carefully to see if they could detect what he thought was wrong and try and fix it."

Langstroth had the same sense of Don's unwillingness to cause friction or to be confrontational. "He didn't express himself very often. His frustrations would cause him to splutter, but they wouldn't cause him to burst out. I sometimes wonder whether that didn't just take its toll on him."

What was bothering Don was his fear that the CBC was trying to get rid of him. He had never felt secure, always wondering whether the show would continue for another season. The astute businessman that he was, he could feel the tides of change, not in the fans, but in the administration and politics of the CBC. He truly felt that Vic Mullen and Bill Langstroth were sabotaging *Don Messer's Jubilee* in favour of another show, *Singalong Jubilee*, that presented "a younger look and a younger orientation," according to CBC trend seekers.

∾

The day the axe fell was a typical day at the studio. Don and Bill Langstroth were speaking in Bill's office when Bill handed him a tele-gram. It was dated April 14, 1969, and signed by Doug Nixon, the director of entertainment programming. It was short, only eighty-two words, but those words cut deeply.

> A necessary change is the cancellation of the Don Messer series and its replacement in the opening sked for the fall and winter by the *Singalong Jubilee Series*. The reasoning for this is to inject a fresh new element into the wintertime sked and provide a program with a younger look and younger orientation. While we recognize the values of Don Messer in the past we feel quite definitely that this change will be in the interest of the overall sked.

Enough room for three repetitions of the word "sked" but no thank you, not even the courtesy of getting the name of his show right. The very brevity of the message hurt. After thirty-five years with the CBC, Don was being dismissed with not even the courtesy of a face-to-face meeting or the softening touch of a phone call. The fact that the person who had to deliver the blow was his producer — the same producer whose new program, *Singalong Jubilee*, would be replacing *Don Messer's Jubilee* — was awkward for both of them. In effect,

Don was being fired by his replacement, someone he had worked with in a collegial relationship for thirteen years, ever since his first television show.

The day the telegram was actually handed over is uncertain. Langstroth remembers it as the day of the final taping, May 8, 1969. That is impossible, however, for Don did an interview two days earlier, on May 6, 1969, with *Weekend Magazine*, which had sent Ernest Hillen to the set to cover "the funeral," that is, the rehearsal and taping of the last show. That show would include a bilingual performance by Gene MacLellan of his composition "Snowbird," the song that would catapult him to fame. Unfortunately, Don could not enjoy the presentation of this new talent.

Don was shattered. It was one thing to look forward to retirement, another to be fired so callously. He had received a personal letter from Doug Nixon at his home, thanking him "on behalf of the Corporation for a very fine job over a long period," but it did little to soften the feelings of betrayal. He told Hillen that the "the news took a long, long time to sink in. I would have liked to retire with dignity and honour after thirty-five years, but they didn't leave me that." He felt he was "dropped without concrete excuse or reason." That went against his logical and methodical nature. "They could have let me know last fall, then maybe I could have planned better," he told *Toronto Telegram*'s *TV Weekly* reporter Pat Johnson.

Langstroth saw the cancellation as a business decision. "The show was not as potent as it was in earlier years . . . it had never changed, never accommodated even a bit of new music, it never could have, it wouldn't fit. The CBC needed to move in a new direction." His view on the viability of the show did not mean that he lacked respect for Don. "He was a very bright guy. I don't think anybody ever plumbed the intellectual depths that were there. There was no real opportunity to do so on the show, it was never really necessary in what we did. We were doing a job, and he did it well."

The public certainly thought so. They rose up in anger, they marched, they wrote, they telephoned, and they protested the loss of their program, which many of them had watched for ten years — its entire time on national television. "There was nothing like it before, nothing like it since," said Catherine McKinnon. "It wasn't just by chance that when they took the show off the air people marched on Parliament Hill."

At first, there were just the letters from fans. Don must have felt gratified to receive more than a thousand of them at his home. Then the articles came, as newspaper after newspaper published editorials and cartoons decrying the loss of the show and the callous way in which the people's favourite entertainer had been treated. "Could it be that the show was too popular? Or is this a case of the CBC mandarins deciding to show the people who is boss?" asked the *Moncton Daily Times*.

Next came the personal telegram, so different in size and content than the one he had received from Langstroth. This one measured almost eleven metres in length and included thirteen hundred signatures of fans in Fort William (now Thunder Bay), Ontario. Then, in quick succession, followed cards, poems, and boxes of cookies, all with the same message: "Don't take Don Messer off the air." Fans, friends, and other musicians called Don at home, commiserating with him, telling him how outraged they were with the CBC, exclaiming at how out of touch their national television network was with the common people. It was heady stuff, but it was ineffective in getting the program reinstated.

By May 27, 1969, more than eight thousand people had written to the CBC protesting the cancellation of the show, compared with eighty who had written applauding the action of the CBC. Approximately fifteen hundred people had telephoned to voice their dismay at the decision. In addition, thirteen thousand pieces of mail were received by the CBC, forwarded to them from politicians, newspaper editors, and others. Of that number, eight thousand were protest coupons that stores had sponsored in newspapers, inviting people to fill them in and mail them to the CBC, protesting the cancellation of the show.

Radio stations took up the cause, conducting open-line interviews in St. John's, Sydney, Halifax, Saint John, Montreal, Kingston, Sault Ste. Marie, Regina, and Vancouver. The formidable display of protest fell on deaf ears.

So the show's supporters ramped it up again. In Winnipeg they made signs for their cars that said, "SAVE THE DON MESSER SHOW." They called on their politicians. In June, Premier Robichaud stood up in the New Brunswick Legislative Assembly and offered to write to the CBC and request that the program be kept on the air. Don Messer, after all, was New Brunswick's most famous son. He, too, was ignored. Three other provincial legislatures condemned the cancellation of the show.

That finally elicited a response from Don. He knew the matter of the show's cancellation had been raised in Parliament, and the fact that this had not resulted in a rescinding of the decision caused him to lash out. "The governments have handed over too much power to agencies. What's the sense in sending 265 members to Ottawa if they are powerless to act on such things as programming? When the head of the CBC can rebuke the people who pay the shot, it's time for a change." He wasn't finished lambasting them. "You'll see great strides in electronics, space, and communication in the next thirty years. What's the sense in having better means of communication if you don't hold the programs you have? Unless the CBC keeps more closely in touch with the people, they better quit."

Meek, mild-mannered Don had gone over the top. Previously always respectful, he now referred to the CBC executives as "dunderdinks," as people who had "replaced their brains with beads." Certainly the unfairness of it all had pushed him to such fervent heights. He had a popular show that had never scored lower than eleventh in the ratings in all those years, yet he had been discarded like garbage. He couldn't understand the unwillingness of the CBC to negotiate, to at least consider the idea of offering *Don Messer's Jubilee* specials.

If the CBC would not listen to reason, then it was time to take to the streets. Graham Townsend, the fiddling prodigy and friend of his mentor, did just that, holding a music festival on Parliament Hill. Crowds marched on the Hill, waved placards demanding that the politicians "Save Don Messer," and they cried, "Canada needs Don Messer, not the CBC," to the delight of print journalists but with no effect on the judgment. It seemed somehow that there was more at stake than a harmless television program.

"Simple down-home goodness with plain music and clean humour was the package Messer offered — one which the Canadian public was only too eager to embrace," said Johanne Devlin Trew in her article "Conflicting Visions: Don Messer, Liberal Nationalism and the Canadian Unity Debate." She believed the cancellation of the show was brought about "by the new vision of Canada which emerged during the 1960s as projected by successive Liberal governments of the period; a vision generated not only in response to the threat of Americanization, but also due to new political challenges at home."

Those political challenges included the demands of Quebec nationalism and the design of a new flag that spoke to Canada as a separate entity from Great Britain. Don was not a fan of bilingualism: he believed all people in Canada should speak English, even if they retained another language for cultural reasons. He had refused to use the bilingual posters supplied by Festival Canada for the Centennial Tour and had purchased English-only posters out of his own funds. Nor did he accept the need for a flag other than the Union Jack, and no one would deny that he was a tireless promoter of the traditional tunes of the country's Scottish and Irish heritage.

Don was seen as "too traditional" and his show as "not projecting the image of Canada envisioned by the Canadian government." Trew concluded, "It begins to look as though Messer's tremendous popularity may, in fact, have worked against him and led to the cancellation of the program."

Closer to home was the change in CBC's cultural climate. Geoff Pevere, himself a CBC radio host, remarked that "one of the most revealing contradictions in Canadian TV culture [is] the fact that while Canada's viewing public has traditionally had a large rural, conservative, and working-class base, most of Canada's broadcasting executives have been well-heeled, urban, hipster wannabes."

∽

Don already had a tour booked for the summer following his TV show's cancellation, and it became even more important that he see it through. There would be no more money coming from the CBC, and he had no pension. He had savings, but he also had expenses, and he worried about the future of his family and his band members. Even the Buchta Dancers would be affected by the cancellation of the show. So while he prepared for the tour he looked for another home for his show, for the security that it would provide. He found it in Hamilton, Ontario.

In June 1969, a mere month after the broadcast of the last show on CBC-TV, CHCH-TV, a CTV affiliate, announced that it would be carrying *Don Messer's Jubilee* on Mondays at eight p.m., a time slot that had always worked very well for Don and his audience. When Don was asked for a comment, he expressed hope for the future and said he "looked forward to the challenge."

The production of the CTV version of the show would be vastly different. It would in truth be exhausting: all twenty-six shows would be filmed in five or sometimes six weeks, in contrast to the filming of one show a week. Everyone would work from early in the morning until late at night, but this was the only practical way to do it because the entire cast would have to move to Hamilton every summer for the taping. Other adjustments would have to be made, too, such as discontinuing the program themes. Instead, every program would have to be suitable for broadcast at any time of the year. There was one exception: *Don Messer's Jubilee* would still have a Christmas program.

The faith that CTV producer Manny Pittson put in Don was well and speedily rewarded. Twenty-two television stations across Canada signed on to purchase the show for the 1969-1970 season. It wasn't a hard sell: obviously a huge audience was waiting for the show. To make the situation even better, the cast liked Manny Pittston very much and appreciated his faith in them.

First, Don had to do the summer tour. His extreme stress became apparent several days before departure, when he developed a rash

"The Peoples Choice"

Photograph sold at engagements during the 1969 tour, after the CBC had axed *Don Messer's Jubilee*. Fans had called Don and the rest of the cast "The People's Choice." Back row: Charlie Chamberlain, Waldo Munro, Marg Osburne, Johnny Forrest, Warren MacCrae, Don Messer, Duke Nielsen, Rae Simmons, Cec McEachern, Gunter Buchta; middle row: Joe Wallin, Gary Copp, Don King, Hugh Ballem, and Gary Eisenhauer; front row: Lynne Donahoe (Sheehan), Jane Edgett, Marilyn Boyle, Judy Edgett, and Linda Clinton.

Courtesy: John Clifford [CBC Still Photo Collection].

covering his face and had to send the others on ahead. Thereafter he flew to Ottawa, where three thousand people attended his opening performance.

The *Don Messer's Jubilee Farewell Tour*, as it was dubbed, "because I am sixty and because I've been at it since 1949," probably did more to heal Don Messer than anything else could have, other than the return of the show to the CBC. It vindicated everything he believed about his band, his music, and people's love for *Don Messer's Jubilee*. As they travelled across Canada to Whitehorse and back, their audiences told them over and over again how much the show had meant to them through the years.

"The thing that has given me the greatest satisfaction is this sea of upturned faces in the audience, all showing appreciation for our efforts," Don told Lloyd Sellick, who published his biography of Don that year. "It has to be seen to be understood. It just keeps you going on and on, even though you are dog tired."

Fans gave him presents. He received drawings of Marg, Charlie, and himself from schoolchildren. He was given gold coffee spoons in the Yukon, coloured glass in Alberta, handmade canes, and a carved moose. Totem poles from British Columbia and a mile post from Dawson Creek were carried home to Halifax. It seemed the fans could not do enough for him, could not try hard enough to let him know that the CBC did not speak for them.

The Buchta Dancers, who had been part of the show since 1959, were included in that farewell tour. They had reacted with shock and hurt at the cancellation of the show and had thought at first that was the end. Dancer Joe Wallin explained, "We felt we had a summer tour to do, and our sadness and the love and respect and admiration from the general public overwhelmed everything. Everywhere we went, the crowds had picket signs: 'Don't Take Don Messer Off the Air.' It was a phenomenon. It's something that I think I was extremely lucky to be part of."

The dancers were used to crowds on tour. There were always people waiting for them at the hotel on their arrival, and at the end of the show there were always people wanting autographs. That year, there were three or more times the number they would usually have. "The people were very upset at CBC for dropping us, for dropping the show, and just seemed to show us more admiration and love than normal."

For Gunter Buchta himself, it was a sad time. He respected Don, his musicianship, and his management, and it hurt him to see him humiliated. He spoke out, uncharacteristically for him. "The people are beginning to realize his greatness. You may have noticed that the feelings expressed in the papers are more for Don than for the band. They don't like the way he has been treated by the CBC."

As a treat, the dancers paid for the Royal Suite in the Capri Motor Hotel in Red Deer, Alberta, for Don and Naomi. "The bed was so big, I swear it would hold nine people," said Don. He was touched by the gift and felt that the band and the dancers had pulled a little closer to him and Naomi on this tour.

There were of course the same old grumblings on the road, the fatigue and stress, and the hard feelings about the cancellation were not eliminated by the future with CTV. Don took it in stride, "It's human nature to do the odd little bit of grumbling. You beef a little if conditions are not good. You know, travelling on the road, come mealtimes, the bus may be in the middle of the desert. You can't just stop and have dinner. You've got to keep going." That was almost a summary of his philosophy of life.

&

Taping *Don Messer's Jubilee* in Hamilton had an unforeseen advantage: over the next three summers, Don and Naomi could see more of Lorna and her family, who lived nearby in Burlington. They had always had a special relationship with Lorna's daughter Brenda (Brenda Hill Hudson today). For as long as she could remember, Brenda had always spent her childhood summers in the Maritimes: six weeks with Grampie and Nana Messer and then one week with the Hills. When *Don Messer's Jubilee* moved to Hamilton, just a few kilometres away from her home, she had the opportunity to do something special for her grandfather. "Grampie was a diabetic and he needed to have fibre supplements, so as a little girl, I would make him bran muffins and take them to the studio and play. He used to call them 'Bren's Brans.'" Lorna would get up early with Brenda and help her make the muffins, and then the little girl's father would drive her to the studio for the day, picking her up on his way home in the evening. "I got to learn pretty early that when the On Air sign was on I couldn't run and get up on Grampie's knees," she said.

In more relaxed moments, he would go out to his daughter's house, sit by the pool in his undershirt and short pants, have a bit of whisky, and relax. That would only last so long, until word got out that he was there and the neighbours started peeking over the garden fence. He was never comfortable with such an invasion of privacy.

When the taping was over, the entire crew would go to the Wiener Schnitzel Restaurant for a celebratory meal, and then Brenda would travel back to the Maritimes with them and stay with Naomi while Don was on tour. It was like going back in time to when she had lived next door.

"We lived up the hill on Grosvenor and Nan and Grampie lived on Kearney Lake Road. The houses backed on each other and there was a steep hill between our homes, and when we were little kids, we knew that we had to wait until the kitchen window curtain was half-way drawn, because if it wasn't, that meant Gram and Grampie were still sleeping, and we weren't allowed to knock on the door. Nana used to say it took her a long time after we left [to move to Ontario] to clean the window of the door."

"Nana" was much more relaxed with her granddaughter than she had ever been with her own children. Brenda recalled Naomi's taking her to the mall and asking her if she wanted a record "from that boy with the big fat lips." Mick Jagger was no hero to Naomi, who loved music, except for "that foolish rock and roll: that about drives me up the wall." Whereas her own children had found Naomi's quick temper a fearful thing, Brenda was in awe of it, thrilled that her grandmother had such attitude. "She had an intuition that was sharper than a razor. She could take one look, have one conversation with you, and she knew immediately if you were down to earth, had an agenda, or were a snake. She didn't put up with garbage from anybody. She was very, very quick with words and very loyal toward those who were genuine, rather than wanting something."

Brenda recognized when she was quite young the protective role that Naomi played with Don. "My Nana took it upon herself to really look out for him, because he was shy and giving and not the kind of person who liked any kind of confrontation or anything ugly. She was definitely the 'bad cop' in the relationship."

Jack Gray, Naomi's nephew, saw another dimension to their relationship. When he was stationed in Halifax with the Air Force,

Naomi and Don would come over to spend the evening with him and his wife in the married quarters in Dartmouth. "He loved his bottle of Scotch," said Jack. "When he used to come over to visit me, he always brought a bottle of Scotch. He carried it in a bowling bag, you know, the kind you carry your shoes in. He was totally different than he was on television. He would talk about anything. I remember at the time they were integrating the Armed Forces into one, and he certainly didn't agree with that. Naomi was quick tempered, but Don could stand his ground with her. I don't think she was the total boss of the house, but she shared in it."

If Naomi had known what was occurring in the Hill home, "she would have torn my father to shreds," Brenda said without hesitation. It seemed to her that Don Hill and Nana Messer did not like each other one bit. "She had his number from day one, and he knew it. They couldn't be in the same room together." Even as young children, she and her brothers had sensed that tension.

Brenda was unsure when Naomi and Don learned of the abuse that her family had suffered, but she believed that "they suspected a long, long time. In those days, my mum felt, I'm married, I have four children, my job is to be a mum and take care of them, and I just have to suffer through it. I'm sure that she was humiliated and embarrassed. I am sure that she would have loved nothing more than to run to her mum and dad and say, get me away from all of this, and they would have moved heaven and earth if she had done that. I think she was afraid that if she did she would lose her children. In some ways, her family's status exacerbated the fact that she couldn't say anything."

Janis, too, was in dire straits for a time. She had been delirious with joy when Kirk was born on March 19, 1972, and there wasn't a more beautiful baby on the entire planet in her opinion. Three months later she was pregnant again, but David was never there; he was off in his cabin cruiser.

"She just lost her grip," said Brenda. "Here she was with one baby and pregnant with another, and she just lost it." Janis started drinking. Dawn would stop by to check on her, she resented that, and,

Brenda said, they fought like cats and dogs. "It didn't matter what Dawn wanted to do, or what her intentions were, she saw it as Dawn questioning her ability to handle her family." For Dawn, it was terribly painful to watch her sister destroy herself. "It broke my heart," she said. She didn't discuss it with her parents, feeling that Janis was an adult and it was her private business, but she did everything she could to try and help her.

~

In June 1972, the cast of *Don Messer's Jubilee* was in Hamilton for the taping of the show. Charlie was not well; his legs were swollen, his breathing was laboured, even after the short walk from the hotel to the converted movie theatre where the taping took place. He showed up at rehearsal every day, never missed one, but his friends worried about his obviously failing condition. One day, Charlie collapsed on the set and was taken to hospital.

Don seems to have thought Charlie's condition was a temporary setback, or perhaps his own brush with heart attacks made him unwilling to consider that his friend wouldn't necessarily recover. When he was interviewed on July 1 by the Halifax *Chronicle Herald*, he said "This has been a terrible shock for all of us. Charlie and me have been together for nearly forty years. The show would go on, we'll all have to work that much harder until we find a replacement for him." Charlie's doctor had reported that Charlie would be unable to sing again, so Don planned that Charlie would make an occasional guest appearance, which actually might be only a walk-on. Don went on to say that he wanted people to "remember him as they knew him last year."

There is no question that Don knew Charlie was loved by the audience; he was "dear old Charlie" to millions. Still, Don was accustomed to replacing people that were no longer able to perform. One has only to look back at photos of the group to see the changing faces, some gone due to illness or death, some replaced because they couldn't fit in or follow the rules. Charlie himself could never be replaced, but filling the position of male vocalist was another matter. Don hired Tommy Common to replace Charlie on the show.

On July 8, 1972, members of the core *Jubilee* cast drove out to Hamilton Civic Airport to say good bye to Charlie, who wished to return to his beloved Chaleur Bay, in New Brunswick. On July 10 he was admitted to Bathurst Hospital, where he died six days later. The family telephoned Marg Osburne in Hamilton to tell her about the passing of her dear friend, and Marg, in turn, went to producer Manny Pittson. He gathered the cast together and broke the news. Of course, they were devastated.

They remembered Charlie's exuberance, his eternal gratitude to Don. "That was the biggest break I ever had in my life, when Don Messer took me in, tucked me under his wing. I gave him a lot of hard times," Charlie had said. They recalled, too, how as frustrated as Don would get with Charlie, "when Charlie would get Don's goat, he'd say only, 'Damn and tarnation, Charlie, would you smarten up.'" But they also remembered Don and Charlie sitting and having tea together, just discussing things, two people with different personalities and different jobs enjoying each other's company.

"We knew he was dying," said Jane Edgett, one of the Buchta dancers. "We knew he would never be back." All the same, his death hit them hard, and many of the cast wanted to attend his funeral. "We could have gone home for one day and recognized Charlie's passing and returned the next day to the studio. We would have made the time up."

Instead, the next day, the cast was back at work taping the fall season. When the Halifax *Chronicle Herald* interviewed Marg Osburne, she told the reporter, "We're taping some music today, but it's all a bit unreal. But it's best that everyone keep busy, rather than sit around and think about the bad news."

Thirty-six years later Jane Edgett still felt upset that they weren't allowed to attend the funeral. "We were all very angry, the dancers particularly, very angry that Charlie had given his whole life to the program and Mr. Messer wouldn't allow us to respect that. He told the station, we're not taking a break. It came from him. Half of the station would have gone to Charlie's funeral. It was lack of respect for Charlie, that's how we read it."

The situation was far more complex than they realized. Don may have made a mistake in not attending the funeral of his most loyal band member. Certainly he would have been wise to let his cast go. His far bigger mistake was in not sharing with the cast the shattering news he had received that same day. Jannie Clifford, his adored eldest sister, with whom he had lived after his mother's death and again when he began his radio career, had died within hours of Charlie's death. Don was dealing as best he could with that overwhelming loss.

Don's absence from Charlie's funeral may be explained by the simultaneous death of his beloved Jannie, or it may remain a mystery. One thing is certain: he loved Charlie Chamberlain like a brother. Jim Morrison, of the All Star Band, met with Don at Woodstock, New Brunswick, during its Old Home Week in the summer of 1972, about a month after Charlie's funeral. They knew each other well for they both stayed at the Hammond House on Chapel Street every year during the annual event. When Don learned that Morrison had been at Charlie's funeral, he asked him to describe the service in detail. He wanted to know who was there and what hymns were sung, even what Charlie had been wearing in his coffin. It was as if he were trying to place himself at the funeral, to attend long after it was over. Another evening, when he and Johnny Forrest were watching an old tape from Hamilton with the antics of Charlie doing the step-dancing routine he had learned in the woods, embellished with shillelagh, bowler, and mischievous smile, the tears poured down his face. He missed Charlie dreadfully.

∽

Back home in Halifax, following Charlie's and Jannie's deaths, Don and Naomi were around home a lot more now that Don had slowed down. They would spend hours together, the two of them. He took her grocery shopping and to the dentist. He drove her to hair appointments and waited in the car for her. She seldom spent an evening by herself or did an errand without his companionship. They spent time with Kirk, Janis's son, giving Janis a chance to rest. Don was the same calming presence he had been with his own children. When

Kirk climbed out of his crib and fell to the floor, Don picked up the screaming child and said calmly, "Well, that first step was a big one."

He had a Ford Thunderbird, a car he was immensely proud of, and, carrying Kirk, he would walk around the car, admiring it. That car was about the only trapping of fame he had ever acquired. Finely tailored suits, a larger home, or expensive vacations seemed to hold no appeal. The Messers never travelled far, never bought a cottage. Don had a leather jacket, he had Wallaby shoes, and he had several suits, light gray, nothing black. He had a watch that he loved; he had bought it in Alaska, and it had a band studded with gold nuggets. He wore a black onyx ring, nothing flashy. The only thing he never had was a pair of jeans.

In 1972, Don and Naomi decided to go away for Christmas. For years, Lorna had invited her parents to spend Christmas with her and her family in Burlington, but they never would; they said they didn't like to travel at Christmas. They would send gifts instead, including, once, a John Deere riding mower for five-year-old Scott because he had loved to sit on his Grampie's lap when Don cut the lawn in Halifax. "But that year," said Brenda, "Nana Messer called and said, 'We're coming.' I think Grampie knew that he was dying, I really do. I think that's why they came to spend the time with us." She can still remember him, with his wool coat and his wool hat with ear flaps, and the way he hugged her so tightly it seemed as if he never wanted to let go. That was the last time she saw him.

In March 1973, Don was getting ready for another trip to Hamilton for the taping of twenty-four *Don Messer's Jubilee* shows. The cast, with the exception of himself and Gunter Buchta, had been asked to take a twenty-per-cent salary cut because the station was unsure they would be able to sell the show as successfully as they had in the past. By March 3, Manny Pittson, the producer, was pleased to report that they had already received commitments from eighteen stations, and everybody's salary would be reinstated. Irma Buchta was making new costumes, and Johnny Forrest was working on some music selections.

The show would not be what it had been in the past. Tommy

Common was adequate, but he wasn't Charlie Chamberlain; he didn't have Charlie's following. Then there was the strain among the cast caused by the hurt and anger over missing Charlie's funeral. Don was determined to give it his best for one more year.

He was looking forward to the arrival of Janis's second child. He loved having his children around, loved having his grandchildren close by, and he was glad that she was due before he would have to head to Hamilton. He was worried about her; she didn't look well lately, but he supposed it was the pregnancy and the worry. She delivered her second son on March 5, 1973, and called him Kris.

Everything seemed fine, and Don relaxed a little, feeling sure that now Janis would get back on her feet. It was almost spring, and he was looking forward to the first of the barbecues in the garden. He had determined that this season would be his last with CTV; it was time to retire and relax with his family. His nephew, Millard Clifford, more like a brother to him than a nephew, had died the month before at the age of sixty-four, and he knew that he needed to slow down. He owed Naomi a lot of attention to make up for the time he had been travelling the roads and making a living for them and a career for himself.

Don spent the month of March preparing more tunes for the summer taping. He liked to have extra music with him so that he could change the program if he wanted, although he tended to plan each taping months in advance. Sometimes a song just didn't work at the last minute. Thinking about that, he went down to his study in the basement. He had a jig he wanted to do some work on. It was called the "Adios Jig."

~

Don Messer died early in the morning of March 26, 1973, just twenty-one days after the birth of his grandson Kris. A heart attack caused his death, the fourth one that he had suffered since 1955. The press release said he was pronounced dead on arrival at the Victoria General Hospital at 9:45 a.m. It didn't say that the paramedics and

Don in his office at home, Halifax, Nova Scotia, 1960.

Nova Scotia Records and Management Don Messer Collection, 1998 – 132/071/291 [Maurice Crosby].

doctor had worked valiantly to restart his heart at the scene. He was a young man, only sixty-three years old, and doctors weren't accustomed to giving up. Dawn was grateful that they had not succeeded in their efforts, for she knew that his heart had been stopped for so long that he would never have been able to play the violin again.

Like the news of Charlie's death, word of Don's passing travelled quickly across the country. Charlie's widow, Lydia, heard about it on the radio, as did Don's brother Andrew, in Saskatchewan. Lorraine Hickey, Don's niece, heard the news in the hardware store in McAdam, New Brunswick. Despite Naomi's desire to call all the family to tell them personally, most of them learned of Don's death from the radio, television, or newspapers.

The papers evoked his talent and his ability to stir listeners and viewers with his rollicking rhythms. They told of the nationwide appeal of his Down East music and gave him credit for making it look easy, never mentioning that he practiced hours daily until he died. They failed to note the integrity that he maintained throughout his life in his dealings with musicians and sponsors and, most importantly, his fans. He helped many Canadian musicians achieve their goals. He didn't make a big fuss, he just quietly corresponded with them, made suggestions, and, on occasion, directed them to a recording studio or invited them onto the show. Most of all, his essence was his passion for the music itself, the need to keep it alive, and his passion for the violin as the instrument that served it so well.

Charlie Chamberlain

Don and Charlie are seated side by side in the CBC studio in Toronto. It is August 22, 1960, and they are being interviewed by the host of *Tabloid*. Though both men are dressed in suit and tie, their shoes buffed to a high shine, their proximity to each other highlights the disparity in their appearance. Don is 5' 6" tall and weighs possibly 130 pounds. Charlie is 5' 10" and close to 260 pounds with a size 20 neck and 10 inch wrists.

Don's demeanour is subdued and he answers carefully, in complete sentences. Charlie responds in short, abrupt bursts, looking all the while as if he is enjoying some private source of hilarity. The topic of discussion hints at what he finds so amusing.

The hostess is a sleek and fashionable blonde, dressed for a cocktail party rather than an afternoon television show. Her tone is slightly patronizing — not enough to cause offence, but enough to jangle the antennae of both men, who long ago became accustomed to being mocked by the CBC intelligentsia. She first refers to them as a "curiosity in the world of show business," then asks them, in a serious and wondering tone, "How, in this age of sophistication, does *Don Messer's Jubilee* continue to perform so well in the ratings?"

"Perhaps because we are not sophisticated," answers Don. He offers no apologies, no explanation other than the obvious, which is that their audience, some four million Canadians, apparently enjoys their brand of unsophisticated entertainment.

Charlie laughs out loud, amused at her discomfiture. She speaks about him as if he is unfamiliar with the complexities and cruelty of the literati. She confides to the audience, "He has violet eyes, girls." She has misread Charlie, as have so many others. He is no rube; he is simply one of the most transparent men on earth.

◆

Some thought Charlie simple because of his total lack of guile, the often self-deprecating way that he presented himself. He was honesty itself at a time when sincerity was derided. This quality cost him dearly in his career, though it made him one of the most loved men in show business.

Charlie drank more than was good for him; however, he never once performed drunk. "Don would never have allowed it and nor would Langstroth," said Don Tremaine. He did drink more than some members of Don Messer's band (though, in some cases, not a lot more). The difference was that Charlie never pretended otherwise. His candour was part of what made him approachable and real to so many of the men and women who attended his performances. He often joked about alcohol because his fans had come to expect it, and with time, it became increasingly difficult to tell where the truth ended and the myth began. Eventually, the myth overtook Charlie, became his inescapable identity and followed him past the grave.

There was so much more to Charlie Chamberlain. Charlie's early years are as much legend as mystery. Family members say that he went to work in the lumber camps at the varying ages of nine, fourteen, or seventeen, depending on who tells the story. They recount how he sang at restaurant back doors for food for his family and at the train tracks for coins to pay the bills. Charlie's own version, as told to *Maclean's* reporter Susan Dexter in 1965, is a little less romantic but no less fantastic.

Charlie Chamberlain was born in 1911 in a small house at the bottom of Village Hill in Bathurst, New Brunswick, one of six children for Elizabeth Chamberlain, a school teacher, and her husband

William. Their marriage in itself was fantastical at that time. He was a Protestant of Anglo-Scottish descent; she was a Catholic and Acadian. In the early 1900s, Catholics and Protestants seldom married in New Brunswick. They seldom even lived on the same street, but it seems that Elizabeth was a woman of uncommon determination, and her husband, who became the Bathurst chief of police, was not interested in being told whom he could marry.

They had little money but a lot of music and joy. Charlie later recalled waking up on winter mornings in a house "so cold, you'd think rigor mortis had set in." A lot changed when his father died in a car accident in 1924 while transporting a prisoner from the Bathurst jail to Jacquet River. He was driving over a bridge when his car spooked a horse, said his son Donny Chamberlain. Trying to avoid the horse, he ran into the side of the bridge and bled to death from his injuries. Elizabeth was left with six children to support, and it seems there was to be no help forthcoming from William's parents. Their initial coolness toward her had not been mellowed by the poverty facing their grandchildren.

Charlie was in grade five at the time, though barely passing. "They near had to burn down the schoolhouse to get me out of the first grade," he used to say. Ann-Marie, his daughter, told how, during the First World War, he would go up to the train station and sing for the troops on their way to Montreal or Halifax. He had been doing that since the age of five and had learned how well they appreciated sentimental tunes like "Good Luck to the Boys of the Allies" and "Never Let the Old Flag Fall." They would toss coins to him for his effort, a sizeable amount of money for a young boy.

Charlie's version elaborates on the basic facts. He certainly did sing for the troops when he was five, but after his father died, he spent his other hours filching chickens and vegetables and stealing coal from the railway. His dog, a Newfoundland-German shepherd cross called Tony, would accompany him. The police were often at his house, and likely their affection for his father and the iron-clad alibis provided by his mother kept him out of jail. That would not suffice much longer; Charlie needed to find legitimate work.

He and Tony left town for a job building timber roads through the swamps at the Rose Hill relief camp. Perhaps because of his age, he was assigned the job of lopping the branches off the downed trees. For this he was paid $3 a week, money that was deposited directly at Kent's store in Bathurst, where his family bought their goods. Tony survived on scraps from the camp kitchen.

After two years, Charlie left the camp, walked 129 kilometres into the woods to a Bathurst lumber camp office, and applied for a job there. He was big for his age, though not yet the large man he would become, and he easily found work, despite his youth. In fact hardship and hunger forced many very young men to work in the woods then.

Charlie started off helping the camp cook, peeling potatoes, washing the pots and pans, and cleaning up after the men. He also washed the long johns that the lumbermen wore for months at a time. The work paid relatively well, but it was not to Charlie's liking. Sometimes he would sit in the cook hut and play his guitar. There was no radio and the loggers made their own entertainment, its variety confined only by the limits of their talent and musicianship. The men brought their instruments with them into the woods: Jew's harps and mouth organs, guitars and banjos, and of course fiddles. They danced the familiar quadrilles and step dances on the tables, and they sang the traditional Irish and Scottish ballads of working men and heartbreak.

Charlie was quite the performer, with a voice that had almost won him a job when he was seven with the John R. Van Arman Minstrel Show. He had wowed Van Arman, but that gentleman was no match for Mrs. Chamberlain, who would not allow her son to join him. Charlie's voice was admirably suited for the songs he learned at the camp. He was such a big hit that, according to Weston Breckenridge, who worked as a woods cook for Billy White in the 1930s, "Charlie didn't do much work. He hung around the camp and played his guitar." Between his singing and his lumbering, he brought in $18 a month for his family.

Charlie would have been a very different person without his Lydia. She was the fulcrum upon which he balanced his life. He called her Ti-Belle, "little beauty," and he showered love upon her. Oh, he could be short at some times, bad-tempered even, but Lydia always knew that she ranked first in the life of this giant of a man.

Charlie met Lydia Doucette one summer when he was working on the road crew building one of the country roads that ran through Belledune, Dalhousie, and Campbellton. Although there were thirty men on that job, Charlie stood out in her eyes, perhaps because he was perched on top of the cement mixer when she walked down the driveway of the farm where she lived with her parents and five siblings. He thought she was the most beautiful woman in the world. She was tall like him, brunette, and slender, and she carried herself with certain flair.

Determined to romance her, Charlie would show up after work with his guitar and serenade her from the garden. She must have reciprocated his interest because soon they were a couple at the dances. She was no pushover. When Charlie would put his head on her shoulder as they waltzed, she could be heard saying, "Straighten up Charlie, straighten up." He was a dashing figure in the reels, when, it was said, he could burn the rubber right off the soles of his boots.

Charlie Chamberlain as he may have appeared when he was serenading Lydia, about 1929.

Courtesy: Chamberlain Family.

They had been going together for three months when, obviously entranced with her, he painted a big heart on his guitar and wrote her name in the middle of it. It was special, this guitar. He had paid $6 for it, and it was a step above his old one that he had bought for $1.50 when he was seven. That one had been purchased from Bob Doucet, the music teacher in Bathurst. After Bob tuned it, Charlie had taken it down to the end of the bridge and started "plunking away on it," teaching himself to play.

When the ground froze, Charlie returned to the woods. He was doing all right, lumbering in the winter and working on the roads in the summer. Lydia didn't want to remain in Bathurst her whole life, and in the spring of 1933, she moved to Saint John in search of a better job. Charlie decided he should do the same before his Ti-Belle found someone else, so he wrote her a love letter: "Sweet lemonade heart, I'm coming down and I want to get married, love Charlie." It was short and to the point, but it had taken him a long time to get the words on paper for Charlie had never learned to write well.

They married in November, and Charlie gave her a ring he'd had made from aluminum piping obtained from the pulp mill in Bathurst. A friend at the mill's machine shop shaped it, and then he placed a topaz in the setting, for topaz was Ti-Belle's birthstone. They had a two-day honeymoon, and then Charlie returned to the woods for the winter.

Separation from his loved ones was never Charlie's forte, so he looked for a chance to work out of Saint John. The trip down to look for a job at the port resulted in Don Messer hiring him instead. In fact Charlie was taken on by both Don Messer and Bruce Holder, another bandleader. Bruce in particular wanted him because when Charlie sang songs like "Danny Boy" and "Sylvia," he sang them as if he really meant them.

⌒

Charlie and Lydia had six children: three girls, Mary, Muriel, and Ann-Marie, and three boys, Don (Donny), David, and Barry. Don was named after Don Messer, a testament to Charlie's respect for the man — as significant on his part as Don's asking Charlie to be godfather to Brenda, his third child. Though the children were similar in age to Don and Naomi's children, they did not often play together. The families lived in different parts of town, and the Chamberlain children went to Catholic schools, whereas the Messer children attended public schools.

The children of the band members would sometimes come to the Chamberlain house with their parents when the group congregated to practice. The Chamberlains had a piano, so the men would gather there when they wanted to go over a new song or practice a new piece. Charlie loved Fats Waller, and Waldo Munro would play "Honey Hush" for him. Sometimes the women would dance, especially if they had had a cocktail or two. "I can still remember Lydia and Naomi getting up in the kitchen and dancing. They called it the Belledune Hop. It was hilarious," said Ann-Marie with a delighted chuckle at the memory of the two women, who had become close friends.

While Ann-Marie addressed the band members by their first names when she got older, Don was never anything but "Mr. Messer." That was her father's influence: Mr. Messer was his boss. They were good friends, often like brothers, and would sometimes go shooting at the shooting gallery in Charlottetown or go to Don's sister's cottage near Saint John, but he was still Charlie's boss. Don was something that he wasn't: Don could read music and play very well and manage a band. Charlie admired these skills tremendously.

⁓

Charlie's love of his home and his family kept him in Canada. In 1936, when an American talent scout spotted him at the New England Sportsmen's Show in Boston and offered him a screen test, he turned it down with barely a thought. He knew that Lydia would not be happy in the States — she was very close to her family and would hate to live so far from Belledune. "I'm going home to Lydia," he had told the scout.

In 1939, he sang at the World's Fair in New York City and was offered a chance to become the next singing cowboy — another Gene Autry or Roy Rogers. He turned that down, too, recognizing by this time that he needed the stability that Don provided. "He's kind of like my keeper," he told a reporter.

There was no question: his voice was unique. Once when he performed at the skating arena in Sackville, New Brunswick, he was heard by Ethel Peake, a professor of music and an opera aficionado. She was enraptured by Charlie's voice and felt he had the talent and the physique to perform the operatic arias. Charlie wasn't interested.

Charlie did leave Messer once. In the early 1950s, he told Don that he was going to Montreal to work, and he'd be coming back "with a car so big it won't be able to turn corners." Lydia had family in Montreal, and Charlie thought that city might provide better opportunities for his own children, perhaps a better education and a chance for more promising jobs. He sang at the Clover Club, near the Forum on St. Catherine's Street. After a year, he returned to Prince Edward Island and the group that had become an extended family to him, at least when they were on the road. The stint in Montreal hadn't been as lucrative as he had hoped, and it looked as if he might fare better back with his old group: CBC was considering a pilot for a television show, and they wanted Charlie to be part of the cast.

⌁

Charlie and Lydia's home was a gathering place for more than the band members. "Mom and Dad fed everybody. In the war years, I remember us having Air Force men from England in our house at Christmastime because they were so far from home that my parents would give them Christmas dinner," said Donny. "RCMP officers stationed in Charlottetown often found their way to our house for homemade bread and smelts. There was always somebody there." That didn't happen only in Charlottetown. When Charlie went to the cottage they built on Chaleur Bay, just across the road from Lydia's family farm, the community would begin to buzz. "Charlie's home,

Charlie's home, Charlie Chamberlain's home." Anyone could drop in, and they did, to sit and sing, to eat fish or chicken stew. They were always made welcome by Charlie and Lydia.

Lydia and the children spent every summer at Chaleur Bay, and eventually so did the grandchildren. Charlie was often away on tour or performing, but the rest of the family would leave Charlottetown the day school let out, returning only for the first day of school in the fall. Though Charlie was not there in person, Lydia would frequently bring him into the conversation. She would say to the children, "Your grandfather, my husband Charlie would . . ." It was as if she tried to keep him front and centre in the life of the family even when he was away, so central was he in her own life.

When Charlie was on vacation, he loved to go to the cottage. It was the only place he truly relaxed, and he would sit backwards on a chair, telling a story. Sometimes there would be a child or a grandchild wedged between him and the back of the chair. "He'd slip us right in between him and the back of the chair and say to us, 'Sing me a song.' I remember being so safe in that place with him. He knew how to hug," said his granddaughter, Sandi MacKinnon.

Charlie and Lydia went to the movies a lot. Sometimes they would take the children with them and go to a restaurant for dinner. Often they would sing together: Charlie strumming his guitar, Lydia singing her Acadian songs, the children singing along. They had a different lifestyle from their school friends in Charlottetown because of who their father was, the travelling they did to Montreal, Quebec, and the summer escape to the cottage at Belledune. The children grew very close. It was important to Charlie and Lydia that their children were best friends with each other, and to this day they have remained so.

The children loved going in the car with Charlie because once they were out of Lydia's sight, he would let them drive. He was great fun on the beach, building a bonfire and roasting hot dogs. Charlie never used a barbecue, but he did love to cook great stews and soups. "He used to make these giant pots of friggin' stew, they'd last for a week," said Donny. Fish and pork scraps were a favourite. He'd boil potatoes, then fry codfish and pork scraps (back bacon cut into little pieces), and pour the grease from that over the fish and potatoes, and serve it with chow, the green tomato pickle that's a staple of Maritime diets. Everyone loved it.

"He was a neat dad," Donny concluded. "People would want to meet him, especially after the group gained some prominence. They would come and want to have their pictures taken with him and listen to him sing. He was always up for that. He'd say, just sit there and be quiet and don't touch anything, and he'd sing the songs. If anybody needed him for a charity, he was there." Even as an adult, Donny enjoyed being Charlie's son. He worked for Woolworth's for a while, and every time his father would come to town to visit him, he would find a way to advertise the fact. People would come into the store in droves to meet Charlie.

Few people knew that Charlie was such a great and fun-loving dad. Ann-Marie spoke of him with undisguised affection and admiration. "There was none better. The most important thing in my dad's life was my mother and his children. Everything else came a distant second. That was my dad's life — my mom and his six children. In those early years there was not a lot of money, and it was always a struggle. He did everything he could to make sure of the comfort of his children. But most of all, before anything else, was the love he showed to us and what he gave to us in terms of the hugging, the 'I love you' before we'd go to bed at night."

That sort of caring and affection for his children extended into their adulthood. When Ann-Marie was a single parent living in Montreal, her son suffered from allergies to trees and grass. There was no Medicare system at the time and his medications cost $120 a month, far more than she could afford. Charlie paid for them.

He was undeniably soft-hearted. "We used to say his bladder was right under his eyelids," said Ann-Marie. "We were one of the first people on the Island to have a television, and it was all snow. He would watch *Lassie* and *Father Knows Best*, and he'd be crying. In those years the lights had to be out to watch TV, so we'd switch on the light and catch him crying."

His devotion to Lydia never abated. He used to tell anyone, "If God ever made anything better than her, he'd keep it for himself." When he travelled, he would phone her every night and buy her fancy lingerie, hats, and red high heels. "They were really something, the two of them. He'd walk in the house and she'd be busy in the kitchen, and he'd grab her and be dancing her around the house," said Sandi.

He was a religious man, raised Catholic by his mother. All his boys served as altar boys, all the girls sang in the choir, and it seemed to the children that they were at church all the time. At home, he was full of song. "He used to make us start every day singing when we were children," remembered Ann-Marie. Sometimes he would get them to sing some of the songs he would have to perform to help him learn the words. If he sang songs like "Lucky Old Sun" and "Old Man River," the house would just tremble.

Christmas at the Chamberlains meant food, music, and company. When there were no toys to be bought on the Island during the war years, Charlie took the train to Quebec City and bought toys there, carrying them home with him. One year he gave his Christmas tree and Christmas turkey to the paperboy, who had told him that because his father was out of work, they would not be able to have a Christmas tree that year. The story goes that Charlie unplugged the Christmas tree and picked it up off the floor — lights, ornaments, and tinsel — and carried it down the street to the boy's house. In his other hand were the Christmas turkey and some presents. Then he went home and phoned the manager of Woolworth's to ask him to open up so he could buy another tree and presents for his own children.

There was never really enough money to go around. Charlie was generous to a fault and would buy a drink for anyone. Lydia would remonstrate, "For God's sake, Dad, you've got six kids to feed." He worked hard to bring in the money to do that. He worked in gas stations, he Simonized cars, and he cleared snow for the city. "He was a really good provider," mused Donny. "He brought us all up and paid the ultimate price by working night and day to make sure we all got an education and had a warm place to live. He was responsible."

Working for *Don Messer's Jubilee* precluded taking a regular job, so he would fit in part-time jobs as he was able. Charlie never got rich doing the Messer show.

Even when the children were grown and on their own, Charlie would pick up odd jobs. In May 1966, he offered to help a neighbour, Gordon Elliott, run his gas station. Lydia came along to work as cashier. In short order, he had overturned the place. "Some of the kids [working there] were as useless as dory plugs," he told *Weekend Magazine* journalist Stewart MacLeod, "and all together they weren't doing enough work to break the Sabbath." So Charlie hired replacement staff, had them paint the station, and then made sure they kept it shipshape. He would take his turn pumping gas, always getting a big kick out of tourists' surprise when they realized that Charlie Chamberlain of *Jubilee* fame was their gas attendant. One time, the customers thought they were being televised as part of a *Candid Camera* spoof.

⌒

Charlie was working when he collapsed. He had not been himself when he reported in at CHCH-TV in May 1972, to start a new season of taping. He was coughing a lot; years of chain smoking had damaged his lungs. He had suffered a number of heart attacks in the previous years, and the band was aware of how ill he was. They had taken turns ferrying Lydia to appointments and visits to the hospital, had seen first-hand Charlie's struggle to keep going. They all knew that it was probably only willpower and a determination not to let Don down that had kept him going as long as he had — that and his love of entertaining.

None of that was going to be sufficient, and when Charlie collapsed, he was taken to St. Joseph's Hospital in Hamilton. The press found him there and took photos of him in pyjamas, two adoring nurses at his side. The doctor made it clear to Donny, Charlie's son, that Charlie would never perform again. His heart was under so much stress that it was like a pump trying to operate in a flood. Don didn't

Lydia lights the candles on Charlie's birthday cake in Bathurst
Hospital on July 14, 1972. Courtesy: Chamberlain family [*The Northern Light*].

appear to be as upset by Charlie's collapse as the others, or perhaps
he simply had to keep his anxiety at bay while trying to ensure that
the taping of the show carried on as normally as possible.

On July 8, 1972, Charlie flew back to his beloved New Brunswick
via Montreal. His daughter Ann-Marie lived there, and he asked her
to meet him at the airport so he could see his five-month-old granddaughter, Kim, for the first time. When the plane landed, the flight
attendant took Charlie and Lydia to a room in the airport where
Ann-Marie and her daughter waited for them. Charlie looked at Kim
and said, "She has beautiful blue eyes like me," laughed Ann-Marie,
who added that the baby's father also had beautiful blue eyes.

Charlie first went to the summer cottage on Chaleur Bay, where he had spent so many happy times. On July 10 he agreed to enter the Bathurst Hospital. Ann-Marie tried to phone him on July 14, which was his sixty-first birthday. She knew her dad loved his birthdays and his birthday cake. She had a hard time getting through. So many people had called wanting to speak with him that the nurses were denying all phone calls. Eventually Ann-Marie convinced them that she was truly his daughter, and they connected her to his room. "He said to me, 'You better come home soon.' I told him I'd be home in August. But he repeated, 'You better come home soon.'"

Charlie had a good birthday party, by all accounts. It was photographed for the local paper, Charlie sitting up in bed, his birthday cake on the table in front of him, an ashtray to the side. He looks happy and carefree and well cared for. Lydia was there, as she had been every day, all day. Later he said good night to her and added a cheery, "I'll see you tomorrow," and she left.

The next day was much the same. Charlie was finding it more difficult to get his breath; he tired easily. Lydia sat quietly by his bed as he napped, her knitting in her lap. Late that evening, she got up to go home and Charlie told her, "Good bye." She didn't notice what he had said at the time, didn't hear the finality in the ordinary expression. "She never would have left if she'd noticed the difference," said Ann-Marie. Charlie died during the night, two days after his birthday. Only after he died did the doctors discover that he was suffering from lung cancer as well as the cardiac ailments.

Jessie Ryan, his niece, was a nursing instructor at Bathurst Hospital when her uncle was a patient there and she believed he knew he was dying. He maintained his high spirits, singing for the nurses. "All you had to say was, 'You're Charlie Chamberlain!' and he would start to sing. That's all it took," said Jessie. She used to go in and say good night every evening before she left the hospital. The night he died, she had gone in as usual and said, "Good night, Uncle Charlie, see you tomorrow." Charlie looked at her and said, "Jessie, you and I both know I won't see you tomorrow." Jessie never thought that he wouldn't be there the next morning.

Lydia was absolutely devastated by his death, by the fact that after all those years together, he had died without her present to calm his fears. It was a terrible time for her, for all of us, said Ann-Marie. Only recently has she been able to listen to recordings of her father singing. It was so hard to say good bye to him, to accept that he was gone, she said, because she could still turn on the TV and he would be there, big and bold and full of life.

The absence of the cast of *Don Messer's Jubilee* at Charlie's funeral seems appalling in light of the close relationship between the two men and the length of their partnership. "In my heart, I would like to think that it was the studio and not Don," said Ann-Marie Chamberlain. "I just can't see Don saying they couldn't go. He might have been a distant man, but he did love his band and his men and his lady. I know how he felt about my Dad. I just can't imagine him saying anything other than, if we had a choice, we'd go. It had to be a terrible time for Don and the band, to have the funeral and not one of them there."

Few of Charlie's relatives were in New Brunswick at the time of his death. Ann-Marie was in the Laurentians with no phone and heard of her father's passing over the radio. Charlie's family in Ontario were in transit and heard the news while they were driving home to visit him in hospital.

More than five hundred people attended Charlie Chamberlain's funeral. Federal Cabinet ministers Bob Stanfield and John Diefenbaker were both honorary pallbearers. Both had more than a passing acquaintance with Charlie. Bob Stanfield and he had come to know each other well when the Chamberlains lived in Truro in 1959 and 1960. John Diefenbaker had invited him to Ottawa to sing "Bless this House" at the opening of Parliament.

What of Charlie Chamberlain's legacy? His family members like to say that it is they — children and grandchildren — who adore him unconditionally. They want him to be remembered for his love of music and entertaining. "He just loved to make people happy, that was his thing," said Sandi MacKinnon.

Ann-Marie recalled a day when she was speaking to her father. He had told her that he wished he had a lot of money so that, when the time came, he could leave it to his children. "But," she said, "that's not what we had with him." She asked him how he felt about his life, about what he had done, and he replied, "There's not one day I lived that I wouldn't want to do again." To Jane Edgett, it was even simpler. "Charlie just seemed to go around grateful to be on this earth."

Marg Osburne

Don Messer is being interviewed in 1971 by David Cobb for a feature titled, "Who's the most attractive woman in the world?" Don doesn't really like answering these kinds of questions. Last summer another interviewer had asked him for his opinion on whether there is a heaven and a hell. He had responded that he felt people made their own heaven and hell right here on earth. The response had angered some of the churchgoing fraternity, but Don, while he tries to be diplomatic, is not about to serve up some platitude just because the interviewer expects it. He is direct — always has been — and he speaks from the heart, perhaps unaware how odd his description might seem.

He responds, "I'd have to pick Marg Osburne. She's been with us for twenty-four years; she has talent, brains, and she's fairly well-balanced, you know. Very easy to get along with. Musically, she can do anything you ask her to, from pop to country and western. Marg has a personal magnetism all her own — the kind of personality that means that once you meet her you'll always remember her. She has all the qualities that go to make up a good female."

~

Verna Marguerite Osburne was born on December 29, 1926, in Moncton, New Brunswick, one of two children for her night watchman father and homemaker mother. They were a musical family, courtesy of her grandfather, who, over the years, had amassed a huge repertoire of hymns and folk songs. Family get-togethers were always an opportunity to gather round the piano, and by the time Marg joined the church choir she was well practiced in singing before an audience.

She taught herself to sing in harmony by singing duets with her brother Gerry, a skill that would become a mainstay. "She was a very, very talented woman," said Jane Edgett, and was one of the first to adopt the technique of recording a second track of her voice over the first, in a sense allowing her to sing harmony with herself. So new was the technology that audiences had no idea both voices were Marg's. She once received a letter from a fan who told her that she liked the "other lady's" voice better than Marg's and wondered why Marg never gave her any credit, never allowed her to appear on television.

When she was sixteen, Marg's obvious talent won her an opportunity to appear on radio station CKCW in Moncton, where she sang old-time Western songs on a weekly program. When she had been doing this for two years, one of the announcers, believing she had more talent than the show required, sent a recording of her singing to Don Messer for consideration. Don didn't hire her immediately, but three years later, when Charlie had a car accident, Don needed a replacement vocalist. Marg filled the bill.

When Charlie returned, Don didn't even consider letting Marg go. She had become one of the group and would remain with them for twenty-five years, until Don's death. Everyone who worked with Marg loved her. Don Tremaine says of her, "She was a lady when being called a lady meant something. She was just the finest kind of person I have ever met." Bill Langstroth seconds that. "Here's a woman who travelled with six or eight men around the country, and they all treated her like a titled lady. She's royalty." Marg never saw herself that way. She was just a girl who liked to sing and was lucky enough to be able to do it for a living. The cast and studio staff even watched their language when she was around. Not that Marg would necessarily have complained; vulgar speech just seemed inappropriate in her presence.

Marg, Don, and Charlie in a Model T, 1960.
Nova Scotia Records and Management, Don Messer Collection 1998 – 132/071/206.

Journalists and critics described Marg as "plump and contented." One went so far as to label her a "frumpy matron." Even her city-dwelling cousin, while not prepared to criticize her style, would moan, "I do wish Marg would spruce up." Her fans didn't see her that way, or if they did, they recognized a kindred spirit and loved her all the more for it. They saw her as accessible, as one of them.

"She was just very down to earth, not a fancy person at all, except when she was on television," says Barb Patriquan, a neighbour in Sussex. That quality was a bit of a problem for the CBC at first. Her wardrobe could at best be described as dowdy, at worst as unflatter-ing. "She turned up initially in her own clothes," said Bill Langstroth. "They were pretty crazy sometimes." Later, Marg would go shopping with Dorothy Payne from the CBC wardrobe department. "It was hit and miss," said Langstroth, "but Dorothy knew what was required for the show." Marg went along with Dorothy's advice, wearing what they bought and agreeing to heavy pancake makeup, even though her sensitive skin would suffer for days after. Whether or not Marg's clothing was attractive by any absolute standard, Penningtons, a company that sells larger-sized clothing, saw in Marg a potential gold mine. She shopped there for her personal clothes, and in the seventies she signed an agreement with them to sponsor a line of clothing.

When she was invited to do a guest appearance on the *Juliette* show, Marg was overwhelmed and more than a little intimidated. "Petrified" was the word she used. Juliette was a beautiful, glamorous blonde with a wardrobe far more elegant than Marg's. Juliette took Marg under her wing, giving her a touch of elegance by lending her a fox stole to wear on the show. Marg was excited, couldn't wait for the "folks in Halifax to see me in this." As nervous as she was, she performed brilliantly, sliding into the more polished show as if she had rehearsed for days. She was invited back on four other occasions.

In a fan letter of October 20, 1971, a woman wrote, "Dear Mr. Messer, Your program is good. We like Marg Osburne's new hairstyle, it's very becoming, makes her look younger too." Men, at least two of them, proposed to her with great frequency. The first, a prairie rancher, wrote daily; the second, an Ontario millionaire, phoned the studio with repeated entreaties for her to become his missus. Neither seemed aware that Marg had been married for almost twenty years.

ᔕ

Marg met Austin Squarebriggs at a bowling alley in Charlottetown in 1950, when she had been performing with the Islanders for three years. Austin, a boxer, had gone down to the alley to speak with his fight promoter about an upcoming bout, and he noticed a group of people there. They seemed to be having a wonderful time and he stayed to watch. He eventually plucked up the courage to speak with Marg. He knew who she was, of course; it would be hard not to in a place the size of Charlottetown. He was surprised at how approachable she was, how genuine and nice. He was eighteen, and she was twenty-three.

The next time he saw her was at a dance, where she was performing. He managed to get her attention after the show, and they started going together. "We did a lot of walking," said Austin. "It was a year and a half before I proposed. I was still fighting, I wasn't settled yet." His proposal was about as romantic as Don's proposal to Naomi.

"We were standing outside where she lived, and winter was coming up and it was getting cold, and I said, 'You know, we've got to stop saying good bye all the time.'"

Marg responded to this somewhat obscure remark with, "What do you want to do about it?"

"I said, 'I think we should get married.'"

They were wed at the church manse in Charlottetown. Marg wore a light blue ensemble and Austin wore a suit that had been custom-made for him as a sixteen-year-old, when his fighter's build made it impossible for him to buy a suit off the rack. "I was 6'2 ½" and I weighed 158 pounds but had a 44-inch chest and a 27-inch waist. The tailor sent the request back, saying nobody was built like that," said Austin, still proud of his physique all these years later. "We had to write back and tell them I was a fighter, so then I got my first 'built-on' suit."

Duke Nielsen and his wife were witnesses, but in his eighties, Austin did not remember whether the rest of the band attended. The newlyweds headed off to Mechanic Settlement, to the old Osburne homestead near Sussex, New Brunswick, for their honeymoon. Marg's dad went along for the weekend, still chaperoning his daughter, then headed back home to Moncton, presumably satisfied with Austin as a son-in-law.

While Marg worked with the Islanders, Austin continued fighting professionally for another four years. He was good. In forty-seven fights, first as a middleweight and then as a light heavyweight, he lost only three decisions; he won the rest. He was a one-time sparring partner for Yvon Durelle, but then a punch damaged a kidney. After surgery to remove it, Austin left the boxing ring for a job doing aircraft maintenance for Maritime Central Airways, the same company from which Don chartered aircraft in the 1940s and 1950s and for which Dawn worked in the 1950s as a flight nurse.

In 1954, David, Marg and Austin's first child, was born with little public fanfare. Marg continued to perform throughout her pregnancy, the cameramen filming her at such an angle that no one in the television audience could see her condition. She quietly went off and had her baby, and then a few weeks later she returned to the set, leaving David in the care of a nanny.

Six years later, when Marg was expecting her daughter, Melody, the situation had changed dramatically. The week before her baby was due, the cast of *Don Messer's Jubilee* gave her an on-camera baby shower. The televising of such a personal event was unheard of in the sixties and demonstrates the unique place Marg held in the lives of her audience. What would have seemed alarmingly inappropriate and intrusive with another performer seemed just fine with someone as approachable as Marg. The audience was pleased with the chance to give something back to this lady who "sang the songs that stick to your heart," and when Melody arrived, she was the recipient of seventy-five pairs of bootees and twenty-seven bonnets and sweaters, all sent to the CBC.

Austin remembered Marg leaving the house with the guitar at eight in the morning. "I'd say, 'Where are you going?' Marg would reply, "I'm putting on a little show at the senior's home." Sometimes it was the orphanage or the hospital, or perhaps the home of a shut-in. Austin could never remember Marg refusing a request, whether it came from someone in her home community or someone she would meet on tour.

Marg and Austin continued living in Charlottetown until 1960, the second season of *Don Messer's Jubilee* on the national network; then they moved to Halifax. Marg was cautious with her money. She wanted to be certain that the income was going to continue before they uprooted their children and moved from the Island. They chose a modest home in Halifax: the rented ground floor of a frame house in Rockingham, with two bedrooms, a living room, and a kitchen-dinette. Although the place was sparsely furnished and cluttered with toys and souvenirs of Marg's tours, it was a home where any visitor felt welcome, and it was within blocks of Don and Naomi's house.

Chatelaine magazine once reported that if people didn't have a TV set, they would never have known that Marg was a celebrity. She hung her wash on the line like her neighbours and prepared meals and washed dishes just like the rest of them. The warmth she exhibited on the show was as apparent in her everyday life. "She didn't have any more than the one face," said David. "She didn't try to hide anything from anybody; she didn't

Marg Osburne and Melody on the cover of *Chatelaine*, 1963. *Chatelaine.*

put on airs, not one dress for one person, another for someone else." Marg was the same person onstage as off. "That's how she was all the time. That wasn't just some way she acted in front of the camera. She was the same if someone came to the door, if she saw someone at the grocery store. It made no difference."

She did have a nanny, "Granny Beaver," which few women of that time could afford, even if they needed one, and she had an unlisted phone number. That was likely Austin's influence. He took strong exception to men approaching her at shows, didn't want them contacting her at home. His new job working in security for the Maritime Harbour Board prevented him from attending as many of her performances as he would have liked.

~

In 1961, Marg's life was turned upside down. Initially, no one was aware of the crisis her family was facing. Marg came to work early as she always did, but one day, she approached Bill Langstroth and told him that she would need the teleprompter — she couldn't remember the words of the scheduled songs. It was an unusual request for Marg. The consummate professional, she always came to work prepared and could nail a song with only fifteen minutes of preparation, even though she had never had any formal vocal training and couldn't read music.

David, her seven-year-old, had been diagnosed with cancer. He can speak calmly of it now as an adult, but the trauma of that time and the treatment reverberates in his voice. "It was a fast-growing malignant brain tumour. There were only seventeen known cases of it when I contracted it, and the only difference between those seventeen and myself is that I survived. The others had all died between two weeks and two months of diagnosis." He had surgery, but the doctors were unable to remove the entire tumour and it quickly grew back.

Waiting in the doctor's outer office, David heard the doctor tell his parents that he was "dead, that he just didn't know enough to lie down." He did tell them about a possible treatment, about the experiments being carried out with cobalt radiation therapy, but he didn't offer them much hope. Marg and Austin jumped at the chance to save their son. The doctor said, "We'll try it. Considering where the cancer is, we'll probably kill him anyway. But since he's already dead there's nothing to lose."

David heard every word. "When you are a child and you hear a doctor say that you are dead, you just don't know enough to lie down, that the procedure is going to kill you anyway, it dramatically alters your perception of things around you. When I heard that doctor, I was even more determined that I was going to prove him wrong."

David had blocked out a lot of the treatment, although he remembered playing quite contentedly and then being violently sick with a reaction to the radiation. Austin remembered those days with great clarity. "His cancer was behind the eye and they usually took both the eye and eyelid, but with David being so young, they didn't want to do that." Instead they made a lead mask, cut a slit in it over the eye, and bombarded him with cobalt radiation.

David responded to the treatment, and Marg and Austin travelled west to join the tour. They left David and Melody with family members in Sussex but were soon called back in a panic. David was in so much pain he couldn't sleep. For five days he writhed in agony until he finally passed out from exhaustion. "But even in my sleep I would whimper. It felt like somebody was sticking a hot poker in my eye."

Marg and Austin arrived home and bundled him into the car for the trip to the hospital in Halifax. "I remember being in the back seat of the car, whimpering and crying, and then, all of a sudden, the pain stopped and I sat up straight. The car stopped and Mum and Dad got out. They thought I had expired. I just looked at them and said, 'I'm hungry.'"

As an adult, David explained what happened. "Basically, the eyeball boiled in my head. They called it a delayed radiation reaction, and the eye was now dead and I lost the vision that I had in it." The cancer never came back.

During this difficult time Marg had the full and heartfelt support of the group. Whenever anything happened to one of them, it was as if it were happening to all of them. They were close-knit; they lived near each other, and sometimes one band member's older children babysat the younger children of another. "It was an extended family," said David. "If anything happened in that extended family, it affected everybody."

Perhaps because of his illness, Marg took David on tour with her in 1964. It was a phenomenal experience for the little boy. He and his mother took the train from Halifax to Winnipeg, where the tour bus awaited them. Then they zigzagged up and across provincial boundaries all the way to the west coast and did it all again in the opposite direction.

There was a strong sense of camaraderie on the bus; everybody seemed to get along. Oh, there were times when someone would get on someone else's nerves, David remembered, but that was hardly surprising, considering the amount of time they spent together and the schedule they kept. Marg's focus on her son was a huge benefit to the group. She was a nervous traveller and sat right behind the bus drivers — first Mel and then Scotty — and imagined all sorts of disasters, from falling over cliffs to having a tire burst on a downhill run.

Marg was always like that, said her daughter Melody. "There were too many close calls. It might have had a lot to do with entertainers dying in plane crashes. There was one time, they were trying to take off or land, and the runway was icy and they skidded. It was traumatic for her."

David's most indelible memory of touring was the amazing talent of the musicians. "They were able to interpret the music, to be the music; they were never just people playing an instrument." Many of them played more than one, and he would watch them become one with whichever they had in hand. "It was almost a metaphysical thing."

On that 1964 tour, David also gained a lot of weight: "I ate an awful lot of hot dogs and drank a lot of pop," he said with a chuckle. The fans couldn't do enough for them. One day, a farmer took David and Catherine McKinnon on a trail ride. "The horse took off with me. It was great!" recalled David.

As exciting as touring was, David saw that it was extremely hard work for Marg and the band. "They'd travel all day to a place, set up, eat, come back to the hotel, change, and do a performance. Sometimes they would do a dance after the performance, and then they would tear down, go to the hotel and get some sleep, get up the next morning, and travel all day to another spot and do the same thing all over again." David was too small to help carry the equipment, but he did help carry instruments and luggage. During the show, he would watch the performance and then go back to the hotel room with his mother.

"I think she really enjoyed having me with her on tour," said David, and for him, it was a revelation. He had never seen his mother perform before he watched her sing in Calgary; he had no idea of the kind of adulation she earned. He wasn't aware that Marg had become one of the most popular members of the group, and he didn't know that the summer before, when the group was touring out west, police escorts had to protect her from the crush of fans and photographers eager to get a glimpse of Canada's most popular female performer.

David went on tour again the following year. He was well into the routine now, the early morning, the quick breakfast, and then the run to the bus for the long trip to the next venue. He had his seat, two or three rows back from the front, next to his mother. Sometimes they would sing songs, play cards, or do jigsaw puzzles. Often, David would sit with one of the band members. Waldo and Rae were fun to be with, and Duke always had a magic trick. Charlie was a big favourite. They all treated him as if he were one of their own children whom they missed when they were on tour. "Oh, when I was a brat, Charlie would tell me to go and sit down, but we all got on really well," David said.

In 1966, Marg and Austin and the children left Halifax and moved to Sussex. She felt more at home there than she did in the city. She had many relatives in the area and wanted her children to grow up with the large extended family that she had so enjoyed in her youth. Austin gave up his job with the Maritime Harbour Board and acted as Marg's manager. They commuted to Halifax every week for the taping of *Don Messer's Jubilee*.

Marg left David at home the next summer. He had met Pat, the girl he would eventually marry, and he wasn't prepared to be separated from her for the duration of the tour. He stayed with her parents, and for two years Marg travelled without her children. Then Melody joined Marg and travelled with her on tour four years in a row — from 1969 until 1972. She was nine years old on her first tour, a sweetly innocent little girl with a brown ponytail and big eyes. Going on tour was an incentive to keep her marks up; that was Marg's condition, though it was obvious that she enjoyed having her children with her on tour.

"Before the performance we would go in the room and get clothes out. Mum would get ready, and then we would have something to eat. If we had time we would go out; I remember the wax museum in Niagara Falls and the Parliament Buildings in Ottawa. We went shopping. At the site of Expo '67, we went to the midway. A lot of

Charlie Chamberlain, Don Messer, and Marg Osburne with a
group of senior citizens at Golden Acres Lodge Home for the Aged,
Lethbridge, Alberta, June 19, 1963.

Courtesy: Galt Museum and Archives, Lethbridge, Alberta [*Lethbridge Herald*].

times, on the road, if she got into a place and there was time, she
would go to old people's homes and play for them. There was never
any charge, she just enjoyed doing it." Sometimes Melody would go
with her. Sometimes Waldo would go along and play the piano. Like
her brother, Melody rarely sat in the audience but would most often
stay backstage.

In fact Melody was often dancing backstage. She was entranced
with the Buchta Dancers, those young men and women who twirled
and waltzed, fox-trotted and square-danced on the show. She knew
every step of their routines. "After the show, as soon as they had finished, I would run up onstage and collect the sequins that had fallen
off the dresses." She had gathered a large number of them in a jar by
the time that tour was over. "My dream was to be a Buchta Dancer
and wear crinolines and sequins," she said wistfully.

She had little contact with Don. "He was very quiet and he commanded respect. His aura commanded respect. He might have been quiet and slight, but he was very powerful, without having to say anything. He didn't intimidate me, but we never connected. He would smile and nod, but he never talked to me. I didn't connect with Naomi either, even though she travelled on the 1969 tour when I was nine. They just didn't socialize."

Marg and Charlie got on very well, something which led fans to think that they were a couple. "They had a very strong and very professional relationship," recalled David, "but they were good friends, too. Oh, sometimes she would be very frustrated with him and she would let him know, but she really appreciated his goodness and his talent." Charlie and Lydia often visited Marg and Austin in Sussex. When they had lived in Charlottetown, Marg and Charlie would sometimes get together at the Chamberlains' house to sit down and strum their guitars and play the songs they wanted to sing. "That was beautiful," said Ann-Marie Chamberlain.

During the fifties and sixties, people who were under the influence of alcohol enjoyed a considerable degree of acceptance; heavy drinking was considered more a social liability than an illness. Even drunk driving was, if not acceptable, certainly recognized as a reality. Marg was the sole member of the group who never drank; although, she chain smoked, as did many of them.

David said that his mother's ability to travel with a group of men who were quite different from herself attests to her "high tolerance for a lot of things. She was a non-judgmental person who went with the flow." Her own husband was a heavy drinker and at times a difficult man, but even his requests for money when she was on tour were met with acquiescence.

"We'd barely get into a hotel, and they'd get a call from the lobby," said Rae Simmons, who recounted the story to Bill Guest. "Miss Osburne, please come to the desk." And there would be a telegram from Austin. "Dear Marg, please send $500. Having a nice time. Hope you are too." She loved him dearly — of that make no mistake, Ann-Marie Chamberlain asserted.

༒

As easygoing as Marg was, she could be very determined when it came to her own family. David and Pat had been dating for ten years when Marg decided it was time they got married. She went out and bought the marriage licence and gave it to her son. "We set the wedding for May," said David, "but one day I came home from college and asked Patsy if she wanted to get married. She said, 'When?' I said, 'This weekend.'"

It would be two weeks later before they married, without Marg present. She was disappointed to have missed the wedding but relieved that it had finally occurred.

David and Melody have vivid memories of their mother. "She telephoned us all the time when she was on the road, and she was always home for Christmas," said Melody. She realized that her children missed her very much when she was performing, and she would keep in touch as best she could by writing letters. The children wrote back, knowing in advance where the band would be staying each day of the tour.

Melody remembers dolls and tea sets for Christmas presents and, when she got older, the beginning of a collection of audio tapes. She and Marg shared a lot of girl-talk about boys, and sometimes they talked about the music industry and whether Melody would follow in her mother's footsteps. "She was always encouraging," recalled Melody, "but she always made sure that I would remember to have something to fall back on because music is not an easy profession."

༒

Marg was a consummate professional. She feared flying, but she would get on the plane anyway. "She knew there was a job to do and she did it," said Langstroth. She sang songs that she loathed, like "Hound Dog," because the audience loved such songs, and her job was to please the audience. Don always said that Marg could perform anything except opera, and she had an amazing facility for learning a piece. Ira Stewart, a CBC Halifax radio producer, was more specific. In a December 1963 interview published in *Chatelaine*, he told of "how he has heard her run through difficult pop tunes one time and then perform them note and nuance perfect." Langstroth said, "She was much better than we gave her credit for at the time. She always had much more to give than you saw on the Messer show. I would be standing beside her when we would start to rehearse for a pre-recording, and she'd start to sing and be pure Rosemary Clooney, for instance. She could sing like so many people and had a terrific music ear."

So good was her ear that Don said of her, "You'll never hear Marg Osburne make a mistake." They wouldn't always agree on the choice of music, though. Marg loved folk songs, and when she was interviewed by herself on television or radio, she would often take the opportunity to sing some of them. Presenting them to Don for inclusion on the show would not always meet with approval. Don had a very particular idea about what suited the show, and if she made a suggestion that he didn't like, he would say, "I don't think that is for our show." Marg always bowed to his judgment because she respected Don as bandleader. "Marg would acquiesce," said Langstroth, "but the next week she would bring up the suggestion again. She was very persistent about getting her type of music some air time."

"Snowbird," the song that would galvanize Ann Murray's career, was not one of the songs that Marg championed. Gene MacLellan, the composer and lyricist, had gone to Johnny Forrest's home one Sunday to ask him for an introduction to Don Messer. Together they phoned Don, and asked if Gene and bass player Blair Doucette could come over with a song that Gene would like to perform for him. Gene said that he had sent the tape to Bill Langstroth some time ago, but it was languishing in a box somewhere, and he was anxious to see whether the song was good enough to go on Don's show. Don immediately invited them over, and Gene performed the song in the front room.

Dawn happened to be home that Sunday and heard her father say, "Let's do a tape of that." They did, and Don gave the tape to Marg to see if she liked the song. "But Marg didn't," said Dawn. "It didn't really suit her style." So Don invited Gene to perform the song himself. His unique performance in both English and French took place on the very last *Don Messer's Jubilee* show that the CBC broadcast. It remains one of the few times that it has ever been performed in the bilingual version.

After Don died and the *Don Messer's Jubilee* group disbanded, Marg would perform across the country with her own successful nightclub act, the Hennessey Trio. She also developed a television show, where she had free rein to choose the music and guests, and called it *That Maritime Feeling*. On July 16, 1977, the fifth anniversary of Charlie's death, she performed before a large audience in Rocklyn, Ontario, and then collapsed offstage, dying later that evening of a heart attack. She was only forty-nine years old and had not yet heard that her pilot had been accepted by CBC for a full-season show.

Undoubtedly there was something special about Marg. David told a story that summed up his mother for him. "They were playing at Old Home Week on Prince Edward Island, and it was a dull, overcast day, with a bit of mist in the air. They didn't know if they were going to go on, because of the possibility of rain or the chance of a lightning storm. But they decided to go on anyway, and Mum came out onstage. For the time she was on, there was a break in the clouds and the sun was shining right down on her on the stage, but on nobody else. She did her bit and then she thanked the crowd and got off the stage, and the clouds closed over again. That's how she was."

Charlie spoke for family, friends, neighbours, and co-workers when he said, "Marg? Aw, she's terrific. There ain't nobody like Marg Osburne. She's a darlin'."

The Buchta Dancers

Don and His Islanders are at the Halifax Forum preparing to go onstage. They are giving their time tonight to play a concert in aid of Walter Callow's fundraiser toward a wheelchair-accessible bus for veterans and shut-ins. One of Don's personal heroes, Callow has persevered against all odds. Despite being badly injured in a jet fighter crash as a member of the Royal Flying Corps, Callow continues to operate a successful lumber business. In the last few years, that business has been located in a suite of offices at the Camp Hill Military Hospital, Halifax.

Callow is blind and paralyzed, yet shows no sign of slowing down. Recently, he has funnelled his considerable creativity and energy, to say nothing of his cash, into his favourite charitable projects. Don is happy to help and quickly accepted his invitation to perform as one of the main attractions of this concert. Ed McCurdy, an American folksinger, is the other main act, and Max Ferguson is doing the honours as master of ceremonies.

Don watches the performance onstage: eight ballroom dancers swirling in a waltz. They are the Corteens, a dance troupe under the direction of Gunter Buchta. Don has heard a lot about the European dance teacher who is making a name for himself in the Halifax area. He suspects there is much depth to the man. Gunter Buchta has a presence about him, a bearing that is enhanced rather than diminished by his limp.

Don continues watching, caught up in the beauty of the dancers' movement, the precision of the troupe, the synchronized music and dance. He wonders whether such an act would work on his show — probably not ballroom dancing, but perhaps square-dancing. He has had soloists on the show, tap dancers and folk dancers, but never a troupe.

The dance comes to an end and the young men and women flash radiant smiles at the crowd and file offstage. Their discipline impresses Don, as does the way they pay attention to Gunter when he speaks with them. He decides to ask Max Ferguson to introduce them.

⸙

In 1957, a year after that first meeting, Bill Langstroth phoned Gunter Buchta at his dance studio and mentioned that the CBC was working on a television pilot for Don Messer, they were looking for dancers. If Gunter were interested, could he and his dancers come down to the CBC studio for an audition with the band?

Gunter carefully selected eight of his best dancers, taking into consideration experience and similarity of physique. They would not only have to dance well, but they must look attractive together. Some of his students had had several years of training, while others were new to the troupe but showed great promise. His wife chose costumes that would transfer well to the television screen.

When Gunter saw the studio, he realized it was smaller than he had anticipated, measuring only twelve metres by eighteen metres. In that space were lights and cameras, eighteen CBC crew members, the band, and their instruments. Gunter recognized the challenge immediately: if his group were chosen, he would have to choreograph dances unique to this setting and space. First, they had to pass the audition.

He chose a waltz for the first set, and the dancers glided effortlessly in time with the music. The Islanders ramped up the speed with a foxtrot. The dancers again performed faultlessly. Don was impressed with them, with their skill, charm, and composure, but could they do a square dance? Indeed, they could; however, it was unlike any square dance Don had ever seen. It had all the elements that he was familiar with, but somehow the result was entirely different. There was no bustling around, and what it lacked in exuberance it more than made up for in grace and elegance.

"That's it," Don said to Bill Langstroth. "That's what I want."

~

Don, Bill Langstroth, and Gunter Buchta would meet long before each season began, and they would map out thirteen shows. Don always picked the tunes and the theme of the show, but Gunter had a lot of freedom in the choreography and would offer suggestions that would involve the band, not just the dancers. Gunter placed some restrictions on the music to which his troupe would dance: the first section had to be 96 bars, and the second was always 128 bars. Forty years later, Gunter described Don as a "human metronome": "We require either 128 bars or 96 bars for our numbers. Over and over again he turns out the 128 bars in exactly two minutes and the 96 bars in one and a half minutes, without the aid of a metronome." Don trusted Gunter, too; he seemed to share his sense of timing. Finally he said to him, "Gunter, you conduct the orchestra. You tell [us] exactly what you want to hear, when you want the rhythm to come in, when you want the bass coming in."

"The only stipulation that Don Messer had was that he had to have the first sixteen bars and the last sixteen bars," said Gunter. Don liked to have melody predominate in the beginning of a piece and drums and rhythm at the end, and thus both his needs and Gunter's were satisfied.

They got on very well, even though their backgrounds were disparate. Messer was a fourth-generation Anglo-Scottish Canadian farm boy with an elementary school education, whereas Gunter was a lawyer and the son of a lawyer, born in Germany of Czech-Slovak parents. What the two men shared was more important than what differentiated them: their vision, their single-minded pursuit of excellence, and the willingness to work hard to attain it. They also took the same approach to discipline. Don docked his men's pay if they didn't perform well; Gunter fined his dancers $5 if they were late for rehearsal.

"We never had a fight, never had a disagreement," said Gunter. "There was once a tiny little ripple when we tried to make the show flow better artistically. Don didn't like this. He said, 'We better sit down and talk about this. I know what the people like, why fix it?'"

Gunter could be as adamant about his dancers as Don was about his show. "I explained to him, I have to also think of my dancers. They have become a household word. Music and dance blends together. He agreed with this, and from then on it was smooth sailing." The advantage Gunter had when working with Don was that he was a colleague rather than an employee. He was also an expert in his own field, and Don had always respected expertise.

❧

The road that Gunter Buchta travelled to reach *Don Messer's Jubilee* was complex. He arrived in Halifax on July 4, 1950, a refugee sponsored by his future wife, Irma. She herself was a refugee from Hungary who had come to Halifax the previous year and was then employed as a domestic in the home of Major General Harry Foster. Apparently, Major General Foster had arranged for Irma to sponsor Buchta herself, which was unusual at the time and would make him the first immigrant to come to Canada after the Second World War without the sponsorship of a Canadian citizen. Irma and Gunter had fallen in love when Gunter had moved to Hungary, although there is no record of how and when they met.

Gunter had limited proficiency in the English language and only $10 to his name. He also walked with a pronounced limp and had little use of one hand, both conditions the result of injuries incurred on the Russian front during the Second World War. At the time, he had been taken to the field hospital, where doctors considered amputating his mangled leg. Gunter had resigned himself to this until he remembered a young butcher's apprentice who had recovered from a very serious leg injury. Gunter declined the surgery and spent ten months recovering in a military hospital before he was considered ready for rehabilitation.

He first tried swimming and then riding a bike. Because his hand was still paralyzed, and these sports required the use of both hands, the doctor suggested dancing as an alternative. "To dance, one has to learn the discipline of rhythm and to perform certain exercises without stopping," Gunter said. Within two years he was winning competitions, helped no doubt by his instructors, among the best in the world — Alex Moore of England, Karl von Markowitzsch of Austria, and Paul Krebs of West Germany.

Gunter grew up in Germany, but fought in the Hungarian army. Though a lawyer by education, it is unclear whether he practiced law in Europe before escaping to Canada. There is also a story of him opening a dance studio in Europe before he was forced to flee to Canada. He had had all the opportunities of his social class and education and he was quickly able to build a future for himself here.

Despite his poor command of English, which prevented him from obtaining a licence to practice law, his resumé was enough to land him a job as a dancing instructor at the Halifax Conservatory of Music, no doubt helped by Major General Foster. Ballroom dancing had not been offered on the curriculum prior to this, and his first class was attended by only one student, a sixty-five-year-old woman. Within a few weeks, he had a steady stream of adults and children who wanted to learn the foxtrot, waltz, tango, rumba, and quickstep.

While he was teaching at the conservatory, Gunter also gave lessons at the Halifax School for the Blind. He would not accept payment for this; he wanted to show that dance could build confidence in those with physical challenges. These lessons were his contribution towards enabling the students to participate fully in the life of their community.

He next introduced folk dancing to students at both the conservatory and the Halifax School for the Blind. Within three months, he proposed a dance recital. Irma made all the costumes, and Ken

Back Row: Jane Edgett, Gary Copp, Don King, Hugh Ballem, Gary Eisenhauer, Joyda Ruegeberg, Joe Wallin; front row: Judy Edgett, Marilyn Boyle, Gunter Buchta, Lynne Sheehan.

Nova Scotia Records and Management Don Messer Collection 1998 – 132/071/291.

Winsby, a Halifax shoe merchant, provided shoes for the troupe. Gunter went a step further and entered both his sighted and his blind students in a provincial folk-dancing competition. That same year, he founded the ballroom dancing branch of the Canadian Dance Teachers' Association.

He was obviously a gifted instructor; within a year, he had assembled a group of talented young dancers who could perform at festivals and shows. He called them the Corteens. Langstroth didn't like the name and suggested to Gunter that, instead, they should henceforth be known as the Buchta Dancers. The troupe remained with *Don Messer's Jubilee* until it ceased production when Don died. Years later, Buchta told an *Atlantic Insight* interviewer, "It came to the point that Don Messer did not want to go anywhere on the road without the dancers. We went five times across Canada [with him]."

〜

There were never more than eight Buchta Dancers on the set or stage at one time, since a square for a square dance consists of four couples, but the troupe always consisted of ten dancers. That gave the dancers one week off in four, and all went on tour in case of illness or accident. The dancers had little contact with Don. "He talked to us, but it wasn't as if we hung out together, unless it was on tour and it was something the whole band planned to go to. He was certainly always very kind to the dancers, but we rehearsed separately," said Joe Wallin, who was with the Buchta Dancers from 1963 until 1972. "After the first few years, we were never there when the musicians were. The whole show was taped, and then the dancers were taped as part of the show."

Jane Edgett, who joined the Buchta Dancers in 1965, recognized a definite social stratification. "We were two groups. There were the musicians and the dancers, which is typically how it works in the artistic world. Singers and musicians are number one, and dancers are number two." She concurred with Joe's recollection. "Don was a loner. He kept himself totally separate from everybody else. He was not very social, but he was definitely in charge of the musicians. There was no question in their minds that he ruled the roost. But our involvement was all through Gunter Buchta."

The advantage of working for Gunter rather than Don was that the dancers were all guaranteed the same pay, regardless of audience numbers. The band members received a percentage of the house, depending on their status in the band and their union regulations.

Certainly the dancers recognized the uniqueness of their opportunity, and they felt they added something important to each performance. "We were a large part of the success of the show," said Jane. "We were a visual asset; otherwise you would just have a group of people playing instruments. The combination of the two made it blossom into something bigger. The fans all had a piece of it that they liked." Some people fell in love with Marg, some recognized Charlie as a Maritime icon, and others watched the show for the music or the dancing. *Don Messser's Jubilee* had a little bit of something for everybody.

There were the naysayers too: not everybody recalled the dancers so fondly. In one Saint John, New Brunswick, home, *Don Messer's Jubilee* was not acceptable viewing. "Flamers" is what one grand-mother called the Buchta Dancers, those young women who danced and twirled and kicked their legs so high, they'd show their panties. "Flamers," she'd exclaim as she turned off the television. "You're not watching them."

In contrast to the distance they felt from Don, the dancers de-veloped almost familial bonds with Rae, Duke, Charlie, Cec, and Waldo. "These guys all had families, and being away from home was very difficult for them. We filled a bit of a family void for them be-cause they were very lonesome," said Jane. The age difference would have heightened that relationship, as many of the dancers were fifteen and sixteen in the beginning, the same age as the children of the performers. And, as most of them remained members of the Buchta Dancers for many years as they worked their way through university, they became part of the extended family.

"We had all come through his [Gunter Buchta's] school," said Joe. "I was the first one who wasn't one of his students, but he knew me because I had danced as a soloist on the show. He needed a male dancer to go on tour in 1963, so he asked me if I was interested in go-ing and I said sure, and then I auditioned for the fall season. He said that whether I got it or not depended on how I got on with the other dancers." They all gave Joe a hard time at first, until they decided he was okay. Then they had a great time together and remained friends. "I don't think there was ever any kind of argument. There were times we'd disagree, but it was never an angry disagreement. There was never any animosity between us, no jealousies that I ever saw." In fact, Joe said that after the gruelling thirteen-week Centennial Tour, the five male dancers decided to vacation together at Expo '67 and spent another week in each other's company.

It was a wonderful experience, but it was still a job, and just like any other job, it had its good and bad times. The tours were definitely the good times. On the 1964 tour, Catherine McKinnon, because of her youth, bunked in with dancer Mary Wile. "We had all kinds of crazy things happen," said McKinnon. "We played to tiny communities and we played to large arenas. I mean, this band was the forerunner to rock bands, they played in arenas because they would fill them. The RCMP used to meet us; one night the RCMP drove us forty-five miles to take us for a hamburger. Communities did things like open the civic pool and let us go for a swim after the shows. Farmers would think nothing of driving four or five hours to come to a show."

At one point, the tour bus broke down and everybody got out and pushed it. On the side of the bus was written, in big letters, "Don Messer Tour," and when a newspaper photographer came upon the scene and saw them all pushing the bus, he mistook their predicament for a publicity stunt.

Some experiences were truly harrowing, and because of one they almost missed a show in British Columbia. On their way to Prince George, they came upon a landslide. There was no room to turn the bus around, but the road crew had cleared a single lane for cars by bulldozing earth to the side. Scotty, the bus driver for this tour, decided to try and forge ahead. The road crew grew alarmed. "We don't think a bus can make it," they cautioned Scotty.

Scotty looked at the narrow road, he looked over the edge of the precipice, and then he looked back at the dancers. "I can make it if you all sit on one side of the bus. We should be able to get through. Do I have any volunteers?" The dancers all came forward. None of the band would take the chance of staying on the bus; they all walked past the slide in the cleared lane.

"We were all saying the rosary," recalled Joe. "Even the non-Catholics, we prayed the whole way across." They were almost there when the bus started to slide. "The volume of prayers increased," chuckled Joe. "It was such a relief to get to the other side."

Scotty was a careful driver, never travelling at night and generally going to his hotel room to sleep as soon as they checked in and had something to eat. After the meal, the musicians would usually go to their rooms until it was time for the show. Not so the dancers. "We'd go and discover the place," said Jane Edgett. She went on her first tour at the age of eighteen, and to this day she says that she would never give up what she gained from that experience.

⌣

The tours certainly opened the eyes of those young dancers, travelling as they did to every nook and cranny of Canada. "We saw places we had never heard of or even realized existed. We went to a little town called Grimshaw, in Alberta, where they still had dirt roads and hitching posts and wooden sidewalks. How many people have gone to a place like that?" asked Joe. The reception in these towns was phenomenal. Grimshaw had a population of five hundred, yet more than five thousand people showed up for the Don Messer's Jubilee concert performance in 1967. Some had travelled more than sixteen hundred kilometres from the northern Prairies and the North West Territories to see the live version of their favourite television entertainment. The appeal? The whole show was down to earth. "We were admired, but we were not celebrities and we never thought of ourselves as celebrities," said Joe. "I'm the same as you, I'm your next-door neighbour. We were just down-to-earth people who happened to entertain the rest of the ordinary people."

The dancers grew accustomed to the adoration while they toured. They didn't get that when they performed on TV, the high that came when an audience applauded. "It was a great feeling when people would want your autograph," said Joe. "My first time was in Toronto, and somebody stopped me and said 'You dance on *Don Messer*, don't you?' The fact that somebody in a big city recognizes you and wants your autograph is pretty powerful. I once got a fan letter from the United States addressed simply to Joe Wallin, Nova Scotia."

Often they were exhausted. The most gruelling trip was the Centennial Tour, during which they had only three days off in thirteen weeks. On some days they did two performances, and the last thing they wanted to do in the evening was attend a reception and sign autographs. The tours were always sponsored, and they were expected to show up as ambassadors of the show. There was no excuse except genuine illness. "You'd get back to the hotel in the wee hours of the morning and you'd have to be up to get on the bus to travel to the next city. We slept a lot on the bus, we were always so tired. Some mornings we had to be on the bus by seven and might not have got in until three a.m.," Joe recalled. When they weren't sleeping, they played cards, read, chatted with each other, simply did their own thing. Sometimes they placed small bets on when they would arrive, just for the diversion.

"If you were late for the bus, they'd leave without you," Mary said, remembering the day she and Catherine McKinnon had to grab their coats and chase the bus. "Those were long, hard drives on the bus from eight in the morning, a half-hour for lunch, and then on the bus until you reached the destination at five, and you did it every day of the week. Even Sundays, which was supposed to be a day of rest where you could get your laundry done and relax a bit; we would do a charity show at a seniors' home. You had to find time to do your laundry. We had dresses that had to be dry cleaned, but your casual clothes that you wore on the bus were your responsibility."

Don always carried a box of detergent with him, but the dancers and band members would save their laundry until they got to a town with a laundromat and had enough time to actually do the job. Irma didn't enjoy the touring, and only travelled with them once, but she continued making all the dancers' costumes. She carried an iron with her on that tour and did her best to make them presentable. She said to Charlie once, "Charlie, your trousers look horrible. You cannot go onstage without a pressing." Charlie responded that he had no one to do it. So Irma told him to get changed and bring them to her and Gunter's room. She did it for him. "From then on my wife could do no wrong," said Gunter.

~

Going across the Prairies, the travellers had a view of a train several miles long. It was the first time they had ever seen an entire train, from the engine to the caboose, at the same time. It gave them all a sense of the grandeur of the Prairies, and the farmers gave them a sense of the importance of their show. "They told us that the only thing that interrupted harvesting and would bring them in off the fields was the weather report and *Don Messer's Jubilee*," Joe said.

Because of people's love for the show, the town of Sturgis, Saskatchewan, put on an extra effort to host the performance. They erected a stage and then surrounded it with benches made of planks on two-by-fours embedded in the ground. "We were up there dancing, and then we heard 'boom,' and all the wooden planks collapsed, they just collapsed and the people went bump. They laughed, we laughed and continued on with the show," said Mary Wile, her voice filled with laughter at the memory.

Following the performance, the town hosted a barbecue at the mayor's house. It must have reminded Don of the barn frolics in his home community, for there was a side of beef barbecuing in a pit and long trestle tables set up with salads, rolls, preserves, and desserts. The weather had been perfect, but then the wind came up, and the show members experienced their first dust storm. Rolls flew through the air and salads tipped onto the ground. Tablecloths were ripped off the tables. The people tore into the house with steaks on plates. Marg, Mary, and Rae headed for the first bedroom and plopped on the bed. It was a feather bed, and all of them sank into the middle, steaks balanced precariously aloft. Catherine McKinnon ate her steak standing in the bathtub, unable to find anywhere else in the crowded house.

Sometimes silly things would happen onstage, like the time that Mary Wile's petticoat fell off when she was dancing. She kicked it off the stage and it "landed on a man's lap, but I just kept on dancing in perfect time. The audience thought it was hilarious."

The cast may have had a lot of fun, but they also worked very hard to make the show. "You cannot choreograph new stuff for every show," said Gunter. "I made a thousand dances, but so often it was taking parts out of here and putting them there. We rehearsed twice a week, on Monday and Wednesday, for two hours. On Monday I introduced the dance to them, and they had to forget what they did last week. Wednesday we tried to tidy it up."

"Gunter was a hard-nosed business man," said Jane Edgett. "If we did a poor performance, we would end up in rehearsals next day. His word was the last word, and there was no question. If he was happy, you knew he was happy. If he was angry, you knew he was angry."

One of the angriest the dancers saw Gunter was in Whitehorse. The performance had been sponsored in part by the local Lion's Club and the girls had to face the misunderstanding that they were a dance group of loose women. "Gunter Buchta threw one of them [the Lions] out of his room for suggesting any such thing," said Jane. "Even in the evening the boys wouldn't allow us to mingle with the audience to sell souvenirs. They wouldn't let us do that because of the situation. They were very protective."

That was Charlie's doing. "He was very protective of the girls," said Joe, "especially in towns that he deemed to have rough areas. He would always give the boys a talking-to and tell us, 'You are not to allow those girls to go out on the streets by themselves, even if they are all together. You are to go with them, and you are not allowed to let them go anywhere by themselves at night.' He would give us this speech, and if, for some reason, one of the girls was off by herself, even if she wasn't on the street, if she was near the entrance by herself, he would get after whatever guy was nearest for letting her go off on her own. He was extremely protective, and he was such a kind-hearted man."

"Having Dad as your friend was like having your own security," laughed Donny Chamberlain, Charlie's son. "He was the same with Don. Don was meek and Dad was a little rougher, and so he was very protective of him."

On Sundays the group would always have to gather and eat Kentucky Fried Chicken for lunch. "That was a must, no question about it. It was Don's treat, he would pay for it," said Mary. Her phrase "have to" is telling and sad, for it was Don's attempt to get close to the others, to thank them in the best way he knew how, through the sharing of his favourite meal. He was aware of how distant they found him, and it must have hurt, for he was not a cold man. Nonetheless, he could never dispel the impression he made. "Don was strong, in that he knew what he wanted and was determined to have it, in a very quiet way," said Jane Edgett.

His inability to get close was due in part to his role as bandleader and his belief that he had to be firmly in control of the band and the show at all times. He never was able to relax with the others as one of the gang. The dancers had a good rapport with Cec; they had fun with Rae and Duke. They adored Marg for her big heart. "These guys did all the socializing, but Mr. Messer was always on his own, he didn't come over and mingle," said Mary. Perhaps it wouldn't have worked anyway, given his discomfort in crowds or even small gatherings. This isolation caused members of the tour to take sides in the inevitable conflicts that arose.

Charlie was often the source of those conflicts. "Charlie had the greatest admiration for Mr. Messer," Jane said. "He had made Charlie a Canadian icon, and Charlie knew that and thanked Mr. Messer every day for it. But Charlie drank, and there would be times when he would not be there. When we were on tour, he was there every day, on every show. He never missed one. But people began to disrespect him for his drinking and for those lapses. He lived hard and he drank hard, and the rift between him and Mr. Messer got bigger and bigger. Charlie respected Mr. Messer so much that Don could really raise the hammer to him at any time and Charlie would listen. He would be devastated, but he would toe the line, as much as he could. He would do it as long as he could; he had a heart of gold." The underlying resentment was due to the fact that the dancers were all fiercely protective of Charlie. "He was the one member of the band who really tried to take the dancers under his wing," said Joe.

"Part of it had to do with not knowing when the end was coming, but being tired of it now," said Jane, reflecting on the tension.

Don Messer playing in Children's Hospital, April 1964.

Nova Scotia Records and Management Don Messer fonds, 1998 – 132/071/249.

That may have been the crux of the matter, the fact that Don was tired of the stress, the frustrations he endured managing this group of sometimes difficult people, living out of a suitcase and travelling by bus all day, being away from his family and his home for weeks at a time. He was worried about his own health. He had had three heart attacks and was by then coping with diabetes as well.

He was also worried about Waldo, his brilliant pianist. Waldo had a little girl, "a gorgeous little thing, daddy's little girl," said Mary. "He was never the same after she died. He perhaps needed some help, should have had it, but the show must go on. It was a very hard life for him, but in those days, you had to ride out whatever bothered you."

Waldo's grief was painful to observe. He would sit on the bus, humming and singing to himself, and then he would get up and go to his suitcase to retrieve the pair of baby bootees that went everywhere with him. Jane recalled that anguished time. "He was so sick about his daughter's death. It changed his whole life forever. Waldo was a musical genius. He could play anything, but when his daughter died, he went into another world. She was young and it set him to talking to her bootees all the time. He never fully recovered. We would go to church while we were away on tour, and you would hear this music coming out of the basement, and he'd be down there playing rags during the service. It would be his way of coping."

He and Don had both suffered the loss of a young daughter, but Don might not have known how to comfort Waldo. He had never shared his own sorrow about Brenda once he was past the funeral; he never even mentioned her name to relatives. He grieved her loss deeply, in a very private way that perhaps only Naomi was privy to. Don was certainly ready for this lifestyle to end, but when the end came, it was not how Don envisioned it.

c⁓

The Buchta Dancers stayed together after Don's death to fulfill a commitment to perform at Prince Edward Island's Old Home Week in August of 1973. Then they disbanded. Gunter and Irma Buchta moved to their house in Grenada but returned to Halifax when Gunter was offered the position of executive director of Dance Nova Scotia. He worked tirelessly to bring qualified dance teachers to rural communities. At a workshop in Bridgewater, Nova Scotia, Gunter noticed an awkward young man standing at the sidelines. "You must have confidence," he told future actor Donald Sutherland. "You can do anything you want if you have faith in yourself."

For many years he was a judge of international dance competitions and was awarded fellowships with the Imperial Society of Teachers of Dancing (ISTD), England; the International Dance Teachers' Association (IDTA); and the Canadian Dance Teachers' Association (CDTA).

He continued his work utilizing dance in rehabilitation, and after recovering from a stroke himself, began working with that patient population as well. For his dedication to the rehabilitation and fitness of others through volunteer work, he was nominated for the Order of Canada, but did not receive it. He died in Halifax in 1997.

"Dear Mr. Messer"

The show is over and Don looks out at the sea of faces. They are smiling and nodding, and he can sense what they are saying: By golly, that man sure can fiddle. And that Charlie, have you ever heard such a voice? He knows what they are saying because he has heard it a hundred and more times, at every show the group has done over the years. He still needs to hear it to know that he is giving people what they want; still needs to know that the sponsors will be satisfied.

Years earlier, a hardware store owner in Saint John had told him, "If you can hold the attention of fifty per cent of the people, that is a hundred per cent effort," but he has never been satisfied with fifty per cent. That is not the way to build a successful career.

He dreads signing autographs. He likes people well enough, but he is not comfortable with the chatter of strangers, with the need to make conversation with them. If he is lucky they will talk about music, and perhaps someone may tell him about a Scottish song her mother used to sing. If that happens, they will probably exchange addresses and likely as not will enter into a correspondence about old-time music and Don's search for more and more previously unknown scores. If he is unlucky, someone in the crowd will push for an audition for his son or daughter, or even for himself. Don is supportive of other fiddlers, encourages their talent, but he does not like to be approached after a concert. He feels cornered then, pressured.

Don has already signed fifty copies of the group photograph. He looks up to try and gauge the numbers still in the line. Another fifty, he estimates. He worries because his hand is beginning to cramp. Don has always protected his hands, dependent as he is on them for his livelihood but the sale of so many photographs tonight is bringing in good money, and Don is grateful for that.

Over to his left are Marg and Charlie. The lines in front of them are far longer than the line in front of him. He wonders how they do it, keeping up a seamless chatter with every person. Marg asks people about their children, Charlie tells a joke, and both enjoy themselves immensely. Don will just be relieved when he is finished.

‿

Not many people knew the private Don Messer. He was neutral in his public image, dressed neatly in a suit and tie, hair combed, his manner that of a small-town banker. To discover him and his very special relationship with his fans, it's necessary to get away from the bright lights of the TV screen. The village of McAdam, New Brunswick, is a good place to start. Just thirty kilometres from Tweedside, it was for many years a railway town, and some members of the Messer family sought work there. Hayes Messer, Don's nephew, tells the following story.

> There was a barber in McAdam by the name of Garnett
> Carpenter, and I sometimes went there for haircuts.
> Like our family, he liked music, especially fiddle music.
> He kept a fiddle at the shop and on occasion would
> play it. He would always ask me about Don, as he was
> an avid fan and would give anything to meet his idol.
> So it happened that one day when Don and my father
> came to visit I asked him if he would visit the shop and
> surprise Garnie, as we called him.
>
>   When we entered the shop he was busy cutting a
> gent's hair while two or three others looked on. He
> turned to look as the door opened, and he dropped his

clippers in amazement.
He was only half-done
the lad's haircut, and he
reached to shake Don's
hand. He was so excited
that he forgot all about
the haircut and the lad
in the chair. I thought he
was going to take a spell.

After a while he got
his bearings. He was so
happy to see Don. After a
few minutes, he went to
his fiddle and asked Don
if he would play a tune
for him. Donald looked
the fiddle over, tuned it
a little, and played a few

Don Messer, 1939.
Courtesy: John Clifford [Craswell Portrait Studio].

tunes. Garnett was so happy, he was grinning from ear
to ear. I am not sure yet if he ever finished the lad's
haircut. Everyone that came into that shop from that
day on heard about Don Messer playing the fiddle in
the barber shop. Every time I went there, he would
thank me for bringing Don into the shop.

Not all fans had the opportunity for such access, and most had to be
content with letter writing. Over the years, Don received thousands
of letters, many predating his success with *Don Messer's Jubilee*. The
reason may have been the way his broadcasts, on both radio and
television, seemed to bring people into his living room; indeed, he
brought families together in their own living rooms.

One of his first fan letters came in 1934 from his cousin Minnie
Cushing of Niagara Falls, New York. Don had been performing on
radio for five years at this point, and it had been twenty-one years
since, as a four-year-old, he had attended her wedding. She thought

Don likely wouldn't remember her, but she is unabashed in her praise. "I have been listening to your old-time programs every time you are on the air. I think you're swell. You play so near like my poor old dad that I feel as if I was sitting in our old kitchen at Tweedside."

Don's scrapbooks tell the story. There are four of them, hunter green loose-leaf albums with gold lettering, each thirty-six centimetres by thirty centimetres, held together with a green shoelace-like cord. The pages are brittle with age and glue, and as one turns the pages, letters and clippings fall out. The first entry is a 1929 photograph, labelled "the first picture ever taken in a radio station of the group." There is a dentist bill, his first ever, and the copy of the certificate of registration for Don Messer and His Islanders, dated May 22, 1940, with a receipt for the fee of $7.50. There are letters from fans: letters in pencil on foolscap folded six times over, letters on dime-store paper, and letters in fine script on watermarked linen.

Many of the letters from 1936 have a similar theme. They are from Canadians living in the United States, missing their home country, and finding comfort in the music that Don Messer performs. From Mrs. Jamieson in Lynn, Massachusetts, comes a request for the New Brunswick Lumberjacks, his group then, to play "Six Person Reel." "I think it is the best tune I ever heard. . . . We belong to Sydney, Nova Scotia. So you see, all us herrings stick together. More power to you." Another from Mrs. H. B. Webster of Brookline, Massachusetts, tells the Lumberjacks that she enjoys their program more than any other, "probably because I am Canadian from Moncton. Would you please play "Turkey in the Straw" on Thursday?" Yet another, from Margaret Hearon, of Maynard, Massachusetts, reads, "Dear Sirs, My birthday is tomorrow and I would like to hear Charlie sing "Red Wing." I enjoy your program very much as I was born and brought up in Saint John, New Brunswick."

❧

The supply of fan letters seems inexhaustible, and equally remarkable is how similar their messages remained over the years. In October

1971, thirty-five years after the above letters were written, came this note from someone who identified herself only as "a satisfied listener": "Your program is good. . . . My cousin is elderly and confined to her bedroom. She likes you program too. When it is convenient, it would please her a lot to have Charlie Chamberlain sing "Home Sweet Home." We know he won't sing it too fast."

The fan letters served several purposes for Don. He used them to meet his audience, to learn what they expected of him, and to gauge the success of his performances. Over and over again, he listened to what his fans told him and incorporated their requests into his programs. More often than not, he wrote back, staying up late at night to pen a response to a fan of old-time music or to sign a photograph for a fifteen-year-old child in the Provincial School for the Deaf in Amherst, Nova Scotia.

Fans sent music to Don, too, scores of their favourite jigs and reels, with a request that he play these pieces on the show. Others knew of his interest in collecting old songs of the Scottish and Irish settlers, and they would tell him about a tune, let him know of an acquaintance who might have the piece, or know of someone else who had it. In this way, Don amassed almost eighteen hundred scores, some dating back to the 1700s. He became a folklorist, a collector of tunes garnered from attics and memories. A letter from James Miller of Peterborough, Ontario, shows how Don was able to build his collection: "You enquired in your letter about the 'Red River Jig.' Well, I never had it, but I met a person last winter who claimed to know where there was a copy of it, and promised to send me one, but so far I have never had a reply. If I get it, I'll send you a copy. I am enclosing a reel, 'Murray's Fancy,' one of my favourites."

Don often maintained these correspondences for years, a costly venture in not only postage but time. He saved on stationery by turning a letter over and replying on the back, accounting for the relatively small quantity of fan mail in the Messer Collection at the Nova Scotia archives, relative to the volume of mail he received.

Other fans requested music from him. They might have heard a particular melody on a show, and to please them, Don would laboriously copy the score by hand and mail it to them. He seems not to have resented the requests, as if the community of old-time music lovers could legitimately expect him to share his treasures freely among them. Sometimes the requests were excessive, like that of a man from Boissevain, Manitoba, who asked Don to send him the music for eighteen different pieces and enclosed $8.50 for his trouble.

Hank Snow, the famous country and western singer, wrote to Don on July 1, 1954, asking for a signed photograph, and he was rewarded with not only the photograph but also with an invitation to appear as a guest on the radio show.

From Woodstock, New Brunswick, came a letter addressed to Marg Osburne in October 1971. "We heard you sing a song called 'Pass the Plate of Happiness Around' last week on TV. We would like to learn to sing it at school and wonder if you could tell us how to get the music and the words. We all look forward to the *Don Messer Show* every week. Thank you from the Peter Pan School." There is a note that the letter was written by Sheila Clowes of the School for Retarded Children, but printed by Hazel, presumably a student there. The students' expectations were exceeded: Don sent the music, and Marg made a guest appearance at the school when they next attended Woodstock Old Home Week.

There were those who would call Don at home, wanting him to hear them play a particular melody on their violin to see if perhaps he recognized it, or if perchance they were good enough to play on his show. "Dad always made the time to listen," said Dawn. "He would get this far-away look in his eyes, and you just knew someone was playing the violin over the phone to him." Of course, there were those that wanted something from him, perhaps an audition on the show for a son who "is sixteen and has a bronze medal and part of his silver medal in Latin and ballroom dancing."

Don had a healthy appreciation and respect for his fans. He recognized that they deserved the best show he and the others could put on, and he realized that his and the group's livelihood depended on delivering just that. He was there to provide not just an evening of music, but more, an evening of entertainment.

How much of this determination was his attempt to recapture the feel of the barn frolic in his home community? He once said that he still performed frolics, he just called them concerts now. Like the frolics back home, he provided the type of entertainment that you took your family to, where late at night you saw children sleeping in the arms of parents or older siblings and tables were laden with food. Certainly Don recognized that his fan base was in rural Canada, but he also offered his performances to support fundraising efforts in towns and cities. Fans responded in droves.

In June 1942, Don Messer and His Islanders drew the largest crowd of the week at the Milk for Britain Fair in Amherst, Nova Scotia. Organizers had to turn people away. Ten years later, the scene repeated itself when traffic in Cobden, Ontario, was tied up for five kilometres as six thousand fans lined up for a performance of Don Messer and His Islanders. The hall where the performance was to be held had a capacity of only six hundred.

Despite his obvious success and his popularity with the people, Toronto newspapers dished out some hefty criticism of the Islanders. In January 1960, Franklin Russell of the *Star Weekly* described Messer's music as "cornball, old hat, stuffy . . . ghastly . . . like a rusted hinge being opened." Then John Ruddy of the Toronto *Telegram* judged the Islanders to be "about as entertaining as a ploughing match."

Neither review had the slightest effect on Messer aficionados. Seventeen thousand fans showed up for a Saskatoon performance in the spring of 1960, causing the sponsor to have to "chase people out of the arena after the show so he could put on a second show for those that could not get in." In August, fans at the Canadian National Exhibition in Toronto, bored with the speech of the chairman of the Electric Commission, booed him until he left the stage and the Islanders could get on with their show. It was clear the fans had little interest in the opinion of Toronto entertainment critics.

The reviews did bother Don. He was aware, he once said, that "there's an awful lot of people out there who might not like our kind of music." One of those people was Andrew Webster, a journalist with the *Ottawa Citizen*. On Oct 5, 1961, Webster wrote, "If my guess is right, thousands of viewers across the country welcomed him back [for the new season] with gurgles of inarticulate acclaim and fond affection. Do what you will to convince me that I should gurgle, too, at this unarresting display of gushing friendliness and sickening adorable musical twaddle, I consider it an effrontery unmitigated by the alternative of being able to twist the dial on the TV set."

Despite the fan support that far surpassed the critics' derision, Don found it hard to believe that two million people planned their Monday evening and, later, their Friday evening around his show. His popularity soared. On July 1, 1967, the people of Killarney, Manitoba, filled the town arena two hours before the Don Messer concert was scheduled to start, and the Centennial Tour shows continued to sell out. Four years later, in 1971, the town hall siren in Strathroy, Ontario, "wailed a ten-minute welcome and volunteer firemen roared their vehicles down Main Street," when Don Messer and his troupe arrived. Don Messer was more than an entertainer, he was someone to be respected, and it seemed as if the popularity of the group was endless.

Such a committed fan base could at times be disrespectful and occasionally downright dangerous. Doug Perrin, of Harvey Station, New Brunswick, remembers attending the dances that Don would perform at Halford Hall, next to the railway tracks in the centre of town. Don's music "sure packed them in." With the heat, the excitement, and the drink that generally flowed, things could get out of hand. The Harvey Station show was well controlled compared to the dances in Saint John. One evening, Don and his group played until two a.m. and were ready to pack up their instruments and head home. The fans had different ideas. "A group of fellows came along and threatened to beat us up if we left then. They wanted us to go on playing, and we did," said Duke Nielsen.

Even so, Don seems to have genuinely enjoyed his fans. His live performances often took on the dynamics of a giant kitchen party, with fans being invited up to call the square dances. One such fan at Pilot Mound, Manitoba, in a state of great excitement, called the dance and promptly keeled over, dead of a heart attack. Then there were the fans that brought their fiddles to the dances, keen to play along with the great Don Messer. Don loved these opportunities to get down and do some step-dancing himself, for he was an excellent dancer; although, the audience didn't like it if it went on too long. They had come to hear Don Messer play, not cousin Herbert.

There were fans of legendary proportions. Unable to walk, Mrs. K. Starr, of Vanguard, Saskatchewan, would crawl on her hands and knees to a neighbour's house to watch *Don Messer's Jubilee*. Her neighbours took up a collection and bought a television set for her, and a businessman made arrangements for her to travel to Moose Jaw to see a live performance.

The record for the most arduous trip to attend a performance of Don Messer has to belong to a man who lived 500 kilometres north of Winnipeg. Marg Osburne recalled that he had "portaged from the woods three hundred miles north. Then he had taken a canoe downriver to a lake. There he boarded a plane which took him to a railway. And he finally came in by train. And he had done all that because he had heard that Don Messer was going to be in Winnipeg that night."

In 1968, the organizers revamped the Ottawa Winter Fair around Don Messer: "Don Messer and the Islanders will be the feature attraction at the 1968 Ottawa Winter Fair. The Messer show will combine with the horse show to form a twin bill attraction in the 9,500-seat arena each night of the show. In former years, feature attractions were worked around the horse show, but this year, the horse show will be built around Don Messer, and he will appear at a set time each evening."

Ron Noiles, of Dartmouth, Nova Scotia, knows what it is to be a fan. "He has a picture of the Lord above his bed, and right next to it is a picture of Don Messer," says his friend Stewart Romans. Ron is a fiddler. A long-time fan, he has albums and copies of sheet music, a Don Messer souvenir coin from Charlottetown, programs, souvenir trays, and photographs. In fact he has dedicated a whole room in his house to Don Messer memorabilia.

Leading Aircraftsman Scott MacGillicuddy was not that besotted. He admitted that on first hearing Don Messer and His Islanders when he was stationed with the RCAF at Summerside, Prince Edward Island, during the Second World War he thought it "the worst music I had ever heard. When I left the Island I thought I'd be happy if I never heard a square dance again in my life." Like the rest of the boys, he danced to it at the time. In 1949, when Don Messer toured in Ontario, MacGillicuddy attended the show and admitted to reporter Helen McNamara that he'd "like to hear 'Rippling Water Jig' just once more.

In 1943, that cultural recorder of all things Canadian, the National Film Board, travelled to Charlottetown to make a film about the group. It seems that Don Messer had become a legitimate icon of Canadian culture, one worth recognizing and sharing with the rest of the nation. To top that, in 1951, HRH the Princess Elizabeth and Philip, the Prince Consort, visited Canada, and to give them a taste of Canadian culture, the Governor General held a square dance at Rideau Hall. On October 12, the *Ottawa Citizen* reported that "the Princess and the Duke pitched into the fun with great gusto," the Princess appropriately attired in a brown checked blouse with a white Peter Pan collar and cuffs and a steel blue appliquéd flared skirt and the Prince in blue jeans and a white checked shirt. Don was thrilled to learn that "the last dance on the program was the recorded version of 'Don Messer's Breakdown.'" Safely packed in luggage, Don Messer's music was on its way to Buckingham Palace.

∽

The "mystery" of the appeal of *Don Messer's Jubilee* continued to provide fodder for reporters who just could not seem to accept Don's popularity and made no effort to understand it. In December 1969, an article in the *Ottawa Citizen*'s *TV Times* insulted Don and his fans. "It's not for the sophisticates, goodness knows, and there is nothing particularly accomplished about the featured instrumental and vocal work . . . they're very aware of the low brow nature of the show, but it doesn't seem to matter. No glamour, no gimmicks, no quality.

Just a bunch of people doing what they like to do, and doing it in their own homespun way. Apparently they'll always be a market for that."

Don didn't need to apologize to anyone, least of all to a self-important journalist. His true impact was on the personal lives of his fans — lives that would never be shared with reporters who took such glee in dismissing his music and style of performance. Barbara Vincent of Dorchester, Ontario, recalls teaching in a tiny Muskoka community during the Second World War. She boarded with a local family who had no electricity.

Don, while uncomfortable with fame would take time to pose for photographs, as he did here in Guelph, Ontario, in 1949.

Glenna M. Wilson.

> The old couple had never had a radio before my time, but my board money provided them with the where-withal to buy one. There was no electricity there at the time and they had to use a battery to power it. Their favourite program, listened to with almost religious fervour and enjoyment, was *Don Messer's Jubilee*. The old fellow played old and folk dance tunes on the fiddle, and their pleasure listening to familiar and new tunes, was a joy to be part of.

It was also apparent that Don was truly a mentor for those in his audience who played the fiddle. He inspired those who wanted to learn to play at the same time as he encouraged them to treasure the tunes of their heritage.

Valerie Lee is one of those people. She grew up in the sixties listening to Don Messer with her parents in rural Prince Edward Island; *Don Messer's Jubilee* was a family focal point.

> My parents were mixed dairy farmers, and as such worked fifteen hours a day. One of the few times they rested was while watching the program on TV. I looked forward to it for this reason, and the music became associated with the family times, even more so as dad began to play, and I learned some basic chording on the piano to accompany him. My paternal grandfather somehow obtained a catalogue violin made by the Wurlitzer Organ Co., in Cincinnati, Ohio, circa the Depression years. After my grandmother went to live with one of my aunts, my father discovered the fiddle in pieces in the house. He lovingly put it back together to the best of his ability and taught himself to play, with the help of a few community school sessions and Don Messer via the TV. It never occurred to any of us that I might learn to play his fiddle, but these tunes are now a connection for me with these past generations, and I treasure them. Don Messer inspired my dad to pick up my grandfather's fiddle and learn to play that wonderful distinctive music. For many years we had the enjoyment of playing music together during family gatherings. When my dad passed away in the fall of 2006, I knew I had to do my part to keep this music alive, so I am learning to play it, too.

For others the connection is much simpler. "My favourite memory of all," says Ethel Jack of Dartmouth, Nova Scotia, "is when I was still a very young child, probably only two or three at the outside. Even though it was past my bedtime, all I had to do was curl up on my father's knee and snuggle, and I would get to watch the show with the big guys." Inevitably Don Messer became a celebrity, interviewed by *Chatelaine*, *Maclean's*, and *Liberty* magazines. He was sought after by sponsors. Pillsbury jumped on board and then Massey Ferguson and Canada Packers, for Don embodied the best of comfort and rural Canada. A smoker since the age of ten, he did briefly advertise cigarettes, but he stopped when it became apparent that it upset his fans. Anticipating a similar negative reaction if he supported advertisements for alcohol, he declined an offer to do so.

In an apparent break with its usual posturing, *Front Page Challenge*, a Toronto panel show popular with the intelligentsia that loved to hate *Don Messer's Jubilee*, invited him onto the show. The evening must have been uncomfortable, for Gordon Sinclair, one of the regular panellists, had accused Messer in a Toronto *Daily Star* column of "stinking up the TV network." After the show, Don was taken out for dinner with the cast. The *Front Page Challenge* cast walked into the restaurant first with a famous American actor. "None of the diners reacted to him, and then Dad walked in," Dawn said, "and there was a buzz in the crowd. Dad got a big kick out of that."

⁓

While Don could appreciate the recognition, he was very uncomfortable in crowds. Sometimes after the dances, the audience would surge up to the stage to get autographs. Don would talk to a few people, usually other fiddlers, and then he'd leave Charlie and Marg, both adept and comfortable with the crowds, to handle the autographs. Even with this public display of affection, he never stopped worrying over whether he had given them good value for their money. "Did we go over all right?" he would ask a sponsor after a performance.

He went over better than all right. It turned out that his special brand of entertainment appealed to a great many Canadians. Ratings indicated the show was more popular than *The Ed Sullivan Show*, that bright star of American television, bringing in 2,500,000 viewers a week. An additional million listeners tuned in to his tri-weekly radio show. Still some reviewers continued to mock his particular brand of entertainment. Sonya Covertly of *Liberty* magazine called him "Canada's musical cornball king." Jack Scott of the *Vancouver Sun* described his show as "unsophisticated as a can of beans."

"He never would have lasted so long if there wasn't a love affair between the show and the fans," says Lorne Perry, an announcer at CFCY in Charlottetown from 1955 to 1965. Fans rewarded him with honorary citizenship certificates from places as far apart as Winnipeg and Halifax. They bestowed on him the gold Canadian National Exhibition medallion in 1967 for thirty-five years of entertaining Canadians, and they gave him proclamations like this one, from Strathroy, Ontario:

> WHEREAS - Don Messer has developed a truly Canadian medium of entertainment:
> AND WHEREAS - *Don Messer's Jubilee* has created an individual Canadian identity and content from coast to coast in Canada:
> AND WHEREAS - *Don Messer's Jubilee* portrays in a very realistic way the community entertainment it has developed from pioneer days in Canada.
> NOW THEREFORE - Be it proclaimed, and it is hereby proclaimed:
> 1. That Don Messer, including the members of *Don Messer's Jubilee*, be established and identified as part of Canadian Heritage.
> 2. That *Don Messer's Jubilee* be declared to truly repre-sent the development of entertainment in the Canadian family and community from the earliest pioneer days.
> 3. That *Don Messer's Jubilee* be endorsed and encour-aged as a most desirable type of family show.
> 4. That an excessive amount of television and radio programming is directed to the teenage and younger audiences only; therefore *Don Messer's Jubilee* should be maintained and encouraged as a continuing link in Canadian heritage.
> Signed: J. L. Condon, Mayor, May, 2, 1969

Unfortunately, the above proclamation might have been much more effective if it had been made prior to the CBC decision to remove *Don Messer's Jubilee* from its fall television lineup that same year.

&

Don Messer never had an unlisted phone number. He didn't believe in them. How would he hear from his fans and fellow music lovers if they couldn't telephone him? F. Vincent Clark of Truro, Nova Scotia, learned that he also answered his own phone.

> In 1963, I was in charge of the entertainment committee for the National Convention of the Canadian Institute of Forestry being held in Halifax. At that time, Messer and his band were the number one show on TV in the nation and loved by everyone from coast to coast. I had to get a band to play for our closing dinner and dance. I thought about calling Messer, but I hesitated for some time because I thought, no, he will be too busy to bother with us or just too expensive.
>
> Finally, I decided I had nothing to lose and phoned him at his home in Halifax. He was very polite and, to my surprise, asked me to hold while he checked his calendar. To my shock and delight, he came back and said yes, the date was open and he would be glad to play. I then asked for his price and expected the worst. He floored me again when he asked if $300 would be okay. Now $300 in 1963 would probably be $3,000 today, but it was still far less than I expected for this great band. It was then that I got the distinct impression that this was a very humble person and that he made me feel as if I was doing him a favour rather than the other way around. . . .
>
> After the dance, I went up to Messer with the $300 cheque, my first face-to-face meeting with this great

person. I thanked him several times, which he acknowledged, but apologized for not playing as well as he
once could as "the old fingers were getting stiff." . . .
There was no ego here. He was simply a country boy
who was only satisfied with having people enjoy his
music and not just a big star making money.

There was a price to pay for the adulation. Don was an intensely
private man, especially about financial matters, and it pained him to
hear public reports of his income, particularly because they were inevitably wrong. He and Naomi were invited to a lot of events, "but it
wasn't pleasant for Dad. It was like he was onstage," said Dawn. Even
dining in restaurants became uncomfortable as other patrons would
approach their table seeking autographs. "They were always polite,"
said Dawn "but they were still strangers." Don Tremaine said that
Don was "terribly uncomfortable with fame . . . he was just as average
Mr. Canadian as anybody else." He even endured tour buses driving
past his house. The first time it happened, he wasn't aware that he
was the attraction. In response, he dressed more carefully when he
dug up his dandelions, feeling that he wouldn't be giving the audience
what it expected of him if he appeared slovenly. All the same, he took
care to lock things up, as souvenir hunters from across Canada and
the United States scrambled for "something of Don Messer's."

For one so private, his very public firing from CBC must have
been humiliating, played out as it was in the national press and radio
and television talk shows. He received supportive letters from fans,
first a trickle and then a flood, as a thousand people wrote to his
home address. A telegram containing thirteen hundred signatures and
measuring eleven metres in length was sent to his house, perhaps in
fear that the CBC would not acknowledge the existence of the identi-
cal one sent to CBC headquarters. His home took on the appearance
of a busy post office, with letters, parcels of cookies, collections of
newspaper clippings, cartoons, and poems written by anguished fans
piled on the dining room table and sideboards.

The phone never stopped ringing as irate and heartbroken fans called from across the country, from five different time zones, to commiserate, berate, and offer support. Open-line radio interviews were aired on stations in St. John's, Sydney, Halifax, Saint John, Montreal, Kingston, Sault Ste. Marie, Regina, and Vancouver. Naomi, in desperation, took the phone off the hook for periods of time so they could get some rest.

At the taping of the last *Don Messer's Jubilee*, Don was subdued, even for him. "I didn't want the people to feel too sad, but I thought they would like to know how we felt about them." He was worried, too, that when the show went off the air, "our kind of music just won't be around anymore." "The CBC broke his heart," said his daughter. "He felt he was letting his fans down. Sure, he got another show [with CTV], but it was never the same. He never got over it."

Don Messer's kind of music was still in demand for performances when he died. There are letters in family files from Woodstock, New Brunswick, Old Home Week organizers requesting Don's presence from July 23 to July 28, 1973. Another one from the Old Boys and Girls Reunion at Elmira, Ontario, hoped that Don and his band could perform on June 26, 1973. The band might have kept going without him under a different name, but nobody thought that was possible.

They did try to keep *Don Messer's Jubliee* going, but Manny Pittson, the producer, wouldn't agree to do so. Just three days after Don's death, Rae wrote to Pittson to enquire about the future of the show. Pittson responded on April 4:

> I can tell you now that the Management of CHCH-TV has decided not to proceed with production this summer. They believe that any attempt to keep the show going would reflect badly on both the station and the cast and that any such series would not constitute a fitting tribute to the memory of Don Messer.
> I should add that I agree with this decision and indeed voted in favour of it since it's my belief that a new series would stand a good chance of appearing hasty, ill-conceived, and in bad taste. I realize this turn of events

The fiddle in Harvey Station, New Brunswick. One thousand fans showed up for the unveiling of the fiddle, crafted in metal by master welder Rollie McLean.

Bruce Pendrel.

will disappoint a good many people, but I sincerely believe it to be the best move.

Pittson sent copies of the letter to Naomi, Gunter Buchta, and Jane Edgett.

Don's fans have long memories; they did not forget him or his music. In 1979, a compilation LP "The Good Old Days" (MCA) sold one hundred thousand advance copies. You can still meet people who are angry that the show was taken off the CBC, angry that Don was treated with so little respect by an organization with which he had worked for thirty-five years. Those same people are angry and bemused that Don Messer received few awards for his work. In his lifetime, he was honoured to be asked to send a fiddle to Nashville, but it was not until after his death that he was recognized for his musicianship.

Don would be the first musician named to the New Brunswick Country Music Hall of Fame in 1983. Then, in 1985, he was inducted into the Canadian Country Music Association Hall of Honour. Four years later, he would be named, with Charlie Chamberlain and Marg Osburne, to the Canadian Country Music Hall of Fame. In 1998, twenty-five years after his death, Don was awarded a Lifetime Achievement Award from the East Coast Music Awards.

In June 2000, the village of Harvey Station, New Brunswick, proud of its local boy and his achievements, erected a four-metre high fiddle in his honour, a fitting tribute to this man of music. One thousand fans showed up for the unveiling, proof indeed that many still remembered him and his music twenty-seven years after his death. More honours were to follow in 2007, when the MasterWorks Award for television was given to *Don Messer's Jubilee*, and the MasterWorks Award for radio was given to Don Messer and His Islanders. There is a street in Halifax, Don Messer Court, which keeps his name alive there.

In May 2008, I received an email from Khris Weeks, of Grand Prairie, Alberta, about his memories of Don Messer.

> I was immediately brought back to my childhood living in Mohannes, outside St. Stephen, New Brunswick. My father's ritual on Friday at seven p.m. was to turn on the radio and listen to Don Messer. My dad played the violin and there was nothing he liked better than to listen to *The Don Messer Show*. I recall how faithful my dad was about turning on the radio when it was time for "his show," and it was his time . . . our family time really. We had to be relatively quiet as kids and listen up. No matter what he was doing, he came in from the fields, or milking, or whatever, to hear Don. We didn't have a TV in those days — late fifties — the radio was our entertainment. My dad played the fiddle by ear; he wasn't a trained musician, so he would listen and then try it out on his own. Of course my mum liked the program, too. My sister and I would dance around the kitchen.

For Khris, those memories are as fresh as last Friday, as vivid as if he were in the kitchen listening to the radio, waiting for his father to raise his fiddle and take his bow to play along with Don Messer.

To Chip Sutherland, Halifax entertainment lawyer, Don Messer was more than a pleasant memory. "Don Messer did more than play the violin. He pioneered the idea of convergence of media, with radio, and television, and live concerts, and he did it fifty years ago. That was groundbreaking stuff."

Dawn Messer Attis sits quietly by herself in the waiting room of the ophthalmology clinic in Halifax. She is waiting for Dr. Alexander Tan, the surgeon who will perform the cataract operation on her right eye. Her left eye had been operated on in February, and the results have given her hope that her vision will be restored.

Three other women share the space. They are similar in age and have appointments for the same procedure. Their conversation is animated. They speak of children and grandchildren, and then they turn their attention to the topic of music.

It has been thirty-seven years since *Don Messer's Jubilee* went off the air, but the women talk as if it were as immediate as last Monday night. They miss the show — the quiet dignity of Don Messer, dressed in a suit and tie, playing the old favourites on his violin; the twinkle in Charlie Chamberlain's eyes as he dances a jig; and the warmth of Marg Osburne's voice and smile. The show was as predictable as the days of the week, and they miss that familiarity, too. They could always count on the music and entertainment that made their Monday nights something to look forward to, made their hearts light and their feet tap.

The women's voices rise and fall, excited with reminiscence. Dawn says nothing, doesn't identify herself as the daughter of the man they are speaking of. She is content merely to listen, warmed by the obvious affection these three strangers still hold for her father.

~

Don Messer never made a fortune; it is the treasures he acquired that are full of richness. He didn't intentionally keep them a secret; he just quietly went about gathering music his entire life, and then just as quietly asked Naomi to bequeath that huge and unique collection to the Nova Scotia archives. The collection reinforces Don Messer's unique place in the history of traditional music of Canada. He was far more than "just a fiddle player" from Tweedside.

While there are some who underestimated Don's abilities, Naomi was never guilty of that. She adored her man, and they became inseparable as the years passed, accompanying each other as they did on even the most mundane tasks. After he died, she would seldom leave the house on Kearney Lake Road, but she would happily welcome visitors who took the time to come. Occasionally, she could be persuaded to travel to the Island to visit Jeannie Miller at her cottage, where she would spend hours sitting on a swing on the porch, staring at the ocean. She seemed absolutely lost without Don, terribly alone without the man who had always seemed to remain contented in spite of anything that happened.

They had always been a very close couple. They were opposites in some ways — he the quiet, gentle man, Naomi the straight-talking, sometimes sharp woman. Jeannie said, "I don't think I would have ever done anything to displease him or Naomi. I wouldn't dare displease Naomi, but Don I wouldn't want to, because I wouldn't want to hurt his feelings."

Dawn and Mickey looked after Naomi as best they could. They would try to take her out for dinner, and when she would decline, Mickey would go home and fix her a big bowl of seafood chowder. He would bring it back to her, and sit with her until she had eaten. She relied heavily on this man whom she had been so unwilling to accept and became dependent on his goodness and his kindness, though Brenda, her granddaughter, doubts that she ever told him so. For a time she lived with Dawn and Mickey, but she missed her house full of memories and moved back to live alone.

Brenda continued to come and spend the summer with her Nana, but she found her changed. Naomi still loved to spend time with her granddaughter, but the spark that had always been such a part of her personality was missing.

On January 9, 1976, Naomi died at the age of sixty-four. After a funeral service at Calvin Presbyterian Church, Halifax, officiated by the same Reverend MacLean who had buried her husband, baptized two of her daughters, and married her youngest, she was laid to rest beside her husband. The band members all attended the service, keeping up the tradition of honouring each other to the end. Then they all went their separate ways.

On May 17, 1979, a stone monument was erected in Tweedside, just kilometres from the old Messer homestead. It is barely noticeable as you drive along the road, placed as it is where your eyes are drawn instead to your first sighting of Oromocto Lake. There are only a few words inscribed, their brevity in keeping with the unassuming nature of the man they honour.

Don Messer.
Born May 9, 1909
Died March 26, 1973
Born in Tweedside, NB.
In recognition of his contribution
to the musical heritage of Atlantic Canada

The Don Messer Archival Collection

In 2000, at the invitation of the Provincial Archivist Brian Speirs, I had the rare pleasure of appraising the Don Messer archival collection for Nova Scotia Archives and Records Management. I was excited to have a chance to spend some quality time with the multiple media archives of a Canadian musical giant. It opened my eyes to how sophisticated and worldly but, at the same time, just how Canadian Messer was in musical terms.

There can be no doubt that Messer was a pack rat. Thankfully, because of his penchant for collecting, historians, biographers, and musicologists will be able to reconstruct much of his life and career. It will be a larger, more complex life story than we previously would have accorded him. More importantly, Messer did not accumulate material relating solely to himself. There are depths to this collection that I think will not be fully appreciated for decades — source material that will help to rewrite the history of Maritime and, indeed, Canadian music.

A number of series stood out from the overall collection. The first was the amazing assemblage of sheet music, both published and unpublished. Much of it was undoubtedly used by Messer to supply himself with new and different material for his ongoing radio and television programs, but also much was collected just for the sake of preserving it. He appeared to be fascinated with the isolated "backwoods" folk music tradition of the Maritime region and its roots. Not only did he actively seek out these practitioners, but musicians, composers, and folklorists from all over North America and Europe would regularly send him tapes and sheet music reflecting this. In a private capacity then, I am convinced that Messer was carrying out an activity similar to Marius Barbeau at the National Museum of Man (today the Canadian Museum of Civilization) and Alan Lomax at the Library of Congress.

The sheet music spanned approximately six linear shelf metres. There were scores for almost eleven thousand individual songs and just over five hundred songbooks. A good five thousand items were transcribed and annotated in Messer's easily identified handwriting, a feat that speaks to his intimate knowledge of the material.

The breadth of the sheet music is equally staggering. The published material ranges from: fiddling (Andy DeJarlis, King Ganum, Graham Townsend, Jean Carignon, Ned Landry, Doug Kershaw), to country (Alberta Slim, Bob Nolan, Calgary Kid, Gene Autrey, Hank Snow, Wilf Carter, Stu Davis, Roy Rogers, Hank Williams, Chet Atkins), to bluegrass (Bill Monroe), to jazz (Joe Venuti, Tommy Dorsey, Bobby Gimby, Moe Koffman), to hymns (*Negro Spirituals, New Canadian Hymnal*), to polka (Frankie Yankovic, Gaby Haas), to popular (Kurt Weill, Buddy Holly, Gene MacLellan, Burt Bacharach, Paul Anka, Lionel Bart, Irving Berlin, Gordon Lightfoot, Delaney Bramlett, Jerry Leiber and Mike Stoller), to classical (Ernest MacMillan, Eldon Rathburn, Franz Wohlfahrt), to folk (Fred Neill, John Sebastian, Tom Paxton, Sylvia Tyson), to rhythm and blues (Duke Ellington, Ray Charles), and to the entertaining but indefinable (the Korn Kobblers).

The manuscript scores include well-known composers alongside both traditional or unknown composers and the above-mentioned Canadian composers generally unknown outside their own rural communities. Therefore many of the songs are unique and will never be found in any form elsewhere. Messer's collection of scores, because of their very obscurity, could well be one of the finest repositories of rural, folk, Celtic, and old country music in Canada.

As an audio-visual archivist, the second series that stood out were the musical recordings of which there were over six hundred discs and one hundred audiotapes. This is perhaps not a huge number compared to the holdings of other music archives and libraries, but it was the choice of the recordings — a definite "curatorial approach" if you will — on Messer's part that makes this series absolutely fascinating.

There were amazingly eclectic choices from such international artists as Louis Armstrong, Gene Autry, Hoagy Carmichael, Rosemary Clooney, Cowboy Copas, Bing Crosby, Doris Day, Denver Darling & His Texas Cowboys, Benny Goodman, Stephane Grappelli, Lionel Hampton, the Ink Spots, Dean Martin, Frank Sinatra, Patti Page, Sons of the Pioneers, Fats Waller, Paul Whiteman, Bob Wills & His Texas Playboys, the Big Bopper, June Carter, Everly Brothers, Connie Francis, Les Paul & Mary Ford, Elvis Presley, the Sandpipers, Bobby Rydell, and Petula Clark. Messer's scope was wide, and touched on all points of the musical compass during his lifetime.

Of personal interest to me was the large percentage of Canadian content in the recordings. Long before the CRTC radio regulations "forced" us Canadians to listen to our own performers, Messer was actively and thoughtfully gathering and appreciating recordings by both well-known and obscure Canadian artists (in both official languages). These include Joseph Allard ("Le Reel Jacques Cartier"), the Andrews Sisters ("Red River Valley"), Joe Bouchard ("Les Joyeuses Quebecoises"), Gary Buck, Al Cherney, Mac Beattie, Ward Allen ("Maple Leaf Hoedown"), June Eikhart, Olaf Sveen, Stompin' Tom Connors ("Bud the Spud"), Jerry's Hayshakers ("Cape Breton Breakdown"), Eddie Chwill, Dick Damron, Mart Kenney ("When I Get Back To Calgary"), Henri Lecroix ("Marche de Dorval"), Guy Lombardo, Hank LaRiviere, Fred McKenna ("Plain Old Three Chord Hurtin' Country Songs"), Walter Ostanek, Frankie Rodgers, Marg Osburne ("Shenanigans"), Graham Townsend ("Buckwheat Batter"), Wilf Carter ("My Prairie Rose"), Winston Fitzgerald, Ned Landry

("Hillbilly Calypso"), George Hamilton IV ("Canadian Pacific"), Catherine McKinnon, the Quid ("Mersey Side"), the Rhythm Pals ("B.C'ing You in B.C."), Keray Regan, Billy Stolz ("Queenston Heights"), Scotty Stevenson ("Keep Canada Strong"), the Travellers, and the *Singalong Jubilee* gang.

Of course, there was a comprehensive collection of his own recordings in all formats with his various ensembles, the New Brunswick Lumberjacks, the Don Messer Orchestra, and the Islanders. My personal favourites were "Little Burnt Potato," "Belfast and Cock-of-the-North," "Three Men and a Horse," "Hudson Bay Breakdown," and "Dill Pickles."

The discovery of thirty acetate discs and test pressings was also exciting. Acetates were recordings that were cut directly to a disc live, on the spot. They are truly one-of-a-kind items and were used extensively before the widespread acceptance of audiotape. My jaw dropped to see, for instance, totally unique recordings of Messer with the New Brunswick Lumberjacks, a band that goes back to the beginning of the Depression years. The test pressings were also rare — they were the next-to-final pressings of a recording before it went into mass production. Usually at this point they were "tweaked" for sound balance or sequencing of tracks, so this gives enormous insight into editing and mastering decisions.

The audiotapes were also interesting. Some were obviously dubs of commercially released recordings. Others were more rare: audition tapes (especially one from fiddler Dougie MacPhee), composer's demo tapes of original songs for Messer to consider performing, rehearsals, live tapes of fiddle competitions such as the famous Shelburne Contest throughout the 1960s, radio interviews, Charlie Chamberlain appearing in 1940 on CHSJ (Saint John), and numerous air checks of Messer's radio and television shows, some from as far back as 1938. There was even a tape of Messer playing a tune that spoke to my hometown roots: "Saskatoon Breakdown."

Of course, the other material in the collection was also priceless: four boxes of contracts, royalty statements, newspaper and magazine clippings, programs, advertisements, older music periodicals, posters, photographs, and several scrapbooks. This, plus three decades of Messer's correspondence — with record companies, music publishers, fellow musicians, and fans — all contribute to a more complete picture of Messer as a person and an icon, and to a better understanding of how the Canadian music and broadcast industries operated during his active period.

Although there was no written evidence of Messer's aims in assembling this material, I certainly came away from this appraisal with a greatly amplified appreciation for the scope of his knowledge, and especially for his commitment to appreciating, performing, and preserving all kinds of music. This was not an accidental collection of ephemeral interests; it was a record of one person's musical, intellectual, and even philosophical growth. Those who think Messer was a one-dimensional, modest, unassuming, naive fiddler from the backwoods sorely underestimate the man.

Brock Silversides
Director, Media Commons,
University of Toronto Libraries
November 2008

Sources

Every effort has been made to procure as much bibliographic detail as possible. Don Messer kept many newspaper clippings, but they are not fully noted. The audiovisuals include many tapes that I watched at CBC Archives in Toronto. Sometimes there were only a name and a date as identifiers. Nevertheless, it is important to credit these sources with the information at hand.

Archives and Libraries

Canadian Broadcasting Corporation Reference Library, Toronto, Ontario.
Fredericton Public Library, Fredericton, New Brunswick.
Harriet Irving Library, University of New Brunswick, Fredericton, New Brunswick.
Provincial Archives of New Brunswick, Fredericton, New Brunswick.
Nova Scotia Archives and Records Management (NSARM), Halifax, Nova Scotia.

Print

Adilman, Sid. "He only wanted to retire with dignity." *Weekend/Showcase, The Telegram*. June 14, 1969.
Alderman, Tom. "Nobody Loves Don Messer but the People." *Star Weekly*. November 29, 1968.

Beaton, Virginia and Pederson, Scott. Notes from interview with Gunter Buchta, April 17, 1991. Located at NSARM, Halifax, Nova Scotia.

Beaver, Bert. "Family Favourites And Their Families." *Weekend Magazine*. No. 38, 1964.

Braddock, John. "The Don Messer Story." *Atlantic Advocate*. June 1967.

Brewer, Jacqueline. "The Real Chamberlain Was The One On Stage." *Telegraph Journal*. July 25, 1972.

Copeland, Gary. *Fiddling in New Brunswick: The History and Its People.* Moncton, New Brunswick: Gary L. Copeland Associates, 2006.

Covertly, Sonya. "TV's Don Messer: Canada's Musical cornball king." *Liberty* February 1961.

Cunningham, John. "Waldo Munro at Messer Keyboard." *Atlantic Advocate*, March 1984.

Dalrymple, Angus. "One Grueling Day in the Life of the Minstrel King." *Toronto Star.* June 25, 1966.

Devlin Trew, Johanne. "Conflicting Visions: Don Messer, Liberal Nationalism and the Canadian Unity Debate." *International Journal of Canadian Studies.* 2002.

Dexter, Susan. "Backwoods Troubadour: Everybody here loves Charlie." *Maclean's.* September 18, 1965.

"Don Messer and His Islanders to Appear in Haliburton June 26." *Haliburton County Echo.* June 21, 1956.

"Don Messer's Jubilee Coast to Coast Centennial Tour Programme." CBC Halifax, Nova Scotia, 1967.

Feniak, Peter. "Fiddling with the past." *Globe and Mail.* April 20, 1994.

Hillen, Ernest. "The Death of *Don Messer's Jubilee.*" *Weekend Magazine.* June 21, 1969.

Johnson, Pat. "Goodbye Charlie . . . and goodbye Don and Marg and the Buchta Dancers and Johnny." *The Telegram TV Weekly.* June 20-27, 1969.

Macfarlane, John. "In the beginning there was Don Messer." *Maclean's.* February 1972.

MacLeod, Stewart. "The Other Life of Charlie Chamberlain." *Weekend Magazine.* November. 1966.

MacMinn, Brenda. "Messer's Memory Lives On." *Fredericton Daily Gleaner*. June 19, 2000.

Mair, Shirley. "Marg Osburne, "The Housewife who is a TV star", *Chatelaine*, December 1963.

McCall Newman, Christina. "What Makes The Don Messer Show Go?" *Chatelaine*, January 1961.

_____. "Meet the Children of Canadian TV Stars." *Chatelaine*. May 1964.

McCrae, Doris Messer. *The Descendents of William and Margaret Messer 1837-1985*. Fredericton, New Brunswick: Self-published, 1985.

Messer, Don and Naomi Gray. Correspondence. NSARM. *Don Messer fonds*, 1998-132/047-048.

Neilson, Donna. "Tribute to a native son." *The New Brunswick Reader*. June 17, 2000.

Porter, McKenzie. "Doh-si-doh to your Partners All." *Maclean's*. October 1, 1950.

"Radio, TV veteran Chamberlain dead." *The Chronicle-Herald*. July 17, 1972.

Rimstead, Paul. "Charlie Can't Stop Working." *Toronto Telegram*. January 15, 1971.

Robbins, Li. *Don Messer's Violin: Canada's Fiddle*. Toronto: Canadian Broadcasting Corporation, 2005.

Rogers, Keith. CFCY "The Friendly Voice of the Maritimes." Island Radio Broadcasting Co., Ltd., no date.

Russell, Franklin. "This band won't believe it's famous." *Star Weekly*, January 23, 1960.

"Second Protest Hoedown Staged." *Evening Times Globe*. April 23, 1969.

Sellick, Lester. *Canada's Don Messer*. Kentville, Nova Scotia: Kentville Publishing, 1969.

_____. "They'll Never Replace You, Dad," *Halifax Suburban Mirror*. September 10, 1969.

_____. "Tribute to Don Messer." *Free Press Weekender*. April 11, 1973.

"The Maritimes – Hillbilly Hit." *Time*, September 14, 1959.

Weisz, Marnni. "ECMA's will honour Don Messer with Life Achievement Award." New Brunswick *Telegraph Journal*, January 23, 1998.

White, Nancy. "From under a dirty desk." *Dartmouth Free Press*. February 13, 1969.

Whittaker, Rhonda. "He made us tap our feet." *Moncton Times and Transcript*. January 29, 1998.

Audiovisual

Audiotape of interview by Gary Copeland with Emma Treadwell, Tweedside, New Brunswick,1995. Messer family collection.

Canada Vignettes: Don Messer, His Land and His Music. Directed by Martin Defalco. Produced by Andy Thomson. National Film Board, 1979.

Don Messer, His Land and His Music. Produced/directed/written by Martin Defalco, National Film Board, 1971.

"Don Messer in conversation about his life and radio shows from the 1930s." Ken Reynolds. Paugan Music Inc. Studio. March 13, 2007. Audio recording.

NFB Shoots East: Don Messer, His Land and His Music. Vol. 11 and vol. 12. National Film Board, 1943.

"Sit Down and Shut Up, Don Messer's On." Video recording produced/ directed/written by Andy Gregg. *Life and Times*, CBC, 2001.

[Excerpts from:] *Tabloid, Sunday, Telescope, Barris and Company, Inquiry*, and *Jubilee Years*. CBC productions: 1960-1967. CBC Reference Library, Toronto.

Web Sources

Television Station History, Canadian Communications Foundation. http://www.broadcasting-history.ca/listings_and_histories/television/histories